Chestnut Review

VOLUME 5
2023-2024

Chestnut Review
Ithaca, New York
https://chestnutreview.com

Chestnut Review appears four times a year online, in January, April, July, and October, and once per year in print in July.

ISSN 2688-0350 (online)
ISSN 2688-0342 (print)
ISBN 978-1-965158-04-3

Chestnut Review

CONTENTS

Year Five in Review

For some arcane reason—perhaps having something to do with the fact that each of us has five digits on each limb—reaching the five year mark feels more significant than, say, four or six. Certainly, the constant slamming sound of magazines closing their doors, especially college- and university-supported literary magazines in this past year——can be deafening. Reaching five years feels like a moment to pause and reflect, and, especially, to thank our submitters, staff, and readers for enabling this achievement.

It also invites comparisons. While Year Five did not exceed Year Four's numbers, when we compare them to the first year, the differences are striking. We received almost 39 pieces a day, on average, this year, while in the first year, it was only 13. For this reason, our staff hovers between 40 and 50 at any given time. The challenges of administering this many people across the world is significant, but also inspiring, as we all come together to create something new.

We returned to the AWP conference in Kansas City and again had an incredible time visiting with friends, contributors, readers, and staff who made the journey. We invited independent literary magazines and presses to join us in the first-ever "Literary Scavenger Hunt." Participants were invited to visit fourteen different booths and/or tables to have their cards marked before entering them for a chance to win one of four $50 prizes. This was a great success, and drove plenty of interest in all the participating litmags, as well as creating wonderful conversations with people who might not have otherwise stopped to talk.

We repeated our Mexico retreat in January and were delighted to collaborate with a hard-working group of eleven writers, many of which have continued to meet in small groups to motivate each other forward in their writing and submitting. As a magazine that holds no physical meetings to do our work, making connections in person with writers like this means the world to us.

In chapbooks, we closed our final contest with Erin Little's *Personal Injury* and Dacia Price's *This is for the Naming*, bringing our chapbook catalog up to eight titles. Our focus going forward is to spend more time promoting these excellent books, with a website refresh and more attention paid to promotion. This will be facilitated by recent additions to our communications team, helping to tell the story of our artists and bring their work to the world.

Year Five Statistics

5/15/2023-5/14/2024

Submissions received:
10,934

Pieces Published:
71
(20 prose, 19 art, 32 poetry)

Acceptance rate:
.6494%

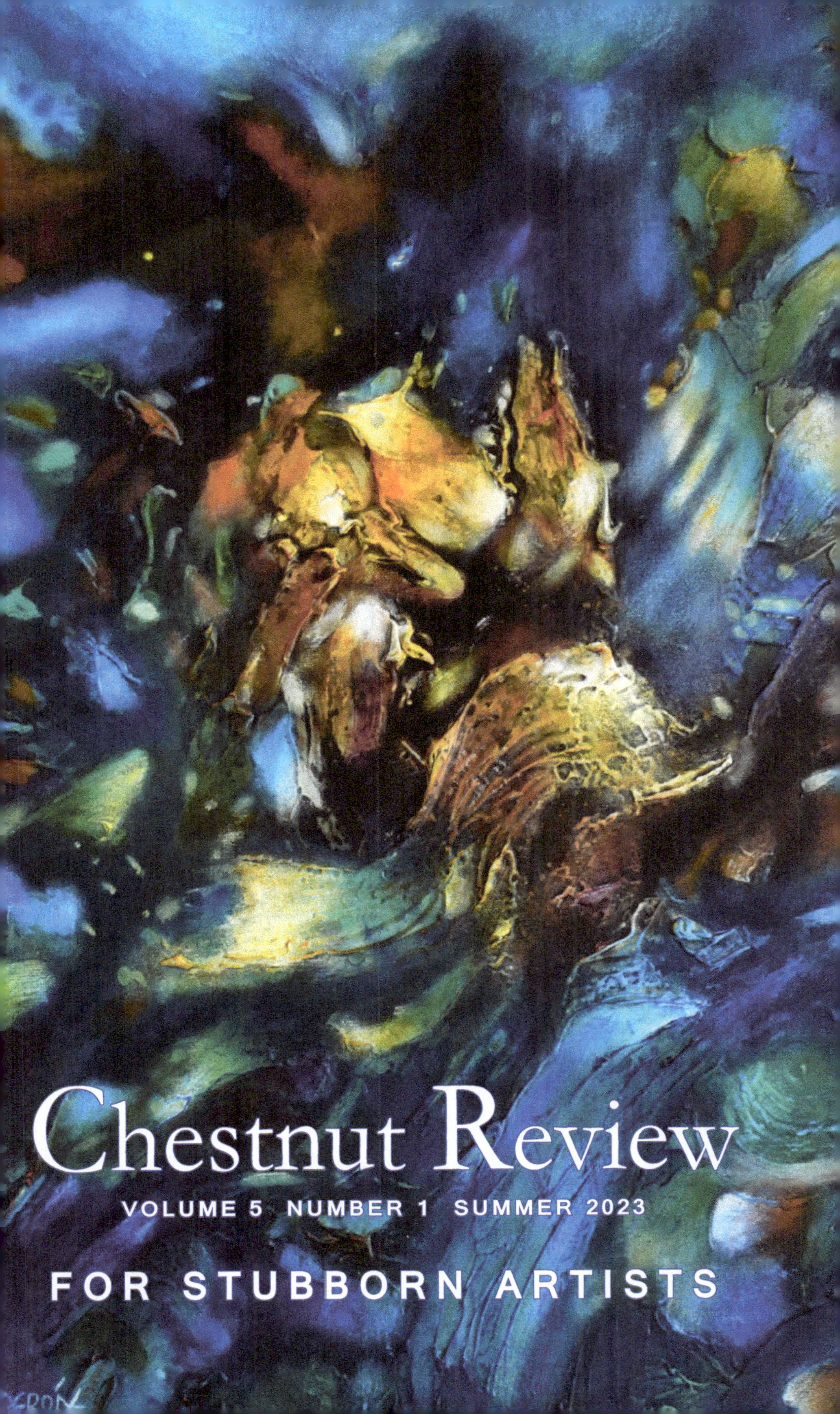

Chestnut Review
VOLUME 5 NUMBER 1 SUMMER 2023
FOR STUBBORN ARTISTS

VIVIAN CALDERON BOGOSLAVSKY

Vertigo de la soledad

Acrylics over canvas, 46x60cm, 2012
(Cover Art)

Vivian has spent the last years investigating The Prints of the Earth. As expressed by the artist: "During this investigative process I have come to the realization that these prints reflect my most intimate and profound feelings, emotions, wishes, sadness and life experiences. My intention behind painting is to create magical worlds that move people, that makes them look within and explore their feelings when confronted with my work. The Prints are related to an extraordinary universe, filled with color, texture, sand and ashes. I try to translate my own path into the canvas and in the process a Print is left behind, filled with all of what makes me."

Chestnut Review

VOLUME 5 NUMBER 1 SUMMER 2023

Chestnut Review LLC, Ithaca, New York
chestnutreview.com

Chestnut Review appears four times a year online, in January, April, July, and October, and once per year in print in July.

ISSN 2688-0350 (online), ISSN 2688-0342 (print)

CONTENTS

Introduction

Summer in the Northern Hemisphere has come to our Chestnut community, starting with the glory of seven perfect weather days in Llanystumdwy, Wales at our second ever retreat. Taking inspiration from the fields, forests, and beaches around us, we spent time sharing our writing and ourselves. We are looking forward to unveiling more retreats in the upcoming year. These trips are magical distillations of what we hope to build leaf by leaf with each issue.

To mark our fifth anniversary, we have started a new feature: Tales from the Queue. Readers will shed light on the process that drives our journal and how we choose pieces for publication. We also welcome comments and notes from the wider community. If you read a piece you like, let us know. We're always happy to hear about it and pass along word to the editors and readers who loved the work as well as the artist or writer.

We're thrilled to mark this entrance to summer with our newest issue. Come; sip a cool drink, and rejuvenate yourself with the talent of our artists.

B E T H   H A H N

Paul Finds Himself in Miniature

But Kay is still regular-sized, asleep in their bed as big as the sea, the raft of her breath carrying her away while Paul jumps to the nightstand, hooks his legs and shimmies down into the rough forest of carpet. He will escape the house—find a corner where rain has made the dead rot of plaster soft in his hands, or a crack beneath the door large enough for a mouse to slip through.

He finds the crevice in the kitchen, near the back door, past the cat who sleeps in the nursery-turned-storage room that contains abandoned things: StairMaster, embroidery projects, unfolded laundry. Dodging a hip-high spider scuttling across pale linoleum, Paul spelunks through the unknown of architectural framing, wishing for a pickaxe or cleated shoes, not the felted moccasins he shuffles the house in: Bedroom. TV. Kitchen. TV. Bedroom.

Outside, Paul climbs across the silvery carcass of cicada, skirts the concave home of a vole. The air is thick with night blooms and the edge of rain.

A Matchbox ambulance, parked haphazardly on the curb, starts right up. The tinny radio and snap of emergency calls mingle as he rolls the windows down and pulls out—the wind whipping in, the music loud, the neighborhood asleep.

He drives the rain gutter at top speed, pushing the toy to capacity, avoiding the pebble boulders and the disaster of fresh leaves. He thinks of Kay asleep, one arm extended toward his side of the bed—reaching, and the indentation his body left in the mattress, his full-sized imprint— empty. This size, he'd barely leave a mark. His footprints would whisper across the bed like the cat's. He could curl into Kay's hair, nestle in the space behind her ear, rub his face along the curve of her upper lip.

The brake pedal sticks beneath his slipper, and for a moment, panicked, he swerves. Where am I? What's happened? The ambulance straightens. The neighborhood falls away, and Paul turns onto the road that leads to the ocean.

At this hour, the pier is lit up and customers, small as he, spill out over a popsicle-stick boardwalk. He guides the ambulance into the lot. There are other ambulances parked nearby. There are dented cars and tow trucks. Still in his pajamas—the ones Kay gave him for Christmas, navy blue cotton, white piping—he stoops to roll the hem. He feels respectable enough. Paul's slippers are old and betray his rolling ankle, his low arch. The heel cap is flattened. His legs are pale. He is bruised from the blood thinners his doctor prescribed when he came home from the hospital.

He stretches, forgetting the long days of inhabiting a big, heavy body, of waiting for results. He forgets the walker and the blankets, the afternoons sitting in the sun with Kay while she knitted an endless scarf, and how even then, he was cold. But in the ocean's air, he is nothing. He is as thick and warm as air itself.

If he focuses, he can move drone-like through the crowd. He searches for Kay's face—though of course she won't be there. He dances with a man wearing parakeet pajamas, who rolls his shoulders and juts his chin to emphasize the beat of the song, which Paul appreciates. He dances with a woman in yoga pants and a striped t-shirt. She leans towards him between songs. "Would you like something stronger than cough syrup?" she asks, but he doesn't understand and shakes his head no. They do a slow twist, but she's distracted by the man in the parakeet pajamas. Soon she hip-bumps her way to him, and the two dance together, their fingers tucked into their armpits, moving their elbows like short wings.

Once, Paul and Kay drove over rolling hills of sage and lavender, through a low valley and along a serpentine road to a place like this, where Kay took off her shoes and cart-wheeled along the surf. He rolled up his trousers and ran into the waves. On the boardwalk, after a late lunch, he took a crooked photograph of Kay while she leaned on the rail and laughed, the birds flocking around and around her on that other pier as she held out fistfuls of bread, letting the birds' wings brush her arms, her cheeks.

When the music stops, Paul is standing in the surf, looking up at the moon. The dancers arrive around him, one by one, smiling and pointing.

"That's the biggest moon I've ever seen," the cough syrup lady says. "Is it because I'm yay high?" She holds her hand up, an inch between her thumb and forefinger.

"Maybe," Paul says. "Are we getting smaller?" he asks, because the rush of the surf is to his hips.

"The moon feels so near, but it's also so far away," the man in the parakeet pajamas yells. He struggles to stay upright, staggering against the rising water. Paul vows that when the surf comes for him, he won't struggle.

"What's your name?" the cough syrup lady asks Paul. "I never got it. And you look familiar, like someone I met at a conference."

But before he can answer, she is gone, swept into the tide. And anyway, he can't remember what a conference is—or his name. There is only the bright night sky and the water carrying him in unknown passage—the departure and drag of the tide, the rising of incandescent sea spray. How marvelous it is to depart in such a fine, silvery flux.

Our reader describes what it was like to find Beth Hahn's "Paul Finds Himself in Miniature"

I've read this story about ten times since it's been submitted to *Chestnut Review*, and each time, I choke up (and I'm not the type to cry during movies).

When we step into Paul's world, we might understand that he shares a home with his wife, Kay. But before long, the ordinary gives way to strangeness: How is he shimmying down the nightstand or slipping out of their home through a crack small enough for a mouse?

We're taken on a surreal adventure that is punctuated by anecdotes from Paul's life with Kay—her arm reaching for him across the bed, the photograph he took of her on the pier once upon a time. Paul is *here*, but these moments of joy and tenderness he's shared with Kay seem to be slipping away from him. It is this dreamlike quality that moves the narrative along—and the reader with it.

By the time the story concludes, the reader understands that Paul is going somewhere else, to a world where he is free—of weakness, pain, and fear—no matter what awaits him.

—*Christina Yoseph*

Our reader describes what it was like to find Ellen Zhang's "Snapshots of Grief"

In my notes, when recommending it to be reviewed by the CR poetry team, I said: "I really like this piece, its central image, its rhythm, its building around the idea of grief." Simple as that might read, it still rings true. I have been dealing with my own grief and its ripples for a couple of years now, having lost my grandfather, my father-in-law, and my grandmother in the space of two years. This has made me gravitate towards poetry which might explain the jumble of feelings inside of me, or at least provide a sense of companionship. A title like 'Snapshots of Grief' immediately told me this would be a poem speaking to a part of me. And it really did. In here, death is a type of "predator"; in the same way in which we can see those we love slowly leave us, grief can also be "all wait and decay," both sudden like a snapshot or "gunshot" and permanent like an "aching" wound that lingers. The idea that even when our bodies have become nothing but "bones" and we have "nothing left to give" and yet, grief lingers—it is a haunting image that will remain with you in the same way this poem has with me.

—*Francisca Fernandez Arce*

Snapshots of Grief

—after Ronan Donovan's photograph

All that remains is a carcass, feast
for the wolves. They come by every
year gnawing on splayed bones.
Chests heaving. Fur knotted with gore.
Every single one all howl and bite.
Even the pups innately know
how to spot and chase the most
worthy of prey. Understanding
what it means to be weak and old.
How death knows in ways
that I have yet to come to terms with:
the muskox's high horns, attacking
and protecting, are all wait and decay.
Ribs fanning out as if in release.
The camera is placed inside where its
heart would have been throbbing if it were
guzzling the milk of their mothers or
galloping across the arctic tundra or
grazing on creeping willow. Strength in
charging their own, gentleness in protecting
their young—still carrying forward and on.
If you were to put a camera inside my heart,
you would understand that my grief is
persistent. Death is no predator, but
it knows how to find and seek its prey.
Neither tender nor bearable, time is
the opposite of a gunshot. It was time

for you to go. Still, I mourn for you
with all of my aching self even
when I am all bones. Even when I have
nothing left to give.

Walking My Grandfather's Garden Gone to Weeds

Feel tomorrow like I feel today,
I'll pack my trunk, make ma git away.
—St. Louis Blues

That black dirt mattered those days
when there was someone tending it,
      hoeing weeds, disking gnarled clods back

to the surface. Blight cost something. We'd pick
before dusk, him singing *I hate to see*
      that evening sun go down, a bushel of peas gathered,

a five-gallon bucket of yellow squash dangling
from his hand, raking across the leg
      of his fouled overalls. Summer money mattered,

him bear-hugging mayhew trees, shaking down berries
onto a bedsheet I spread out under its limbs,
      bringing that bounty home to make jelly

we'd sell by the jar. We could smell rain coming as it doused
all the dirt roads of LaSalle parish, mingled
      with the exhaust of the pumpjacks and the wild wisteria

and jasmine, and that mattered, too, how the next morning
we'd check the rain gauge threaded through
      the hurricane fence wire. He'd document

the inches and pour out the cylinder
into a three-gallon bucket of hose water
            for the mutt yard-dog. Nothing went to waste then.

The soft mush of squirrel innards and organs,
the hounds ate; Ma Peg would stew
            what was left, sop the juice in cornbread.

I'd watch him nap those summers
when he'd come home from his first job
            at noon, crumbs from a tomato and mayo sandwich

on the arm of his recliner, his eyelids flopped over,
puffs of air parting his lips. Granny would wake him
            with coffee we'd take to the porch, a clump

of chewing tobacco wadded into a ball
on the handrail from the morning he planned
            to reuse that afternoon. Everything with its uses

and reuses. The night sky taps its dead light down
to these fields now unworked, light with memory
            of a world that's past or to come, soft light

that can find the years' melody singing,
feelin' tomorrow like I feel today, light that knows
            how to hold that moment in a way you almost believe.

HANNAH GLICKSTEIN

And Is It Too Late Now To Learn Hebrew?

When my father was busy dying on the third floor of the North Middlesex, Edmonton, he said I could ask him anything I wanted. I wanted to know if he was about to stop existing like a tap turned off, but I didn't want to upset him, so I asked if I could get him more tea. He said they put the milk in at the same time as the bag, which makes it weak like dishwater and anyway it tastes mostly of Styrofoam. Which didn't make any sense because the cups from the vending machines were paper.

He only bothered complaining about the tea because that's what Mum always did. I looked at the cup of cold tea waiting pointlessly on the side table, next to the wilted yellow roses she had shoved in a plastic jug with the plant food packet still Sellotaped to the stems. Next to her roses was a wizened geranium cutting I'd encouraged in a jar of water then settled in compost while intensely bored and avoiding homework over half term. But the root could never get a hold of the soil. His geranium was also dying.

I remember a loud pigeon on the guttering outside the window by his bed. Puffed up and cooing. My dad said the poor guy was only trying to impress the ladies. When Dad came back from visiting his friend Saul in Arizona, he used to tell me about tiny hummingbirds competing for the biggest flowers. 'The little bastards beat the crap out of each other!' That always made him smile.

I wanted to ask him about being a kid during the war, but it didn't seem like the right time to remind him of the Holocaust. He wasn't strictly in the war—his father and other relatives made a fortunate exit from Hungary in the '20s, before he was born. I asked if he thought Mum was stuck on the Victoria Line again. He said, 'Probably. Just a little late.' There should have been more to say about it, but there wasn't.

An old man in the next bed was breathing like his lungs were filling up. Between painful breaths he was trying to sing what sounded like a children's song in Chinese.

My dad said, 'When I met your mother, I was crazy. She was the most beautiful woman I'd ever seen.' My face went hot. I watched the pigeon outside getting right up in the lady's beak. I wanted a cigarette badly but couldn't smoke anywhere outside the hospital in case Mum came and saw me.

My dad pulled himself up a little bit and reached painfully for the cold tea. He was looking into the cup. 'When I took your mother back to the States for Sonny's wedding, my uncle Adolf asked me what was I doing marrying another non-Jew. But Aunt Ester set him straight, 'You? Adolf? What do you know about marriage?' Adolf didn't marry till late. When his wife got sick, they said, he never visited her in hospital.' Dad smiled at his hands. 'Ester was smart like you.'

I looked at him for a second. His eyes were bloodshot; his lips wet with cold tea. Some was running down his chin. I wanted to say, Please! Don't die yet.

He said, 'You'll be alright,' then reached out carefully, wincing, and put down the cup, spilling nothing. He asked if maybe I could get him some coffee. From downstairs. Or even, somewhere else. You don't have to put milk, he told me again, if it's *real* coffee. I had money from Mum, so there was finally something I could do for him. But I didn't want to leave in case he died while I was queueing for an Americano. He was the kind of person who'd wait for everyone to leave before dying.

He made a little noise of pain when he slid down the bed, and I was thinking how I'd never met any of those relatives he talked about back in the States. They were long gone before I was even born—their jokes and memories of life in the Old Country. I said I'd get him some coffee.

* * *

With a cup of coffee in his hand, he was a whole being again. There was a future in the coffee. I was afraid it might burn him. Some had spilled on my hand in the lift and left a painful red mark. A nurse came to help him sit up. He called her sweetheart so she couldn't pretend he was a child. She took the cold tea away with a look on her face like he was a bad smell.

I pulled a petal off a rose and sat in the hard chair. He said, 'You'll be alright, kid.' He was talking about himself dying of cancer when I was still so young. 'You've had a harder time than most.' It was dusk. The pigeons had gone somewhere more private. The man in the next bed had stopped crooning and gasping, though his chest still sounded like a blocked drain. At least—in the fading light—the skeletal outline of his profile was peaceful.

My dad lowered his voice. 'Try to work harder at school and don't go places without telling your mother. It worries her.' He put the cup down beside the geranium and smoothed the sheet over his legs. Somewhere an alarm was going off. Someone died. I didn't tell him about being suspended for falling asleep in German after getting wasted at lunch. German verbs always make me feel sleepy anyway. But when they woke me up, I'd wet myself in the lesson. A slowly expanding river ran under the desks. They didn't need to suspend me. Mrs. Kateck said the weeks off would give me time to rest and re-think my behaviour. She thought she was being nice. I wanted to tell her to re-think her own fucking behaviour.

My dad was whispering. His throat suddenly slightly blocked. 'It's a pity I never taught you any Hebrew.'

I shouldn't have got annoyed. 'But we aren't even Jewish! We never went to any synagogue.'

He ignored me. 'I'd like a Hebrew Bible to read now. Maybe you could find the hospital rabbi for me and ask. There must be one. A lot of old Jews die in North London.' He turned over his leathery hands like there might be a message written in the lines. I nodded and looked about as if a rabbi would pop out from behind the blue curtain across the ward. Dad had been reading a Hebrew Bible at home recently—holding it right up close to his face—as if he might find part of himself lost inside those empty square letters. If I could read Hebrew, maybe I'd find something there, too.

I wanted to ask if he thought he would see God when he died.

I made my voice respectful. 'Why *didn't* you raise me Jewish?'

He reached for the coffee. It was too far. 'Your mother wouldn't have liked it.'

But *he* was the one who made fun of the priest and the neat stack of baked beans tins every harvest festival. He was the reason why in Year Five I drew the speech bubble out of Jesus' mouth saying, 'Peter. Peter, I can see your house from here…' They stapled that to the Easter display before some parent noticed and complained so they had to take it down. I nodded as if that was all Mum's fault. Closed my eyes and tried to imagine the old Jews back in America switching between Yiddish and Hungarian to keep secrets from the children, listening to news of the war with warm wind blowing through the open windows of their safe American apartments. I passed him his coffee.

I wanted to say I would learn Hebrew. But it was too late for that. I wanted to pray with him instead of walking about the miserable corridors asking nurses if they'd seen any rabbis anywhere. There was a nondescript multi-faith prayer room—I'd gone past it with Mum on the way to the café. No one was ever in there. My father's eyes went out of focus. He allowed his head to rest and gently lowered his arm. The expression of intense pain on his face sent a shiver through me. I snatched the cup.

I was thirsty, but his roses had all the water.

Nothing actually changes when somebody's dying. Though a part of your brain expects the whole world to break in half at least for a minute.

When a nurse switched on the lights, it was suddenly apparent we'd been sitting in the dark. One decaying yellow petal dropped onto the filmy surface of my father's coffee. He slept. Relaxed, but breathing with effort. I willed him not to die yet. I was still trying to figure out what I needed to ask him.

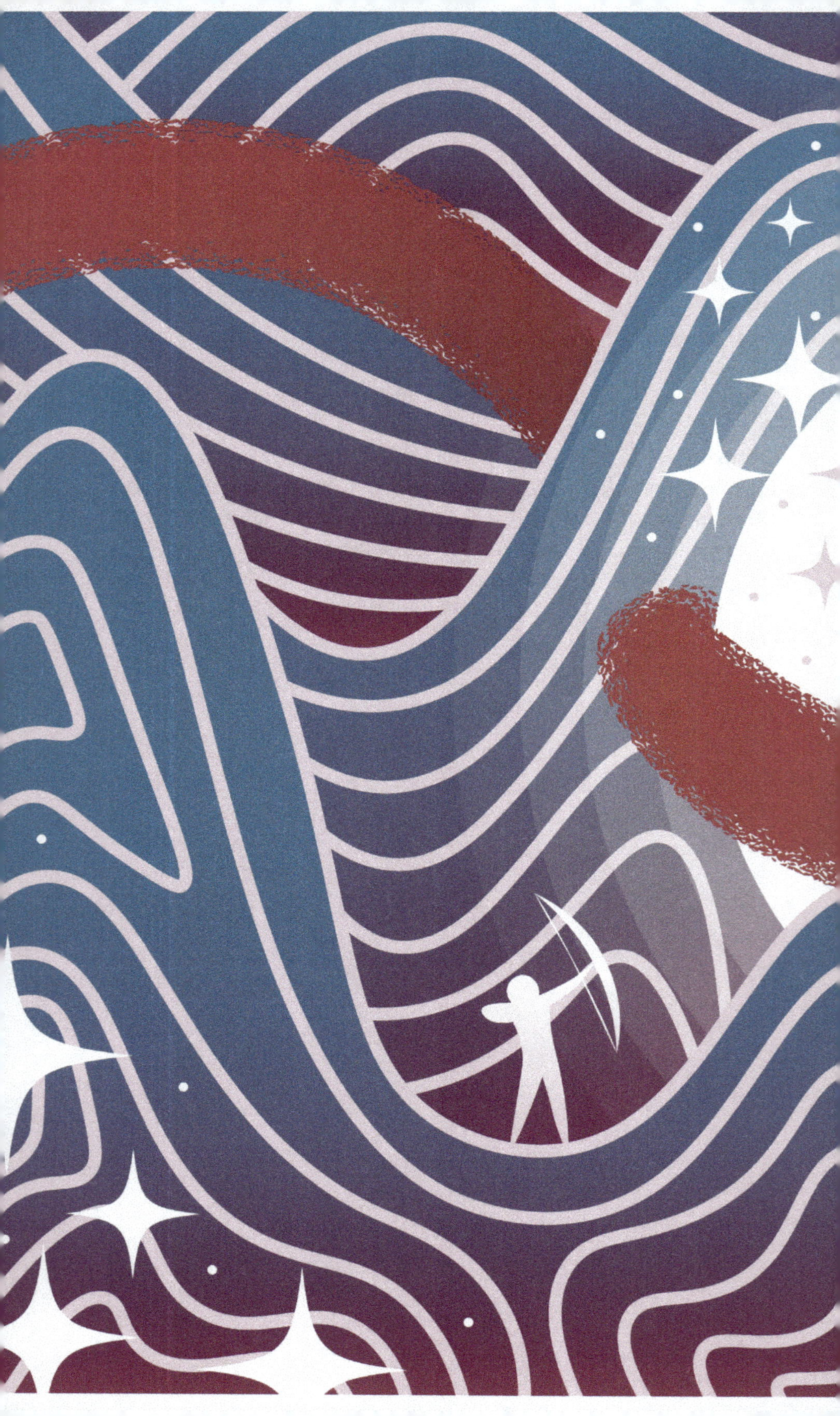

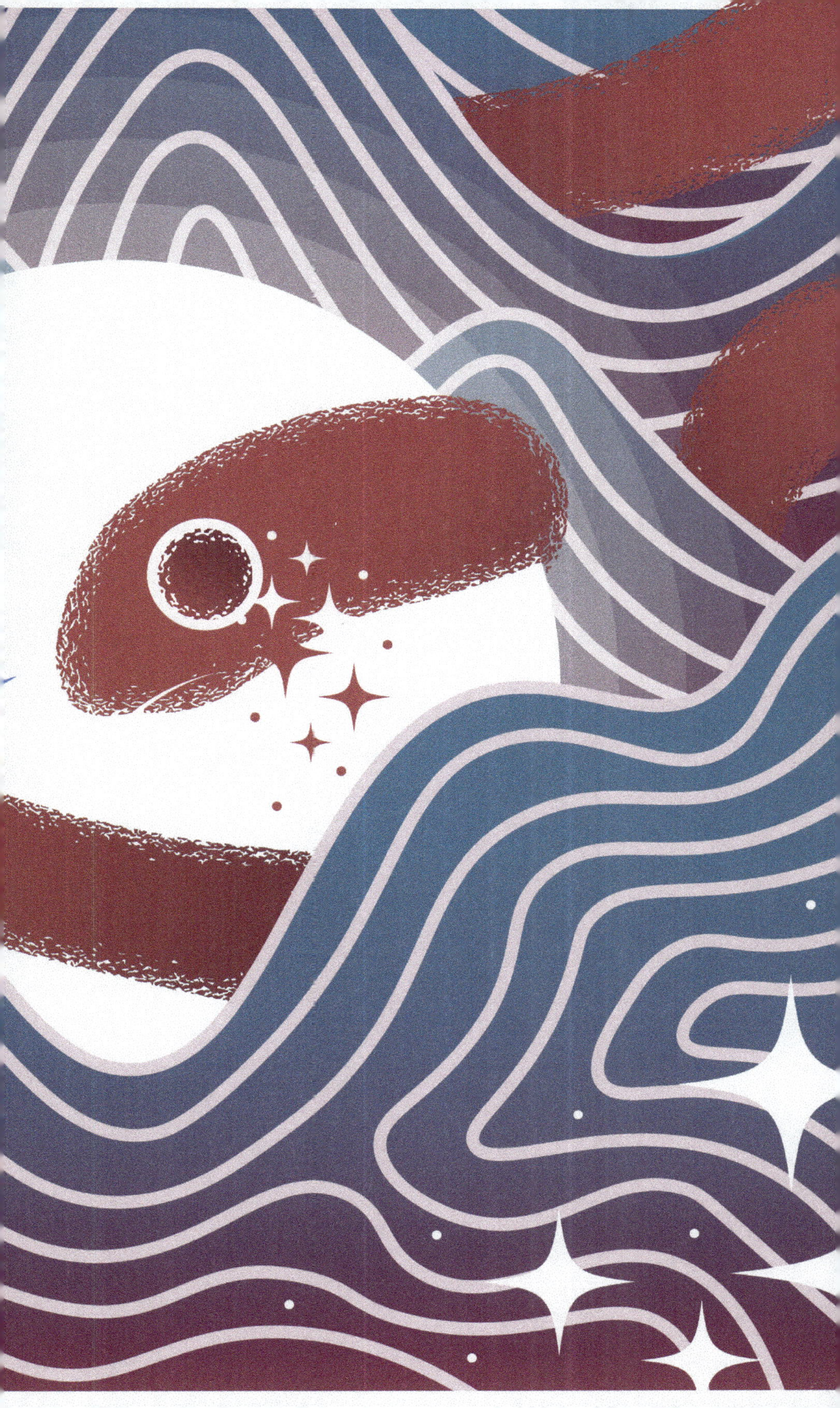

Jormundgand-01

Digital Illustration, 297x210 mm, 2022
(Previous Page)

The Jörmungandr is known in Norse Mythology as the World Serpent
and it encircles the Earth. I first learned about it when I read Jormun-
gand, the Japanese manga. In both stories, the serpents were slain (by
Thor and Koko respectively), thus preventing the transformation that
the serpents represented and were to usher in. In my illustration, I've
portrayed the serpent in a children's fairytale style, just as it is about to be
slain.

How to Drown a Kraken

Friends think I must have had so much fun growing up at an amusement park. They remembered Sea Land from the hooded eyes of their childhoods, how everything was big, how the kraken lowered its prey under the algae-soaked water as gleaming turtles basked their black backs under the Oklahoma sun. That was when the animatronics still worked.

Sea Land. Such a silly name for an amusement park built around a shallow landlocked lake. There was a small-scale railroad. A rattlesnake pit. Alligators fed with the naked bodies of plucked chickens, a spectacle for the visitors.

A rattlesnake bit my dad and he showed off the scar to every boy I brought home. One day, an alligator pulled Mom into the lake. She beat its snout until it released her, but walked with a limp ever after. They carried the alligator away, its nose wrapped in silver duct tape. I don't know where it went.

Dad clucked his tongue. "She knows better," he said. "Can't take your eyes off them bastards."

* * *

I could see the lake in the distance from the porch of our house. Cicadas droned in the darkness as yellowed lights clipped the pirate ship anchored near the shore. Its stern pointed to the sky, a googly-eyed green octopus holding tight to the body and the masts.

I was twelve and learning about myths and legends at school. "You should have built a squid," I told my parents. "A kraken is a squid."

Dad laughed over the dinner table as we ate pan-fried catfish my mom caught from the lake. "People love a story," he said. "It's even better when it's not true."

He told me he built the kraken for their tenth wedding anniversary as a token of his love, deep as the sea. She told me she wanted to go to France. But instead she got a kraken, and she named it Odysseus and dreamed of lands far across the ocean where the water shone in shades of turquoise and tourmaline, not brown.

When Dad walked the grounds after dark, Mom and I watched *Fantasy Island*.

"Would you go?" I asked Mom one night as the plane soared over diamond-flecked waters.

"In a heartbeat," she said.

Dad came home, and she turned off the TV. He said the ringing of bells and PA announcements and laughter all day long was enough. Home needed to be quiet. So quiet, I kept my voice like a firefly in cupped hands, glimmering unseen in a tiny cave.

* * *

Mom never left Oklahoma. I sent her postcards from Paris. The spire of Notre Dame. The Eiffel Tower, angles and rivets against an aquamarine sky. For her birthday one year, I made her a card with a shaky line drawing of the Arc de Triomphe. I wrote, "Trip to Paris, on me. Anytime you want."

Mom opened it and smiled. Dad frowned and she held it to her chest and thanked me. "Your dad needs me here," she said. "Next year maybe." After five years, I quit asking.

* * *

They closed the park, all but the lake. Dad patched together an asphalt parking lot and dropped in a Tuff Shed with a hand-painted sign reading "Ice Cream Shack." He sold orange push pops and Nutty Buddy cones all summer from an electric cooler that moaned like a sick cow. People came to see the kraken of Route 66. He sold them keychains shaped like octopuses and showed them where the rattlesnake bit his wrist. Dad repainted the kraken and the ship. The paint peeled and Mom hardly ever left her bed anymore.

"She's fine," he told me when I came to visit. She told me the same thing, but she looked away when she said it.

* * *

I came home for Mom's funeral in springtime as shining bluestars lit the overgrown banks of the lake with tiny tentacled flowers. The wood dock had slid half under the water, its posts decayed. The kraken held the ship to its chest. The final tatters of the sails hung limp from the masts.

I paid a guy to let me use his tow truck overnight. In the darkness of a half moon, I waded the hook out to the kraken, its rusty red eyes staring down at me. The cable slipped under the one-way mirror of the water. I put the chocks under the truck's back tires and turned on the winch, watching the cable reel in like I was some deep-sea fisherwoman battling her catch. The line went taut. The beast in the lake screamed in metallic tones, and it was the same sound I heard in my head when Dad called to tell me Mom died. I thought it would make a wave as big as a building, but it fell so slow. The kraken slipped away under the silvery black of the water, just rust and metal pulled back toward the center of Earth.

* * *

Dad and I stood on the shoreline in the humid slick of morning. A decaying catfish rotted at the water's edge. Dad worked a push pop with the palm of his hand. The air smelled of fake oranges and ammonia.

"Well," he said, looking over the flat water. "Don't suppose you know anything about that?"

I had gone back and scrubbed away the tire tracks, worked the soft dirt, spread last year's brown and broken leaves over the ground.

"You know what a kraken is?" I asked him.

He looked at me like I was a stranger. "I loved her."

"A kraken is a myth. It never was real."

"I loved her deep as the sea."

Deep as a lake. But I didn't say it. The words decayed in my throat as I walked away, the asphalt crumbling under my feet. I thought of Odysseus and the exquisite pain of the siren song. How blue. How sweet the cold, pale water.

Painted Lady

Inang puckers her lips at the sight
of the uncapped tube.
It's the color of raw ube,
a shade too bright for skin
as pinched as the bark of an old banyan.
But she lets me paint her anyway.

She does not complain as I sweep
the rouge across the apples of her sunken
cheeks or fill in the faded outline of her eyebrows.
I mix the pigments like memories, hoping
the hues bring her a clarity she has lost

a glimmer of an old routine,
some habit that has not yet died,
the name of the grandchild beside her
she has long forgotten.

When I am done, she smiles at the reflection
staring back at her from the mirror
with just a faint hint of recognition,
nodding as I say

Nagpintas.
　　So beautiful.

And she believes my words
even after I wipe
all the paint away.

IHEOMA J. UZOMBA

The Kitchen as Slaughterhouse where Crucifixion is just another Permutation of Loss

Today, the messiah lays life down before a kitchen knife
& I see God in the yolk beaten into a pan, whisked

till angry-yellow, an evening sun. There is glory in the moment
murder segues into martyrdom, as the knife slits with devotion,

as the blood spills & the kettle whistles in prayer, as the fire
throws open its lips to wring & swallow. I believe all knives

are bloodthirsty & the stove, devil's blue crown, is just one flicker away
from hell. When I stir the Banga soup with a ladle and it sours, I realise

how salvation impairs the soul too. When the buttermilk meant
to sweeten the dish spoils it, I learn how lactose-intolerant grief is.

All my years, I have never seen anything walk into the kitchen
& make it out alive—not the hen, not the lamb, not my mother.

Beneath my meal, I find a grave where something once alive & bristling now lies,
buried, beneath pressure pots & bellies—say animal, say my mother's dream.

Late Afternoon Railroad

Photograph, Brookline, Massachusetts, 2022.
A Samsung model SM-G988U (Samsung Galaxy S20 Ultra 5G) smartphone,
aperture f/stop of $f/1.8$; shutter speed of 1/892s

I shot this photograph looking west from the Reservoir MBTA Green Line Station in Cleveland Circle, Brookline, Massachusetts, on a cold winter afternoon at 3:33 PM on December 9, 2022. It's truly magical when a mundane urban scene is transformed into something magical by something simple like the rays of the setting sun.

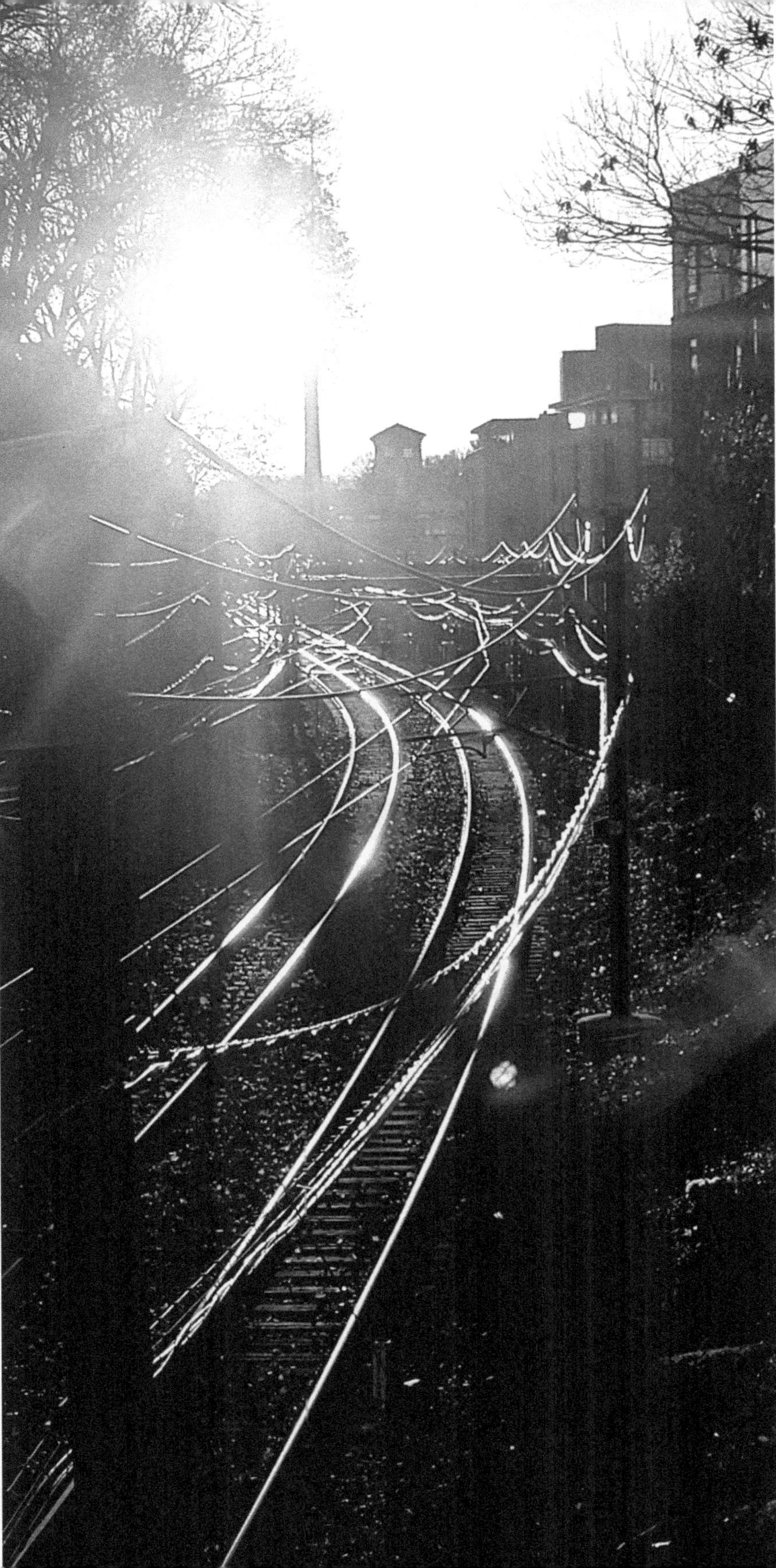

YVETTE A. SCHNOEKER-SHORB

Death by Prime Rib

She ordered three prime rib
dinners because we all have an
other side; hers was not the health-
conscious woman she was forced
to be by circumstances.
When she collapsed at the restaurant,
chunks of meat half eaten on a plate,
they said it wasn't suicide,

that she choked on something
she couldn't swallow, but nothing
was found in her esophagus,
and the emergency room
doctor didn't know her well
enough to determine her death
was an accident—a heart attack
from lack of breath and panic.

But she was a depressed vegetarian
who simply gave up, meal-planned
to kill herself; she always said
she would one day take advantage
of her genetic liabilities
to carefully take herself out
of a world that clogged arteries
and a weary heart couldn't handle.

Tired of metering glucose levels,
monitoring blood pressure,
conforming to caloric restriction,
the metabolic mess that was her body

craving fatal foods, her mind
became intrigued by the forbidden,
shadow side indulging until satisfied
with the inevitable result.

Sparrow Arm

My arm died one afternoon while I dozed under the old bird feeder. Or, it flew off.

They told me I'd have to pick a side, no room in unilateral theology for ambidexterity. Just biology as the lord intended, the scientist-priest lectured me. Up or down, left or right, aerial or ambulation: these were the terms of my religion. Still, the shock of it nearly killed me, waking to find the absence of choice, my limb an amputated ghost. With the right palm flopping a dead fish in my lap, bird-calling the left back, an empty bowl of nuts and fruit at my feet, the panicked heartbeat of wings in my ears, I didn't blame the holy guides, that brutal summer, or my tilted chair.

I cursed the birds.

You're too quick for your own good, the scientist-priest said when I filled my mornings sprinting up and down the open fields, collecting femme insects as they mated with each other, snapping photos of bifurcated vines that split in two only to find themselves at the root again, new.

We're assigning you work detail, the scientist-priest said. I didn't mind at first, toiling over crooked signs and leaning posts and caved-in roofs under tree boughs bent with sticky sap. Trailing my finger along open joints, ruptures, holes.

Except we were supposed to hammer every bent nail straight and force the warped boards back into a rigid shape, even if they cracked. I missed jogging through the free grass with my camera beating against my sternum.

After the sunset, when the moon swelled our flesh plump, a few of us clustered on the cabin porches. Not the men crammed in their shacks and shouting gruff. Not the women tucked and veiled down the rise in the dense shade of pine, huddled on their rugs tittering and writing secrets. We few in-between, hoarding our snack treasures, biting gnarled carrot fingers, ripping at jerky tendons with our incisors, spitting sunflower seed pith at the dirt.

Here—swinging in a hammock slung between the oaks,

and here—playing both sides of a chess set,

and I—in this busted armchair dragged outside, leaning sideways with my birdseed to feed the lonely sparrows, reading fictional men dreaming about women like a textbook until I slumbered under Cygnus, distant stars flickering across my cheekbones. Romance writers did not write my story, but the scientist-priest said the lord would save me if I chose.

So, I did.

I sat right here, my arm nestled over my head like a bird tucking its beak under its wing, a specimen worth photographing.

When sensation returned to my left arm in cold pricks, pin-and-needle ice-fire, the boulder of sleep rolled away, lost limb falling into my lap like a friend, greeting the right once again, not dead, just waking up, ghost meeting body, wholly human, both sides of me, I screamed a bloody murder at the bird calls echoing in the trees, at their holy-silly chatter, all their stupid-lovely freedom.

Stolen

Before Papa was my father, he was
a boy on a motorcycle, occupied

by his mother's declining
health, his latest Quran lesson,

his family and their diminishing
savings—all the mundane

worries that occupy boys
in third-world alley-ways—

when a thief reached into his
back pocket, dug out his wallet,

and ran like a Multani wind.
So mad, I jumped off my bike

and chased him down, he tells me, *I couldn't*
believe it. Stealing my wallet? Stealing

from me? The thief threw the wallet
back, yelled that he was sorry,

called Papa crazy. But Papa kept
running, his cricket injuries forgotten,

his disbelief the fuel powering
his out-of-practice feet in close chase

until the man jumped aboard
a train, and the wind roared

in Papa's ears. *Stupid,* he calls
his younger self now, shaking his head.

So stupid. What if he'd had a knife?
What if he'd had a gun?

But he adds, *it wasn't America,*
and he smiles every time

he tells this story.

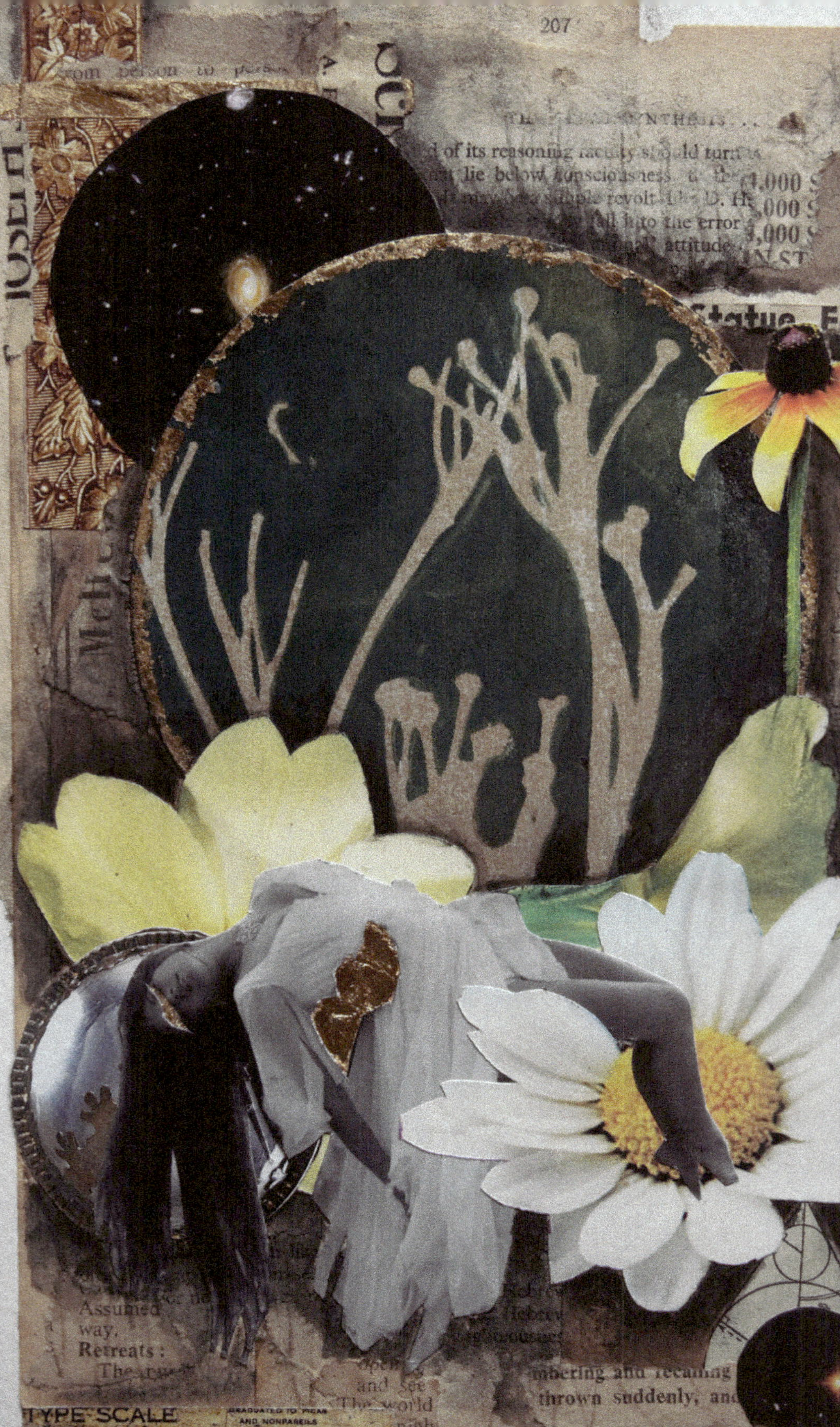

A simple revolt

Botanical monoprint, gold foil, pencil and collage on paper,
8.3x11.7 inches, 2021

This piece, "A simple revolt," is part of an ongoing series named "Anam Orga" (Irish for Golden soul), which is based on the idea of personal kintsugi.

Kintsugi is a Japanese art form where broken pottery is repaired with gold, a process which highlights the damage instead of hiding it, embracing flaws and celebrating them.

In this series, I attempt to do this with the self, acknowledging damage, recognizing the value and growth in these experiences, and in doing so attempting to heal. Much of my work involves layering, using botanical monoprints, found paper and images in a collage ,which I then erode in places. I consider this as a kind of excavation, revealing the hidden depths and core issues which can cause these cracks in ourselves.

Hey, Joe

I kill the engine, frazzled by "Hey, Joe,"
how Hendrix jimmied up this old folk tune
which still gets air time on the radio.

His vocals and guitar cut to the bone
yet something bothers me about the song,
about the man called Joe. I'm not alone

in hearing femicide. Am I wrong
to shudder as he takes his gun in hand
persuaded by the warm notes—slow and long—

as a magician would a magic wand
to shoot his woman down? Unconsciously,
I mouth the lyrics, nodding in sustained

accompaniment, deaf to the grisly
details. I know so many songs like this
which rope you in to their worlds on the sly

then leave you panting with a little kiss
of blood. We worship our guitar gods hard,
permit them anything, but at what price?

A woman's dead—anonymous, unheard.

Three Nights

along the Danube River, 1987

Three nights pass before he wakes. Again
in his own body he oozes, flickers. His tongue is thick—
a black slug lodged in this throat. His head, a cracked
bowl. Next to his face, a pile of broken teeth
and morsels of his own gums,
dirty and shriveled. Three nights he spends
mind outside of body. Three nights. Gone—
where? Three nights pass and his mother unravels, shakes
blood into her bare house. How the son wishes
to have been devoured by vultures bold enough
to eat around the warm tunnel,
around the hot bullet. Three nights pass and his palm
breaks open. For mother, the son's hands move
to a letter. A scrawled language pointed towards a strange,
heavy hope. His hands find nothing
but the glue of blood and bile. His lungs
inflate into a cry. Torn sacks. A sound
like the crushing of a sparrow's bluest egg. Where
has the vapor of language disappeared? A grey fog. In the distance,
gunfire's ghost rings. A bell dies. The son sees
through the jaundiced veil of one swollen eye. He sees the brightest white—
a rib though purple and black. Or a dove. A feather. Then,
ants. Flayed flesh. Pieces of gone muscle ferried into holes. Food.
Another face. The flesh not his own. A forest tall
and full of beasts. A mound. A bear. Black.
He begs. The son begs the black bear's claws to tear
his soul from its bone prison. He begs

but no words escape his mouth. Wordless, he prays
god's tongue cracks open his mother's skull
before she receives the news. Of silence. Of absence. Or worse,
his return. Three nights pass and the son mourns—
even the beasts displaced and starving in comrade-lined trenches
would not pity him enough to eat his body. Three nights pass and the son dies.
He dies a familiar death. How eagerly his mind—the devil
who endures all terror and misery—runs
from the empty corridor of his body.

The Wanting Season, The Rayon Christmas Roast, The Soft-Stained Glass Meal, The Frankenstein Failure, and The Secret of The Sewing Stamina

December 2021, Greenwood, MS

It is the cold, crisp Christmas season, and so many people are in the wanting spirit.

Not one, not two, but all six of her grown-yet-still-children children, wanting.

Make me a quilt, they ask, they tell, they tell-ask.

Because their mama is old and getting older.

While you still can, while you still here, they add to soften the tell-asking, so it doesn't seem like they're making demands. So it doesn't appear like they're stepping out of their place.

* * *

As she steadies herself. Set. Starts. Grandma's hips begin to swoon. When she sews, the needle swims through the cotton depths, plunges beneath the cloudy under-innards, and back up to the clear air again to breathe. Her hand is a shaky ship, stirring the needle upon and through the unsettled blanketed sea.

I am the sewing student, fingertips tapping against themselves rather than making butterfly wind from the fluttering of a pencil, studying my grandma.

* * *

In hoards, the family hunters scythe through the dense jungle of our closets for clothes that no longer fit to our waists, and clothes that still fit to our waists but we no longer use to feed Grandma's soon-to-be butcher hands.

She carves them all up like they are a rayon Christmas roast—the brocade pockets are the breasts, the silk sleeves the wings, and the denim dark meat the leg and thigh.

The zipper is the spine, the plastic-tooth piece that when broken and seam-ripped, unbecomes everything apart.

* * *

Grandma holds the slices up on a white quilt board where the choicest prime cuts hang. Dust flies sprout from the insides, neoprene-nuclear-bomb, and swarm over the fabricated-meat, and around her.

During the butchering, I am reminded of how vulnerable the body is. How the body and fabric are the same. One snick, and it all comes undone.

I am reminded that we are just cross-stitches of strings.

Just slates of skin.

Just something to shed away when a soul can no longer make use of it.

The more Grandma clips through the threaded veins, the more the rayon Christmas roast becomes less and less whole, only pieces of pieces of pieces.

Saintly, she nicks through the snip-strings, shears through their sheer-thin skeletons. Quickly, they join the grave by a merciful hand that is still here, here, here.

* * *

The denim dark meat thigh, silk sleeve wings, and brocade pocket breasts get trimmed into big slices, then those big slices become shapes—big squares, wide rectangles, small squares.

Quilt setting is all about where and how things are placed, and being able to see what it'll be before it even begins.

Grandma serves the shaped-slices upon a blank quilting platter.
Drapes and dresses them like a holiday serving table, and the big squares,
wide rectangles, and small squares are the plates.

The quilting platter gets gifted with soft stained-glass meals to be
swallowed by her children's eyes, and not by their bellies to be digested
away.

When the soft-stained glass meals will fall on her children's boned
bodies, they will not shatter. They will sheath, they will cover.

* * *

Grandma has a sewing stamina that I haven't earned yet.

I intern and do my residency at her home, watch and learn as she doc-
tors the polyester-made patients.

I am a Frankenstein Failure. I cannot make my pattern parts become
alive.

I still stab the pink plum of my fingertips when I try to thread a
needle. Still struggle with tying the knots too small to keep the running
stitch from slipping out.

I am supposed to give the fabric their own veins so that it may suffice
as a clothes-cast to hold other bodies, but all I do is seek the needle into
my very pulse. And though the fabric and the body are similar, though
they are the same, the difference is that they cannot share the same type
of vein.

* * *

As she unsteadies herself. Unsets. Stops. Grandma's hips settle deeply
into the recliner. After its journey, the needle makes a new-world home
of a scarlet-red mountain, proudly pierces the plush flesh to claim the
territory as its own.

* * *

It is a southern warm Christmas day, and so many people are in the
receiving spirit.

Not one, not two, but all six of her children rush to pick out their quilts, drawn to them like flaming-rufous presents beneath the tree. Her hands are a star anise stop sign, and she halts her moving-moth children from their claims because she has already picked out the quilts for them.

They have succeeded in tell-asking her what to do, but she has won by showing them what they will get.

* * *

The children have their quilts where pieces of all the family hunters have been stitched and found themselves, together.

They trace the threads that have slipped and slid between their mama's fingers, marveling at how solid they are.

The children hold their quilts, smile in relief, because they think they have saved the last of it, of her.

Because family is the strongest zipper spine, it is the unclippable vein.

* * *

Like scraps of fabric, there is a scavenging process to save whatever bits that can be found from the body's yard, grasping them with selfishness for the promise of their preservation.

I am a wanter, too. I have been wanting my whole life because wanting seems so easy when so much of getting comes without any thoughts as to who gave it, or how much work it took to give it to me.

Grandma has taught me that giving is never that simple. It is a craft of having to surrender and sacrifice the self, over and over, so that someone else may be able to receive.

Grandma has shown me that giving is the surest way to keep those we love most around forever.

* * *

I have watched as the quilts are made from what held other bodies, made into its own body, by a living somebody.

I have learned the sewing stamina, and like most grand things, it is not as complicated as we think, and it begins and ends in the most simple and secret way—

"I sew a little bit," Grandma says. "I rest a little bit. I do that until I am done."

RAHUL KUMAR

Flower

Digital photo, 2656x3541 pixels,
Bihar, India, 2022

In a world brimming with complexity and chaos, I find solace in the delicate beauty of a single flower. I aim to capture the essence of nature's most enchanting creation—the flower—and invite viewers into a realm of tranquility and wonder and to immerse themselves in the sensory experience that my photographs provide. Allow the subtle fragrance, the intricate patterns, and the gentle curves of the petals to transport you to a realm where time slows down, and the moment becomes eternal.

CONTRIBUTORS

Exodus Oktavia Brownlow is a writer, budding beekeeper, and a rising seamstress currently residing in the enchanting pine tree forest of Blackhawk, Ms. You can find her at exodusoktaviabrownlow.com.

Vivian Calderón Bogoslavsky is a Colombia Native. She holds a bachelors in anthropology with a minor in history and a postgraduate degree in Journalism from Universidad of Los Andes in Bogota, Colombia. She has studied art for over 13 years with a well know Argentinian art master as well as studies in Florence, Italy, and Fine Arts & Design in USA. She was in Madrid Spain for one year painting and having art exhibitions and today she is in Colombia exploring her art. Vivian has shown her work in both individual and collective shows in Colombia, United Stated and Spain. She has been published in various books, magazines and webpages, and has received multiple awards.

Hannah Glickstein lives and works in Stroud, England. She used to be an English teacher and is now a counselor for young people. Whilst teaching, she self-published graphic stories about a skeleton called Skinny Bill. Her writing has appeared in non-fiction publications, including Huffington Post, *The Catholic Herald* and *Spectator Schools*. Her stories have been published by *Platform for Prose, Litro, Bristol Noir, The Corvus Review* and with *Stroud Short Stories*. She was once shortlisted for the Fish Poetry Prize. Her ambition is to write compelling novels, when she can find time. You can read some of her writing at hannahglickstein.blog.

Michelle Granville (she/her) is a mixed media artist living in the west of Ireland. Her current work is a combination of printmaking and collage often using botanical elements. Her work has been published in many magazines, including *The Outpost, Mayday Magazine* and *Perennial Press*. She was recently included in the international collage exhibition "Corporeal Gestures" at Portland University. More of her work can be found on Instagram @beleafmoon and Twitter @michellegranv

Beth Hahn (she/her) is the author of the novel *The Singing Bone* (Regan Arts, 2016) and *The City Beneath Her* (Regal House, 2025). Her writing has been published in *Tiny Molecules*, *DMQ Review*, *Ran Off with the Star Bassoon*, *Small Orange Journal*, *The Common*, *Milk Candy Review*, *Fractured Lit*, *CRAFT*, and elsewhere. Find her at beth-hahn.com.

Amanda Kooser (she/they) is a journalist, rocker and writer. They graduated from the University of New Mexico creative writing MFA program in 2022. Her work has appeared in *Vast Chasm*, *Yellow Arrow Journal*, *101 Words*, *The Twin Bill* and *Conceptions Southwest*. Amanda lives in Albuquerque and plays a pink-sparkle guitar in indie rock band The Dawn Hotel.

Rahul Kumar is an accomplished photographer with a unique eye for capturing extraordinary moments. His photographs evoke emotion, provoke thought, and leave a lasting impact on viewers. Born and raised in Chapra, Bihar, India, he discovered his love for photography at a young age. Each photograph tells a story, offering a glimpse into the diverse and intricate tapestry of life. Through his lens, Rahul seeks to capture the essence of fleeting moments, freezing time and preserving memories. He believes that photography has the power to transcend barriers and connect people from different walks of life. By showcasing the beauty and diversity of the world, he aims to foster understanding, empathy, and appreciation for our shared humanity. Over the years, Rahul has garnered recognition and acclaim for his work. With an unwavering commitment to his craft and an insatiable curiosity, Rahul continues to explore the world with a camera in hand. His dedication to capturing moments of beauty and significance is a testament to his love for photography and his desire to create meaningful art.

Marc Alan Di Martino is the author of the collections *Love Poem with Pomegranate* (Ghost City Press, 2023), *Still Life with City* (Pski's Porch, 2022) and *Unburial* (Kelsay, 2019). His poems and translations appear in *Rattle*, *Rust + Moth*, *Palette Poetry* and many other journals and anthologies. His translation *Day Lasts Forever: Selected Poems of Mario* *dell'Arco* will be published by World Poetry Books in 2024. Currently a reader for *Baltimore Review*, he lives in Italy.

Tamara Panici's works have appeared in places like *POETRY, Muzzle Magazine, Fugue, Waxwing, Poetry Online*, and elsewhere. She was a finalist for the Ruth Lilly and Dorothy Sargent Rosenberg Fellowship, and has been awarded the Margaret Reid Poetry Prize, the Black Warrior Review Poetry Prize, and the River Styx Microfiction Prize. She lives in DC with her partner and their child, and their child-to-be.

Yvette A. Schnoeker-Shorb is the author of the chapbook, *Shapes That Stay* (Kelsay Books, 2021). Her poetry has appeared in *The Midwest Quarterly, The Comstock Review, About Place Journal, Slipstream Magazine, Plainsongs, AJN: The American Journal of Nursing*, and other journals, with work forthcoming in the *New York Quarterly* and elsewhere. She holds an interdisciplinary MA.

Cody Smith is the author of *Gulf: Poems* (Texas Review Press). He is a former Mississippi Review Prize and River Styx International Poetry Prize winner. His work has appeared in *Poetry, Prairie Schooner, The Gettysburg Review*, and elsewhere.

Hiba Tahir is a YA author and graduate of the University of Arkansas MFA, where she received the Carolyn Walton Cole Endowment Fund, the J. Chester and Freda S. Johnson Graduate Fellowship, and the James T. Whitehead Award. She is a 2020 recipient of an Artists 360 Grant from Mid-America Arts Alliance and a 2021 Individual Artist Fellowship from the Arkansas Arts Council.

Phil Temples is a product of the Midwest, but he's lived in the greater Boston area for the past forty years. Phil has published five mystery-thriller novels, a novella, and four story anthologies in addition to over 220 online short stories. Phil also likes to dabble in mobile photography. He is a member of GrubStreet and the Bagel Bards. You can learn more about Phil by visiting his website at https://temples.com.

Iheoma J. Uzomba is the editor of *The Muse Journal*, No. 50 (a journal of creative and critical writing). She is a winner of the Lagos-London poetry prize, a longlistee of the Poetically-written prose contest and a fellow at The Undertow program. Her poems have been published and are forthcoming on *Palette Poetry*, *Rattle Magazine*, *The Shore Poetry*, *Kissing Dynamite*, *The Rising Phoenix Review*, *Ake Review* and elsewhere. Find her on Twitter @iheomauzomba.

Erin Vachon is a gender-fluid writer and editor living with invisible disabilities. They are 2023 Recipient of the SmokeLong Fellowship for Emerging Writers and a 2023 Writer-in-Residence at Linden Place. Their multi-Pushcart, Best of Net, and Best Microfictions nominated work appears in *Black Warrior Review*, *SmokeLong Quarterly*, *DIAGRAM*, *Hayden's Ferry Review*, *The Pinch*, and *Brevity*, among others. An alum of the Tin House Summer Workshop, Erin earned their MA in English Literature and Comparative Literature from the University of Rhode Island.

Jacelyn Yap is a digital illustrator from Singapore. She started focusing on her art proper, having persevered through an engineering major and a short stint as a civil servant. Her artworks have appeared in *adda*, *Sine Theta Magazine*, *Olney Magazine*, *Barren Magazine*, and more. She can be found at https://jacelyn.myportfolio.com/ and on Instagram at @jacelyn.makes.stuff.

Verna Zafra-Kasala (she/her) was born in the Philippines but was raised and still lives in the Pacific island of Guåhan (Guam). Her work has appeared in *Gasher Press*, *Split Lip Magazine*, and *The Tiger Moth Review*, among others. She is also the author of the micro chapbook of poetry *Rites of Passing* (Porkbelly Press, 2023).

Ellen Zhang is a physician-writer who has studied under Pulitzer Prize winner Jorie Graham and poet Rosebud Ben-Oni. She has been recognized by the DeBakey Poetry Prize, Dibase Poetry Contest, and as a National Student Poet Semifinalist. Her works appear or are forthcoming in *Jet Fuel Review*, *The Shore Poetry*, *Hekton International*, and elsewhere.

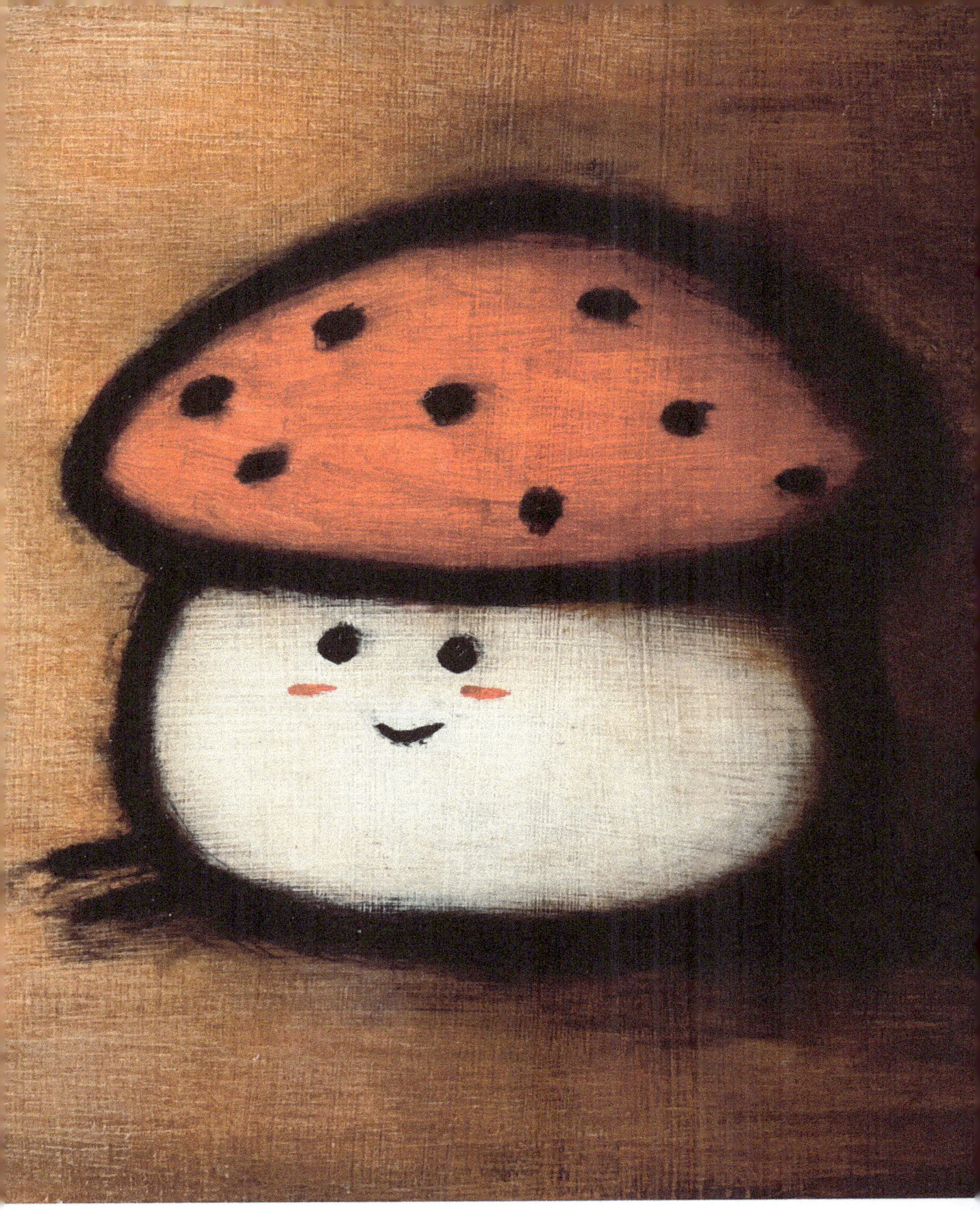

Chestnut Review

VOLUME 5 NUMBER 2 AUTUMN 2023

FOR STUBBORN ARTISTS

DONALD L. PATTEN

Mushroom

Oil on wood panel, 6x6 inches, 2022
(Cover Art)

This oil painting on wood is part of a massive series of over 100 paintings. I feel so much joy making them and seeing others feel joy from them.

Chestnut Review

VOLUME 5 NUMBER 2 AUTUMN 2023

Chestnut Review LLC, Ithaca, New York
chestnutreview.com

Chestnut Review appears four times a year online, in January, April, July, and October, and once per year i
print in July.

ISSN 2688-0350 (online), ISSN 2688-0342 (print)

CONTENTS

Introduction

Autumn is among us, though it's hard to remember amidst the 90-degree late September days. This summer brought the heat to North America and continues to push challenging weather throughout the world. We acknowledge various pressures are building, that the world has destabilized and demands that we accept, adjust, and continue pushing forward. We hope our creative output and community offerings can ease the transition of this time and give you something to continually look forward and come back to.

We are also changing in reaction to the times and our mission to reassess after five years. To that end, we are exploring new programs that will sustain us in the future, including more retreats and workshops, more chapbook publications, and other opportunities. Behind the scenes, we have created a training program to help our staff achieve their goals in the wider literary world, hopefully spreading our ethos and mission to other literary outlets.

We have been here since 2019, and we will keep growing and entrenching, to better reflect our world and serve the people who nurture our *Chestnut* tree and give it the meaning of family.

ERIN LITTLE

2023 Poetry Chapbook Contest Winner

Sonnet for Queer Longing

We walk down St. Charles late one night after the parades.
Street sweepers are out, their open maws rake in go-cups,
beads, sludge. It's 4am and we are so very eighteen, wobbling
on cheap heels around potholes of green wetness.
You ask for my definition of love and I take a block to think.
We're still in it, cross-legged on the bed, barreling through yawn
after—my roommate's voice after saying, "You light up around
her." Thoughts accrue like weeds with oak tree
mothers who live centuries in one sustained embrace.
Endless green canopy, flowering thatched roof. I disappear
the weeds, invasive species that they are. Zephyrs roll
off the Mississippi, dead leaves ride the gust. My roommate drops
the subject. Next Mardi Gras I will drink less,
wear better shoes, walk home alone.

A Conversation with Erin Little, Poetry Chapbook Winner

NB: This conversation has been condensed and is available in full on our website; tune in for more on Erin's MFA program and thesis, how her work is rooted in place, tips for people who are writing into places and moments in their lives, her next projects, and potential next steps.

MP: Hello everybody. So, I'm here today with Erin Little, the author of *Personal Injury*. It's a wonderful chapbook of poetry, but I would say it's kind of hybrid CNF-y in its essence. When we saw it in the queue we were really struck by the presence of place, the real embodiment of different ways of being around health, sickness, and injury, and the way that this has all come together in a chapbook which I really feel like has the scope of a full-on memoir or novel. It is really a pleasure to talk with Erin today.

So, Erin, tell me how long you've been working on this chapbook, and did it start from wanting to discuss these things or did it come together as a cohesive project as you were working on it.

EL: So, great question. Thank you so much for that intro, that was very sweet. I would say that a lot of these pieces have been sort of in various iterations for at least the past five years, if not more. Some of them have been living within me for longer than that, have sort of been in different essays or stories or other poems that I've kept. I think that poets like to keep things, and I've kept them and redistributed them in this chapbook and it's definitely the latter of what you just said, the intent was never to go into a poetry chapbook with this content. I've been learning a lot recently in my last year of my MFA that we don't really ever choose, I don't think, what we write. There's not a lot of that kind of decision making involved. It just kind of happens. As you mentioned, the places that are involved in this chapbook are kind of pronounced and I think that's partially because I've been working through a lot of these questions around injury and trauma and health for my whole life, and they've finally sort of come out in a way that I am comfortable sharing and I'm proud of and that I don't feel in a quandary about. I feel happy with the way that it has come out.

MP: I'm really glad to hear that. I know that it can be difficult, whenever we are talking about something super personal or something that happened, and we are trying to make into art, and it's about navigating that boundary. One of the things I appreciate about our chapbooks in general is vulnerability and honesty, but without spin. If you read some of our former chapbooks, they have that: this is what it is and this is how that has affected me, but it's not played up for drama or sympathy. I really like that element to your work, so that was one of the things that really drew me and some of the people who read it to the chapbook to begin with.

You use a phrase in your answer, "have been living in me" and I think that's such a gorgeous way to put a description of that and a summation of experiences expressed through poetry and art in general. Now, this chapbook also does a lot of archival work. Could you talk about when and how you decided you wanted to incorporate some of those things into the process of this chap?

EL: Sure, that's an interesting piece because it's the most recent addition to this project. I'll put it this way: I was sick from ages six to about eight or nine, from 1999 to about 2001 or 2002, and that was a time before everything was mass digitized. Lots of paper, lots of hard copy things, and so I realized last year around Thanksgiving—around this time, maybe a month later—that I had never actually seen or interacted with a lot of the materials and files that were given to my parents while I was in treatment or were kept well organized because they were about my care. I had never really thought to ask to look at it. I finally did, I finally asked my mom, who I knew would immediately know where it was, even if she hadn't looked at it for years. She brought at this giant binder that is literally right over there. I took it last November and I've had it for almost a year now, which is crazy to think about.

So, I started to dive into this binder that is basically a parent's or guardian's workbook or guide, if there could ever be such a thing, for how your child is going to go through chemotherapy. A lot of it looks like a school binder where there are tabs or handouts or calendars. A lot of it looks like a school binder used by my nurses to keep tabs on me and what was going on. The main material I wanted to work with were these letters that I found tucked into the binder. They weren't given to my family by the hospital; they were actually written by my parents to inform my community about what was going on. I was in a small Catholic school in Dallas, a very tight knit community, and my parents had to figure out how to communicate this to everyone. That's the content of the letters that I found, it's like my parents trying to filter this horrible thing through correspondence. It was so jarring and interesting to find this material because it allowed me to look in the past in a way that I had never been able to.

As a writer and as a person who is still studying and working toward getting better at my craft this was sticky to me, and I wanted to keep going with it. There are pieces in the book that are blackouts of these letters; there's a xerox of the calendar pages for the first month of chemotherapy. These are all things that are very real and tactile. That's part of why— I agree, I think that, although they don't make up a bulk of the pages of the book, everyone I know who has read the current version agrees that they add something really indispensable to it.

MP: Yeah, I agree 100%. Visually and content wise, that was one of the most striking things. From the queue, we receive hundreds of submissions—

EL: I've done the chapbook contest thing before and its crazy!
MP: So, what we do is we have some readers go through, and I go through, and I read, and we narrow down a finalist list and present to other people in the org, the EIC and other editors, and we decide what

we want to do. It's crazy to me that these were added so late, but there's value in that. There's this mining, excavation, that was done maybe as the last step in putting the chapbook together and coalescing the project, but I agree that these pages made a huge, outsize impression in terms of showing what your intentions were as the poet and standing out from the other finalists that we had narrowed it down to. The content's different, it's exciting, its hybrid but not done in a hokey way. Poems like "To the parents" and "Pain Scale" were some of the most visually and poetically striking, especially because they're in the first section of the chapbook and I think those will continue to impress people who read this chap.

EL: I always forget about the "Pain Scale" poem just because those images just come from life saturation. Anyone who has been to a doctor's or pediatrician's office can probably relate to the idea of the face changing and relate that to how much pain is being experienced. That was probably one of the earliest ideas I had when I decided I was going to set myself up to write poems about this experience, and that was something I shied away from for so long.

One of the entry points I had for content that's hard is latching onto the images and archives. I'm working on an essay right now that deals with these themes, and something that I called to mind that I haven't thought of in years is that my parents were sent home with a Charlie Brown VHS special, and it's the episode where Charlie Brown befriends a girl that ends up having cancer. And the doctors gave the VHS to my parents saying, "I think this might comfort her," and they showed it to me, and I remembered it viscerally. So I'm starting to write this essay about something completely different in a CNF class and I end up at this Charlie Brown special. I think it's like, when something is hard, we try to cut it with something else. That's what humor is, and there are moments of that in the chap as well where my voice goes from being more amazed and in wonderment kind of vibes to a harder edged "I'm going through heartbreak and pain" but especially with trauma, it's a survival mechanism to cut that with something that is external.

For me, writing about a prose way about this experience, which is hard in its own way, my brain wanted to ping-pong back and forth between the actual grit of it and the cartoon because seeing that was so nice; it was such a nice reflection. That's another thing that I'm excited for, for this to be out in the world. There are more people than we realize that have gone through cancer or a significant (childhood) medical trauma, and it's not an easy thing to talk about in conversation or at the bar or at the party. I'm hoping that, with finally writing this stuff, it reaches people that need it.

MP: I hope so too, and I think that's a great goal, it's a great mission. One thing that really strikes me about this chap, I like that it's in sections that grow with time. I read a lot of work about childhood trauma or something that happened in childhood, and the entire chap is that. There's nothing that's wrong with that, but when reading your chap there's a sense that the speaker is living, and that's something that's often absent from these narratives of illness and trauma that I feel is necessary. It almost feels like a work in progress, and the speaker's experience is a work in progress that doesn't end when the chap ends. There's a life there. Was that a conscious choice or was there some other way that you played around with organizing it into sections?

EL: I've always loved sections. I love sections across genres. If you read a short story by me, it's section breaks, it's space breaks. I think that there's this inclination toward compartmentalizing for me, at least with writing, because I think it's such a useful tool. One of the reasons I love poetry in general is that it teaches you how to read it. You read a poem on its terms, not on your terms. You come to a poem, and you have to surrender yourself to a poem, and for me I love the vulnerability in that. But as the author you have to create the optimum conditions for someone to do that, to come to the text and lose themselves in it.
I love doing editorial work; it's been a year and a half I think since I was EIC of *New Delta Review* which runs a contest every year, and we do that it teams and it's a lot of work. I can remember and relate to things you're saying when you're looking at the work and thinking, there are poems in here and things that I love, but the organization is not there, or the presentation is not there. It's not as simple as being sloppy or organized— it's that you can't just write the content; you have to find a way to deliver it. I think that's so fascinating when it comes to comedians or standup. They're just saying the same old BS, they're talking about lives and kids and sex and pain and whatever. Its comedy but what makes a standup

good is the way that they deliver it and the cadence and performance of it.

A lot of people get bogged down in the idea that the content needs to shine which it can—that's why I've had so many pieces from the chap published—but there are certain ones that I know better than to submit because they need the structure of the book. They need the juxtapositions around them to work. That's an aspect of putting the book together that you don't know until you read. And the kids are not reading anymore—I can now say that because I'm in my thirties—but you also don't get it if you don't stick with it. I have submitted this chapbook in all its iterations. By the time it got picked up, I had been submitting it for a year. And I know that's not too long—novels can take decades (and story collections), a play can take a decade, it's just that I really resonate with what you're saying in that I've read the slush pile and fallen in love with singular pieces, a story or novella, but the whole thing is not there yet. That's why when you're the editor it can be easy to turn that kind of project away because it's like you're onto something but you're not there yet. Before CR picked up the book, I was on one or two finalist lists, I was on one for Variant Lit, and it can be so affirming and very nice. The first contest I submitted this project to I was on the semi-finalist list, and I was over the moon, but then over the year, over the months that pass, I was like how many finalist lists, how many longlists do I have to be on before somebody just wants it, you know?

MP: I feel you on that, that's happened to my chapbooks as well and I think that what you said, from an editorial standpoint, it's really gutting. Sometimes these chaps have something really valuable to say and you know that and feel what the author intends but there's just stuff around it, and that doesn't mean that it's not good stuff, but it's not the right stuff to bring out those contrasts. I think juxtaposition is a good word because sometimes when we get childhood trauma or familial trauma or something that's trauma-centric you can't make the whole chap trauma-centric because then it's all the same. This chap does a fantastic job of balancing how important that is to the speaker with other things that are going on in the speaker's life. There's romance, there's friendship—I want to steal the way that you write friendship by the way—and it really is embedded in place—Brooklyn, Lake Charles, maybe somewhere else in

Louisiana?—that struck me because the speaker is going through this experience and processing their surroundings in a similar way to how we're being introduced to the hospital wing, the hospital bed, yet at the same time we've moved on from the hospital wing, the hospital bed.

EL: I'm so grateful to you, Maria, to everyone—thank you!

Erin Little's *Personal Injury* is availalble now on our website.

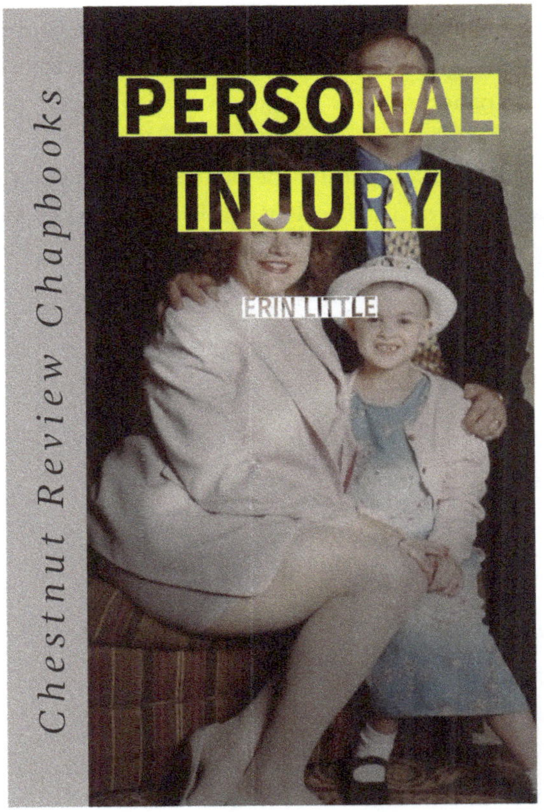

Resonance

Mixed media with acrylic and collage on canvas, 50x70cm, 2022

Resonance: "...state of a system that vibrates at its own frequency, with markedly greater amplitude, as a result of external stimuli that have the same vibration frequency...; The environment in which we live is capable of altering our physical, mental and cultural state. How we reflect and resonate according to these changes that we are subjected to daily in society is the starting point for the creation of this series that emerged in the midst of the pandemic.

Resonance is a series made during the pandemic with eight works painted on canvas + a collage of MRI images kindly provided by a friend of mine.

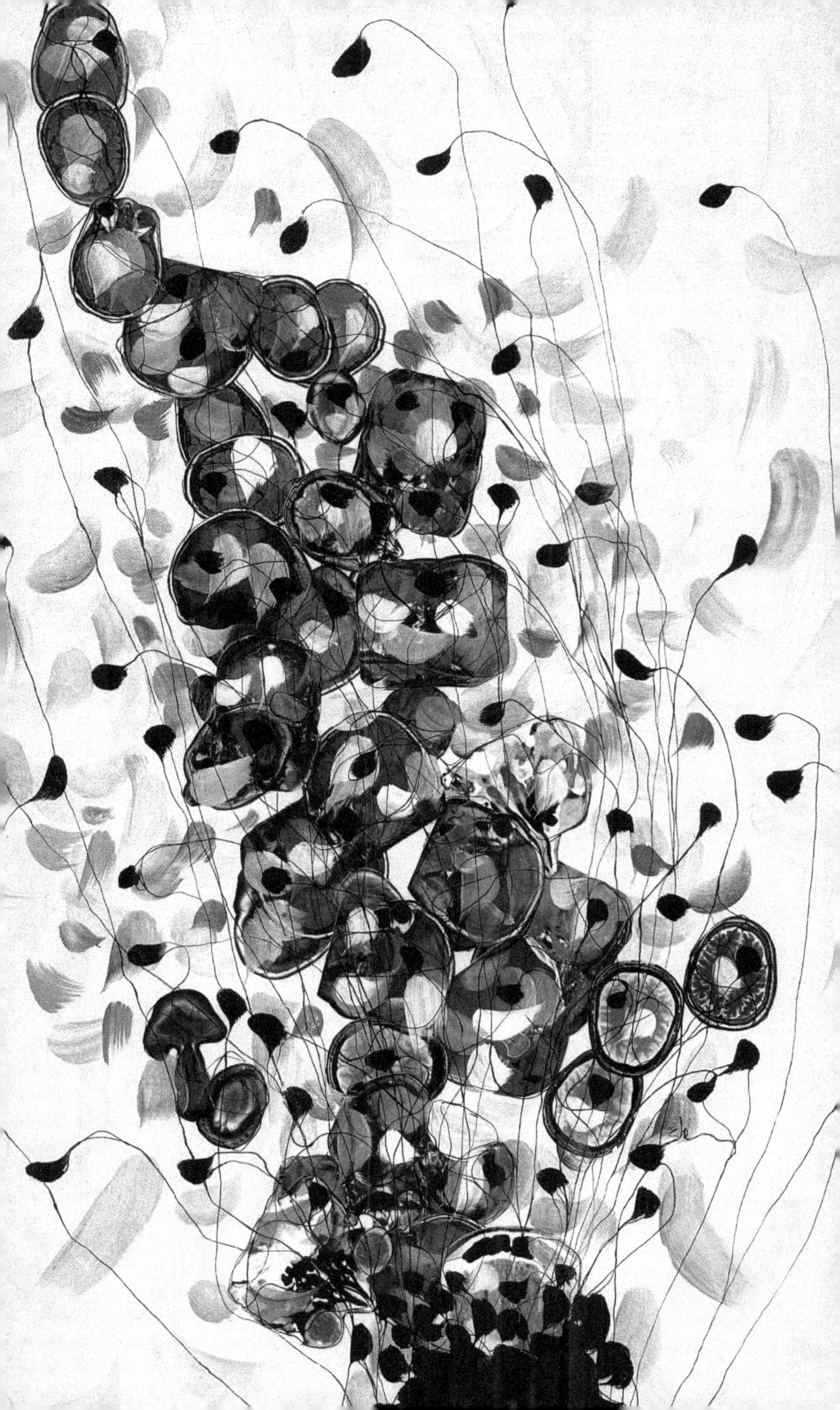

My mother never sang. She watched

those shows where women killed

their husbands in the static night.
Whatever she grew died, or never grew.

The tomatoes not even the blueprint
of a tomato. She would call me

her Eyes. I need my Eyes meant
there was a document with letters

too small, the news scrolling
too fast. I would carry the language

she couldn't. I was in love before
she was. After our father left,

she moved us to the shore where
the ocean was always teething

like a window. I watched it
like it was escaping from me,

like my heart was a room with oceans
for walls. I remember her

in her bathing suit, her knees
disappearing, then her hips,

the bones that roof over
her breath, and her eyes

anchored to my body in the sand
like a blank space. I used to think

she was apologizing for
the water. Then I learned

what we loved about each other
was stillness. Her garden

skeletal. Her garden fruitless
as the sky. The way she loved

the knife on TV, wet with red
corn syrup. The way I keep her

in this metaphor, a wave
in a photograph

Our reader describes what it was like to find Tyler Raso's "My mother never sang"

Tyler Raso's poem, "My mother never sang. She watched" reeled me in immediately, and not because my mother also has the habit of watching *Snapped* in the middle of the night (though this didn't hurt). What made this poem stand out from the many that we read every week at *Chestnut Review* was the care built into the lines. Raso's use of pacing, straightforward language, and understated imagery work carefully to build a 3D image of a mother, and with her, the strange beauty that is familial love. By the end of the poem, we are left with the photograph of the mother, at once still and forever moving. Tyler Raso's poem is the epitome of what makes me excited to read poetry. Like the parting metaphor in its final lines that lingers long after the poem's end, Raso's poem is "a wave / in a photograph."

—*Katherine Shehadeh*

Our reader describes what it was like to find Sara Heise Graybeal's "Direct Light"

"Direct Light" arrived in my inbox a neatly wrapped package. I wouldn't know until I read the story carefully that the experience would be like the eating of a beautifully frosted tiered cake. I was intrigued by this mysterious itching in the first paragraph—one that is certain to lead to some disastrous outcome as it grows—and how the structure of the four theories would uncover the complexity within and between the narrator, Rudy, and Stephen. While disguised as a clear four points, similar to the five-paragraph high-school essay, the prose instead uses the reasons behind the rash as a distraction to discuss the precarity of romantic relationships, both past and current. This is a story where form is closely and cleverly intertwined with a strong narrative. It was by munching through each layer of this flavored cake that the entire experience came together into a meal well worth savoring.

—*Max Pasakorn*

Direct Light

In the days leading up to my partner Stephen's arms breaking out in itchy welts, two things happened: My ex Rudy came into town, the first time we'd seen each other since he was carted off in handcuffs twelve months prior. And, Stephen put his daughter to bed and ate an entire pizza by himself. He felt great at the time. When he woke up, he felt like death. He started itching shortly thereafter and didn't stop for the next six weeks.

Stephen and I developed four theories about the welts:

1. Stress.

This seemed likely. Before Rudy came, I explained to Stephen that when they arrested him a year ago, I was in the bathtub of the house he shared with his uncle and cousin in Toms River, New Jersey. The three of them had been coming at each other's throats all day over some sneakers his uncle said one of them stole. Rudy didn't even like sneakers, but the dispute got so bad the cops pulled up, and who knew Rudy had a warrant out for possession with intent to distribute?

"Jesus!" Stephen said.

"It gets worse," I said.

Turned out Rudy knew about the warrant, and his uncle and cousin did too. I learned the news wrapped in a towel, dripping water on the porch while he hollered through his stringy blond hair, "I'll explain everything, Brooke! I fucking love you!" Then the cop stuffed him in the car and pulled around the corner, and Rudy's uncle went upstairs and started throwing our shit on the street. I mean tampons, cologne, laundry detergent, you name it. The sidewalk stained green, broken glass every-where. A mile into town, at the library, I made a Facebook post looking for a ride south. I was out of there before nightfall.

"And your stuff?"

"I had to get everything new."

"What about your friends? You just left?"

It wasn't only Rudy and his uncle and cousin who knew about his warrant. It was everyone, everyone except me. How do you say hi to people at the gas station after that? How do you look anyone in the eye?

"I told you," I said to Stephen. "I had to get *everything* new."

Stephen had close-cropped brown hair and glasses. He leaned forward when I told him stories like this, elbows pressed against his knees. "Wow," he said. "Just, wow."

My ride dropped me in Richmond, Virginia, in front of a squat gray townhouse whose address matched the crumpled envelope in my palm. My mom had sent me a birthday card from that address last year, and I always figured if I ran out of other options, I'd come down and find her. Turned out I was too late; a *For Rent* sign stood crooked in the grass.

I used the last of my cash to pay for one week upfront at a motel down the street. The next day I got a job decorating cakes at Harris Teeter. I got a new phone and didn't tell Rudy, so he wouldn't start calling and asking for money. I got a beat-up apartment and a car that needed work, which led to meeting Stephen, a single dad who worked as a mechanic but was taking night classes to be a life coach. He seemed like exactly the kind of guy Rudy wasn't, which was my only real criteria at the time.

Eight months in, I spent my weekends with him and his daughter, Zoe. I had every inch of the Richmond Zoo memorized, and my waistline was bulging from all the chicken nuggets and Yoo-hoos. I carried extra life jackets in my trunk. Stephen made me his emergency contact and a copy of his key; he encouraged me to nap in his bed when he was gone. He was always asking how I felt, and I was always trying to think up things to say. He didn't lie to me.

When Rudy emailed to say he was a free man, it was like getting smoke signals from an island I thought had slid into the sea.

"He wants to visit," I told Stephen.

"Why?" Stephen asked.

"Closure?" I said.

"And what do *you* want?" Stephen asked.

Since moving to Richmond, I'd started knowing what I wanted from time to time. Stephen would ask and my answers would spring up, eager and sure:

"I want to make Zoe mac and cheese."

"I want to take a kickboxing class."

"I want to sit on the porch till the moon comes up."

But today, Rudy's request sitting in my inbox, already there was smoke in my eyes.

"You're not getting back together with him, are you?" Stephen asked.

I didn't want to get back together with him. I didn't want to live on Rudy's island. But we'd shared that room in Toms River for a long time; there had been love there, or something. He'd been sitting in a jail cell since I saw him last, and maybe I wanted to know if his island was still there—just that. And if he wanted closure, well, I could just give it to him.

Elbows on knees, blinking fast, Stephen agreed to the visit. And Rudy sped down on the first Megabus he could find, twelve-months celibate with his fingers in my hair before I could even turn the car on.

Hi, Stephen texted as I pulled away from the bus station. *Would love a check-in, feeling a little anxious.*

Rudy had gained weight in jail and had a beard starting. He sat in the passenger's seat grinning at me. I could hear my phone pinging in my lap, but that seemed very far away. "Richmond, Virginia," Rudy said. "I love it already!"

There wasn't any smoke, just fire.

Later that night, Stephen texted again: *Feeling less sure about this whole thing.* Rudy and I had picked up shrimp lo mein and were just starting to dig in. "That dude won't leave you alone," he said, mouth full.

"He's my boyfriend," I said.

Rudy rolled his eyes.

I called him from the sidewalk outside my house, but I wasn't sure what to say. "How are you?" Stephen kept asking.

"I'm good."

"You don't even sound like yourself."

"I'm good!"

The next morning, I woke up to another text: *I'm concerned Rudy is controlling your communication. Send me Zoe's code word if you're okay; otherwise, I'm going to swing by.*

Stephen's daughter's therapist had her choose a code word after her mom left, to signal to Stephen when she was upset. Marshmallow was the word. *Marshmallow!* I texted, scrambling out of bed, but when I eased back the curtains, I saw Stephen's car idling in front of my house.

"He came to check on me," I said to Rudy.

Rudy sat up in the mess of blankets. "He thinks I can't take care of you?"

"He thinks you're controlling me."

"Me? Who's the one stalking you in his car at eight a.m.?"

I guess Stephen got my text then. He pulled his phone out of his pocket and looked at it. Then he tossed it on the passenger seat and drove away. I stood in the sunny window, looking until he was gone. *How do you feel?* he would have asked. I felt like I wished I was in his kitchen, making instant mashed potatoes; I wished Zoe was prancing around singing Moana and I was saying, "Here, try this, you think we should add more butter?"

But then Rudy said, "I'm in the mood for French toast," and I was getting out the frying pan and making it. Stephen and I didn't talk again that day. By the next morning—Rudy's last morning in Richmond—Stephen's texts had frayed into rapid-fire bullets:

I really need him to be gone now.

I don't want to pressure you but I am not handling this well.

I feel we did not adequately prepare for this scenario.

Brooke? Can you answer me?

Please?

All of which is to say, Stephen has been stressed.

2. Soap.

As I mentioned, Stephen's a mechanic. Stephen is one of those good guys who made all the wrong choices: getting married too young, having kids too fast, taking the first job that came his way, and not putting his foot down when the marriage turned bad. His wife spent Zoe's early years hosting Pampered Chef parties online, on which she exerted a lot of effort to make exactly zero dollars. When Zoe started kindergarten, she flew into a panic over her uselessness, which manifested in maxing out their only credit card to replace the furniture, backing their Jeep into the oak tree in their front yard, and then suffering a full-body meltdown for which Stephen checked her into a psychiatric hospital and, six months later, served her with divorce papers. Now she's in sunny Florida remaking her life, and Stephen's in Richmond scrubbing grease off his arms.

"I learned a lot from that relationship," is how Stephen sums it up.

The benefit of dating someone who only divorced his wife when she went AWOL for six entire months is you can be pretty sure that, as long as you fuck up less than *that*, he'll stick around.

Stephen handles the tough cases at Frankie's Imports. That's why they sent me his way eight months ago, when I stopped by with a Honda that kept blowing its tires and shaking at high speeds. It took him six days, but he fixed the car for under a thousand dollars. I was the one to ask him on a date.

All the guys with less experience spend their days changing oil and tires, taking smoke breaks, and making the same hourly rate as Stephen, who comes home with bruised shins and sliced-up arms. "Seems unfair," I told him early on.

"I'm just grateful for the job," he said.

"If you threatened to quit, they'd probably give you more," I said.

He looked at me strangely, like he'd seen something behind my eyes that he hadn't known was there. "I wouldn't use a strategy like that," he said. But then he reached over and took my hand. "It means a lot to me that you care."

The red welts that Stephen developed the day Rudy left Richmond matched the waterline of his hand-washing routine at Frankie's Imports. And as it turned out, a couple days before that, Frankie had put a different kind of soap in the dispenser. So, the culprit seemed potentially clear, until Stephen started bringing his own soap to work and the itching still didn't go away.

3. Gluten, in the form of the pizza Stephen stuffed down his throat the night before the welts began.

It was the last night of Rudy's visit. Stephen had sent me that litany of desperate messages, and I hadn't figured out how to respond. Rudy and I were eating our second round of shrimp lo mein, the sun going down while he caught me up about his uncle, who'd gotten arrested, and his cousin, who got some chick pregnant and followed her to Ohio. The house that had been in his family for the last sixty years was now empty except for Rudy. I felt nothing for his uncle or cousin, but I did feel a pang for that house—how we strung Christmas lights around his twin bed and kept an air freshener plugged in and watched the fireworks from his window on the Fourth of July. My apartment in Richmond was bare, spilling over temporarily when Stephen brought Zoe by and winnowing to a depressing drizzle in her absence. Until Rudy came and stayed put for seventy-two hours, his presence like a soft seal over a leak I didn't even know was there.

We didn't sleep together the first night. You can believe me or not. Stephen didn't.

But that second night, a white-green glow coming through the window, lighting up the stubble on Rudy's chin, his eyes latched onto mine and wouldn't let go.

"Rudy," I said, "let's—"

"I'm sorry," he said, "but you can't expect me to be with you and not—"

"No, but we shouldn't. Because it really fucked me up when you left," I said.

"It really fucked me up when *you* left," he said.

It felt like exactly the closure we needed, until he moved toward me on the sofa and put his palm on the back of my neck.

4. An infestation of bedbugs, scabies, or some other psychosis-inducing pest, that not only turned Stephen's arms into bloody wormholes but split his trust into a thousand bloody threads we'd never put back together.

After putting Rudy on the bus, I drove home and sat in my empty living room, filling my T-shirt up with tears that poured snottily down my face. It wasn't that I wanted to be with Rudy, but it hurt to watch him leave. And it wasn't that I didn't want to be with Stephen, but I kept thinking that the first thing Rudy did after getting out of jail was violate his probation to come see me, and the first thing Stephen would do after getting out of jail was drive straight home and sit on his couch saying, "Wow. Just, wow." And maybe there was something to holding out hope for a person forever. Maybe Stephen's divorcing his wife was more of a weakness than a strength, because even though Rudy lied and never really wanted closure, it felt good, didn't it, to be fought for?

I mean, but Stephen would never go to jail.

The air was hot and hazy. I had to clock in at Harris Teeter. There's nothing worse than drawing balloons on cakes when your heart is tearing open, but I couldn't call out because I'd just taken two days off. Stephen would expect me to come over later and hash out every last thing I'd felt while Rudy was here, and already I could feel my brain dissolving into shadows. I stood up and looked out the window and thought, *All right, folks, let's see how Brooke fucks this one up!*

But then his Toyota Corolla pulled up. Again. He rolled down the window and called, "Mind if I drive you to work?"

On the one hand, there was what Rudy had said: *Who's the one stalking you in his car?*

On the other hand, although I wasn't sure what I wanted, it was nice to know Stephen wanted me. That, and I was in no condition to drive.

On the way there, he held my hand across the seat. "I missed you," he said.

"I missed you, too."

"This week was pretty rough for me."

"I know."

"Would you say you're—resolved?"

"Resolved?"

"You got closure?"

Rudy had texted me twice since getting on the Megabus. Out of the corner of my eye, I saw an undulating strand of his blond hair on my jeans. "Yeah," I said, "I pretty much got closure."

He pulled up to the Harris Teeter and looked at me. *Poor Stephen*, I thought. *Good Stephen.*

"We'll talk about it more tonight," Stephen said.

I squeezed the shit out of the icing, getting ready for that talk. But by the time I got off my shift, he'd texted: *I'm experiencing some painful itching. Are you comfortable being in close proximity to me?*

To be honest, Stephen's welts seemed like a blessing in disguise. A trade-off: I accepted some mild level of risk, and he forgave me for letting Rudy visit. His itching somehow leveled the scales. That night, before he could launch into a Big Talk, I suggested a movie. In the morning, I braided Zoe's hair and cooked scrambled eggs, and pretty soon we were back to our zoo and Yoo-hoo routine.

The next week he made an appointment. Bedbugs or scabies, he told me when he got out.

"*Scabies?*"

"I feel awful. Another of your partners bringing stuff home."

He was referring to Rudy. Years ago, just after meeting Rudy, I started itching like crazy. He swore he cleaned his house too often to have bedbugs, but my arms and legs got torn up whenever I stayed with him, and then, after he slept over, I found one in my bed. I couldn't afford the three-thousand-dollar treatment so we pulled an all-nighter spraying my room down with alcohol, wiping picture frames and scrubbing book spines and cleaning every card in my wallet. It kind of worked for a few months, like we'd at least disarmed them in battle, but then I started itching again. At which point Rudy said I might as well just move in with him if I was going to be itchy either way. I agreed, the way I always did when it came to Rudy, saying to hell with everything—the same logic it turned out he was following himself, until the cops showed up at our door.

By the time I got to Stephen's house to talk about the doctor's diagnosis, his remorseful tone had vanished. "I've been doing some research," he said, sitting down with me after putting Zoe to bed.

"Let's hear it," I said.

It was the last functional moment we'd ever have.

"They came from Rudy."

I took a sip of wine to stall. "What?"

"Bedbugs, scabies, they thrive in institutional settings. Rudy was in an institutional setting. You can get them from skin-to-skin contact or sex, and I haven't had skin-to-skin contact with anyone but you and Z."

My cheeks burned at *skin-to-skin*, but I barreled past it. "I think the turn-around is too fast. And Rudy didn't have symptoms, and neither do I."

"I'm not saying it sounds probable," Stephen said. He was talking quickly, like this was a speech he'd mapped out in his head while turning a wrench at the shop. "I'm saying there are no other probable options." He spread his fingers wide on his knees. "The doctor says you can see the burrows if you look closely."

"The burrows?"

"Yeah, if the scabies got inside me."

I tried to look, but his shoulder was in the way.

"Well, Stephen," I said, "we talked about Rudy's visit. You agreed to it. Just because you regret it later—"

"Did I agree to everything that happened on Rudy's visit? *Everything*?"

He looked at me like he knew, like he could see past my eyes. But he couldn't, he fucking couldn't. Nobody could do that besides Rudy.

"Stephen," I said, "you can't ask me to eliminate everyone from my life except for you and your kid."

Stephen stared. "I'm *not* asking—"

"I mean, I have my own life to live."

Stephen dug his elbows into his knees. "Are you saying," he said slowly, "there's a chance Rudy might come back? To Richmond?"

"He just wants to clear up a couple misunderstandings about the past," I said. That was what Rudy had said on the phone: *I just want to clear up a couple misunderstandings about the past. I'll sleep on the sofa. I'll be in and out. Look up Frontier flights for me.*

Stephen's eyebrows furrowed so hard they formed a straight line. "Brooke, there is something you're not seeing."

"What do you mean?"

"It's like you're sleepwalking. It's common sense you can't bring your ex around without messing up the relationship you're in."

I thought of his wife in a psych ward for a full five months and twenty-nine days before he divorced her. He must be the one who wasn't seeing things clearly.

The clock ticked. Stephen spread his hands out again. He took his glasses off and put them back on.

The night that Rudy and I tried to get rid of the bedbugs, we ran out of rubbing alcohol at three a.m. and drove to CVS to get more. We'd already been there four hours earlier. Walking in, I caught a glimpse of us in the sliding glass doors, in wife beaters and basketball shorts, lips parched, hair askew. The cashier stared. I wondered what she thought we were doing with the alcohol. I wondered whether, if she knew the truth, it would make us more or less crazy in her eyes.

"Let's put a pin in this," Stephen said. "Okay? Let's get lunch tomorrow and figure this out."

But I kept hearing what he'd said before that: *There's something you're not seeing.*

I had thought, back when it was me and Rudy against the bedbugs, that he wanted to make something of himself. My mom said he seemed like a liar; "I know one when I see one," she said. But my mom had cheated on my dad for eight years, so who was to say she wasn't lying about Rudy, liar that she was? Or who was to say Rudy wouldn't stop lying, eventually? Or how could my mom know what was right for me anyway, since she'd skipped town when I was a freshman in high school and only came back to celebrate her own birthday?

And Rudy—Rudy told *me* he was applying to pharmacy tech jobs and wanted to move out of his uncle's house and get married. I didn't know he was skimming percs off the top of every CVS shipment and passing them off to a dealer. I didn't know that was where he got the money he used to treat me to Chili's and Applebee's. I didn't know that was why we got those looks, walking into CVS—the cashier recognizing him and putting two and two together. But did that fact negate what he'd always said, which was that he planned to be more successful than either of us could possibly imagine and he hoped I'd stick around for the ride?

It was confusing.

The next day, Stephen canceled our lunch date. He said he felt itchy when he thought about it.

"Is Zoe itchy?" I asked.

"No, she's not."

"Just you?"

"Brooke, I'm really pretty tired of talking about this."

After we hung up, I tried to think about how I felt and what I wanted, but instead I typed into Google, *can you carry scabies with no symptoms*. After reading for a while, I typed, *how fast can you transmit bedbugs*. Finally, *asymptomatic scabies or bedbug carrier*.

If you can brainstorm something just long enough to google it, you'll discover it already exists.

There were a lot of other things I should have googled then too, but I lost the energy for it. I wondered how much longer I had on the timeline before Stephen ended things. I wondered how to see things more clearly.

Maybe I did give you scabies, I texted Stephen, but he didn't respond.

5. The fifth theory isn't a theory because it never occurred to either of us. It's just the truth.

We weren't on speaking terms by the time Stephen's allergy test came back, but he texted me this: *I know it's been a while, but I just wanted you to know the problem wasn't scabies. I'm allergic to five distinct types of metals, rarely encountered in daily life, but commonly used in car engines. Hope that brings you some peace of mind.*

I responded: *Wow! What kinds of metals?*

But he didn't write back. Over the next day I kept looking at my phone, thinking the conversation might have inexplicably unfurled to greater lengths when I wasn't paying attention. Zoe had turned eight. How had her party gone? Had they taken that beach trip we'd been planning, and was she afraid of the waves? Did she still say *marshmallow* a lot, or did fewer things upset her now?

There was no way that was the final line of our relationship: *Wow! What kind of metals?* There had to be something else.

Finally, late that night, my phone buzzed and I grabbed it. But it was Rudy: *You check those Frontier flights yet?*

I looked at the bright screen. I looked at each tiny letter that formed each of Rudy's words. I typed: *N-O.*

Four seconds later, my phone buzzed again. *You don't want me to come? Or you haven't checked the flights?*

I studied the black squares of sky outside my window, how perfect they were, how precise. Faint trails of smoke circled my head; I sensed the blurriness descending, but I fought to keep it at bay. I glanced at the webs between my fingers, where the burrows would have been if they had ever existed, if it were possible to pinpoint the reason precious things go out of our lives. I didn't see anything. But I wasn't in direct light.

SARAH AZIZ

Matilda, the only thing that escapes this closet

is a teething dua: a prayer you feel flapping
like a bat inside your throat — eyes shrouded
but wings always molding into the spaces
between its Light's fingers. in the support
groups which you scroll through like a greedy
locust, you are told you should swim towards
America because they must not love you anymore
at home. your mother tears off her hair every morning
and your grandfather spills boiling tears over the blank
patches in her dreams. you rest your cheek against your
birthland, its soil creasing into your dark circles like a
cheap concealer. you know then, like your father leaving
home at seventeen only so that he could look behind to check
if someone was kneeling at the threshold. he never gave
you an answer and you knew not to ask. so, you stagger softly,
wondering if a jaanamaz would fit on this dingy
steel floor. it doesn't, but not every believer needs
a praying rug to clutch the air beneath God's feet.

If a Poem

—after Melissa Fite Johnson

If a poem resurrects, how many times
have I tried? I catch an earlier flight,
the day before, two days before—early
enough that he's still speaking when
I arrive. Early enough to know he hears
me when I say *I love you.* Early enough
he can say it back. If a poem is a time
machine, I back up further, to the day
his body plunged to pavement,
to the day his lung popped, his heart
bruised, his spleen tore. I back up to before
the paramedics arrived, before they couldn't
get the IV into his collapsed veins so they
crushed fentanyl and he snorted it. Let's
go back further, rewind a decade or two
or three. Let's go back to the diagnosis,
let's start intervention early, let's tweak
his diet, the drugs, the therapies. Let's
give him more than 73 years, let's give me
more than 41 years with him. If a poem
grants wishes, I want them all to say *father.*

Looking into Sunset

Watercolor, ink & acrylic on paper, 9x9 inches

This piece started with the blue in the upper left corner. My friend and I were playing around with paint and as soon as I put the paint on the canvas, my friend had to leave. I wasn't sure what to do with blue paint in the top corner as I wasn't used to using acrylic in a collage. So, I brought the canvas home and cut out the face of a Madonna from a photograph I had taken at a California Mission. I placed her where she asked to be, and built the rest of the collage around her, using whatever resources I had at home. She ended up "Looking into Sunset" and there she gazes for all time.

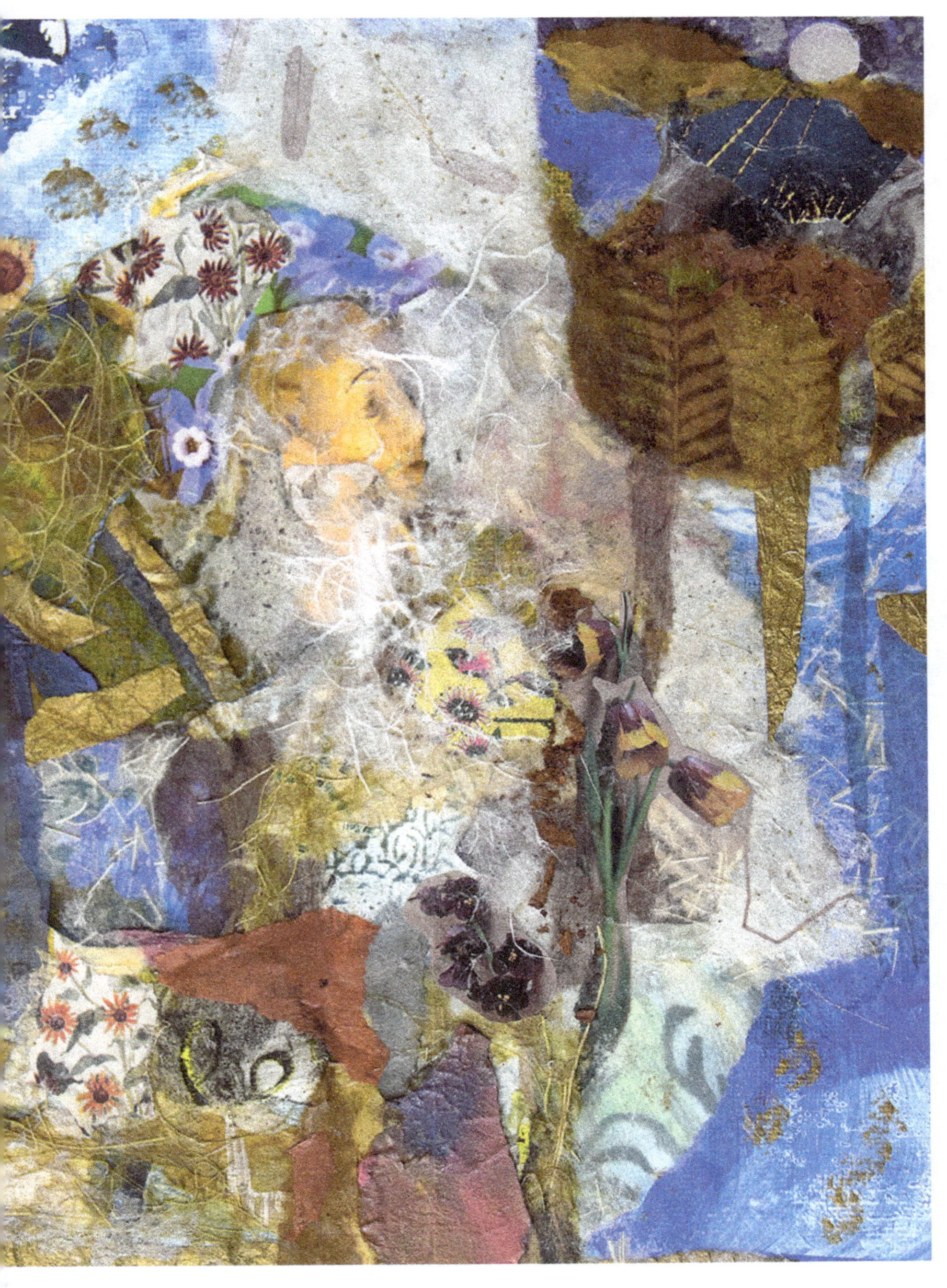

What are the plans for the weekend?

A Kenworth semi jack-knifed in front of me. I ran into it and was thrown from my car. In the air, I was okay. I landed in a ditch below the road and saw that my left leg was lying severed about four meters to the north.

This changes it, I thought. She won't threaten to leave me now.

The Kenworth's truckie came scrambling down the slope. 'Oh God. Oh Jesus,' he said. 'You're bleeding?'

'Your belt,' I said.

'What?'

'As a tourniquet.'

Considering my leg was shredded from above the knee, you'd have thought I'd be screaming. But no, it wasn't like that. What I felt—I felt like a loose plastic bag on the ground being dragged around by the wind.

A doctor arrived. Luckily he'd been passing by. Early thirties, stylish, the kind of guy you'd see on *The Bachelor*. He said, 'Are you allergic to anything?'

'Allergic?' I said, 'No. But I've felt better.'

'The blood,' said the truckie. 'There's so much blood.' The doctor frowned. Pints of me were pouring into the dirt. They can't stop it, theycan'tstoptheblood. Atleasttheyarewithme, at least they are with me. At least, they are with me, I thought. They will wait with me.

'I'm going to die,' I said.

'No,' said the doctor. But the way he said no, it meant maybe.

'I need to call my wife,' I said. 'She should know.'

The doctor looked at me. You know when you see love in someone's eyes? Just a human love, the love for people? He had that. He dialed my phone and held it to my ear.

She was in the car with the kids.

'Where are you?' she said.

I wasn't ready for that.

'Look,' she said. 'I need you to go to swimming and get Jason, okay?'

'Hon,' I said.

'Well, I've got to go to the dog appointment!'

I was going to tell her I was in the ditch, that was my plan, but there was this tension between us, this raw fragility, and the timing was bad. School pick-up was a shitfight. The dog was sick, it had swallowed something. The afternoon witching hour was near. The kids were fighting. In her voice was mild fear and panic, all in a tone reserved for me. But I heard her younger self too, under the tone, the woman I'd fallen for.

'Why are you breathing so heavy?' she said. 'Are you on the toilet?'

The doctor took his shirt off and used it to improve the tourniquet on my thigh. It was MacGyverish. The guy was wise and he looked like he had a great diet, and he was good under pressure, calm when calm was needed, and I loved him. I loved him via an admiration for him. Was it love? It was a kind of love.

'I'm sorry,' I said to my wife 'All the things with us are—'

'Hang on.' She yelled at the kids to shut up. Something about one of them having the pencil first. It was difficult to separate the kids when they were like that, about the fucking pencils, you had to divert them. My wife said, 'Tell daddy about Jane.' Our six-year-old was having trouble with Jane.

I heard my daughter through a filter that was like a five-beer drunkenness. Not all of me was there. Though the part that feared death was; that part was present. 'Stand up to bullies,' I said. 'You'll be scared, but it's not cowardice.' Did she know what cowardice was? She said it was the opposite of being strong.

The truckie was up on the road, watching for the ambulance. 'It's coming,' he yelled.

'Who's coming?' said my wife.

'No one,' I said. 'Keep talking.'

'Huh?'

'What are the plans for the weekend?'

I didn't follow her reply, though I think my promise to stain the porch was mentioned.

'I love you,' I said.

She got quiet.

We hardly ever said I love you. We had a new rule about it though, to say it once a week. A rule I hadn't followed because I thought it was kinda bogus, up until I said it and it became real. Because when you don't say it for a long time, then besides the other person wondering if you love them, you might start to wonder if you do or you might just forget. So it's a good reminder, to say it.

'Here's the ambulance,' said the doctor.

'What ambulance?' said my wife.

But that's all I remember.

At the hospital they gave me a prosthetic leg. A plastic composite. They told me the Kenworth truckie was on speed, and he got fined. I'm not sure who got the money. The doctor visited me and we got to know each other. He was from Iran. He had saved many people from death and he'd learned to let them go after saving them. Because you had to do that, if you were a doctor. We stayed in touch for a while. I loved him, maybe it was only heat-of-the-moment love, but for a moment in that ditch it felt like the engraved love I have for my father. My wife said it was understandable that feelings changed because we had that happen too. Our love was always slipping away and then returning in a rush, we'd remember it and forget it and have to resurrect it again and again. And now when I call her, the first thing she says is, 'Tell me right now if you're dying in a ditch?'

Mouth

I stopped begging my beautiful mother to smile in photos
after I learned that her teeth fell out while she carried me.
The aftermath of genocide, she says. *My starving six year old
body.* Twenty years later, my mother still has to give her teeth
in exchange for my existence. She spends six thousand dollars
on my braces when I am ten. I obsessively brushed
my four front teeth five times a day for years so they
would always be white. This is a life we stupidly think
we can outrun. Still, the dentist tells me when I am twenty
that my white teeth will soon be nothing but nubs
if I don't stop grinding them. In childhood, my doctor warned
she's grinding her teeth from stress! My mother asked, *What stress?*
I am not starving. But from inheritance, I chew holes
through five prescribed mouth guards. I wake and watch
my teeth sharpen smaller by the minute. It's sickening
how this devotion to survival almost feels like devotion to fear.
How I wrap my floss around my fingers every day and see my gums
bleed.

JULIE WEISS

View From Our First Floor Apartment

An unidentified noise stalks
our home, bearded as a freshly freed
convict, wavering on the cusp
of madness, in search of a childhood memory

gasping, as if for air, or blood.
They hear it, too. I tuck them
in protective plush promises
then scuffle until morning with ghost

children, whose windows and doors
once let in more than a breeze.
There are no bodies rotting
in the woods behind our house,

I say nightly in the language
of forehead kisses and fairy smiles.
Boot soles aren't sticky enough
to scale a brick wall,

but my children cling to me anyway,
willing us to the third floor.
When I say *I'll keep you safe*,
what I mean is, I'd move tomorrow.

I want to believe our neighbors
are rearranging furniture.
That the alarm's siren would,
like a baseball bat, shatter

an intruder's stride. That
my children will never haunt
the graveyard of future parents´ dreams.

Young Snakes

My daughters make young snakes
      from the lilac yarn
           they dip into bathwater,
watching them become floss
              and wearing them as if hair

      I scoop each child from the water
and perch behind their blonde heads,
working the brush's bristles through
until I hit a knot
      and do the hurtful work
of separation

I am turned to stone
      with every ratted tangle,
         their small crowns whipping out of reach
from the pulling pain

My hand hovers in air
to release the stolen strands
let loose from their roots,
limp serpents
blending into the woodgrain
      like blonde scales hidden in sand

I imagine their hair as fierce vipers
fanged against the warm-blooded world,
and some days it is impossible
not to feel complicit
in the erosion of power

each girl first holds inside the nest of her body,

until it hardens into stone and drops
from the body like a severed head

I Dream of Produce

Sophomore year I fell in love with Theresa. She wore maroon lipstick, faded black T-shirts that fell short of her belly button. We grew close after meeting in English class. She was the only one who talked to me. I listened with an acute attention. She told me no one had ever listened to her the way I did. I found myself consumed with her, consumed by her. Theresa was a fan of video games and orange gin liquors and was ashamed of her sexuality because her mother would accuse her of promiscuity as a young girl.

She was perfect.

In being around her, I started to become perfect. At night, I woke up from foreign dreams and was confused if I was her or myself. I soon loved the same video games, understood the operatic beauty of distant planets and the plights of ancient alien species. My jaw became larger in the mirror, although I could only see this in certain lights. My hair began to curl, just like hers, tendril by tendril.

When I was a child, I tried to remain separate and distinct, but inevitably, I absorbed the other kids' habits and mannerisms. They thought I was weird, an unwanted presence hovering at the edge of the school yard. I embraced this process with Theresa. My brown irises were flecked with lighter shades, closer to her hazel. I felt lighter and warmer as I shed myself and absorbed her details. Biting my lip just like she did whenever she concentrated. Daydreaming about places I had never been but Theresa had visited; remembering the trickle of Amsterdam's watery channels, the charcoal-damp of Oregon air.

Like the others, she began to sense something she didn't like. I wanted Theresa, all of her. I wanted to jump out of my skin and become her. Spring semester, she stopped answering my texts and calls. It was over. Sinking, I collapsed back into myself.

Three months later I got a late-night text: *I hope you are well. I see you around campus all by yourself. I want good things for you. I was sad you stopped coming to English. I always loved your insights, like what you said about dramatic irony,*

I didn't know how to respond. She wanted understanding, she wanted affirmation, and I provided what she craved and was therefore indispensable. It hadn't occurred to me that what I knew in my heart about her might have been wrong.

* * *

After dropping out of college, I rented a studio in the northwest outskirts of the city, taking the rickety QR train to the suburban supermarket I work in. I manage the fruit and vegetable section. With sheer gloves, I monitor the produce for freshness. Nothing softened or browned, no breeding grounds for the fruit fly larvae. Useless, disgusting insects, burrowing to the core of things and multiplying their tiny bodies and frantic wings.

The QR is unreliable, so I make sure to take the earliest train available. On the cracked leather seats, I watch other commuters in their morning silence, heads nodding to music from tiny earbuds, legs jiggling. My ears perk up, trying to hear their music too. My vision blurs as I briefly see through their eyes, slip out of my skin and into theirs. Sometimes I have the urge to grab these strangers, scream in their faces, reach inside of them and discover what they are made of, so that I can be as real as they are.

There are weeks in which my own body doesn't feel real at all, like these hands are someone else's hands, my face a video game, an alien thing in the mirror. I yearn for the sights and smells of my produce. I am so lonely.

* * *

It's easy to slip out of my skin. I am fascinated with the idea of transformation. Alchemy. Tin willing itself to become gold. The alchemist imagining the very properties of gold itself, understanding it cell by cell.

Learning each chemical reaction required, the right variables and catalysts. Combustion and synthesis and decomposition.

Theresa told me I was like a ghost. Sneaking up behind her without a word, observing silently from corners. Before she stopped talking to me, she claimed she didn't know me at all; what to get me for my birthdays, what movies I liked. I'm not surprised. If we hadn't hung out for a few days, she might pass me on campus without recognizing me, as everyone else did. I am difficult to remember, to notice, to pin down.

* * *

Maintenance of the produce section is not just a matter of appearance. It is about understanding the truest form of the produce. I recheck everything throughout the day. Produce should be not just edible, but bright, bursting; it must perform on the tongue. Temperatures need to be logged, moisture maintained and deterred. There is a constant rearrangement of shapes and colors. These are scientific variables.

I hold the canary yellow lemons, the bristling bloom of broccoli. I am always hungry during my shift, always forgetting to eat breakfast in my rush to get to the store. I hunger for the vibrancy of the produce. Their curves, their feel. Glossy and fuzzed, firm and spiked. Substantial. A furtive sniff of the day's fresh oranges. I want to grow into someone juicy, the best of the crop, something to be painted in still life, consumed, ripe but not yet rotted. Something not human, but grown and plentiful.

I have been buying out all the reduced-price oranges, spending my evenings feeling their textures and topography. After peeling the fruit until my fingertips prune, I eat dinners of citrus. I am enjoying the peace of being away from others. I can focus on beauty and form and physicality. The orange's round, dynamic globe seeps into my consciousness.

My flesh is becoming ridged underneath my fingertips. The underbelly of my arm polishes to a slick shine. My pale brown is now imbued with shades of auburn and ginger and canary-yellow, sometimes like jaundice, other times like the pulsing of a sunrise from within my core. Night after night I stare at the bowl of glistening oranges on my kitchen table, under the single lightbulb, the buzz of the AC unit behind me.

* * *

One weekend, I drive to an orange grove and sneak through the gates at night. It is right before the harvest. There is a buzz unlike anything I have heard before. Lying down on damp ground, surrounded by fallen oranges, I shiver in unison with the tree and its fruit. Water is being sucked from iron-rich soil, seeping through cell walls, up the flesh of the tree, inside the branches and into the dangling spheres. I lie there all night, twisting and expanding. When I wake up, a farmer is screaming at me. I am naked, my belly rounded and firm, and my hips widened. As I run, I reach up and touch plump cheeks. I am light as air, as if my body is made up of tendrils of fiber and sweet juice. A sound like waves pulses in my ears.

* * *

Customers require my assistance. I can imagine their lives as they meander through the bright aisles. Hair still damp from a hurried shower; a shimmering, treasured bracelet; an anticipated call taken; a harried scramble to reel in a child. I believe I can discern if they want cauliflower or peaches, asparagus or zucchini, spinach or a particular apple in the cacophony of varieties.

Garlic, onions, and potatoes fall under my purview. Durable. Earthen. Fingernail underneath the purpling flakes of red onion skin, and I am reminded of my family home. Brittle flakes fall, a slice and a sting in the air, my own tears dripping down into my mouth, salt-wound on my tongue. I back away. Onions last for ages. I should enjoy their layers, demanding to be opened, but there is a brutality to them.

* * *

In the early hours, I am amongst the first workers. Shipments arrive from their long journeys. Picking up yellow-tinged orange, I imagine the produce blooming within its seed, its embryonic expansion; breaking through its shell, towards its tender unripe innocence, unbrushed, unkissed, still on the cusp. Eventually, the fruit is plucked. Sometimes before it is ready, sometimes a bit too late, sometimes just when it is yearning to be separated from itself. Then the long journey elsewhere, waiting to be consumed or discarded. This is the cycle I observe amongst produce and people. People are ripe objects; they eat or are eaten.

It is while repricing produce, saving them as they teeter towards their demise, that I notice the orange blush radiant across my full cheeks in a reflective surface. Usually, these changes rise when I am consumed, then fade after a few hours. Now, I find the orange's qualities lingering within me. The orange is a symbol of something holy, a fertile joy, a citrus complexity. At the end of the day, I usually carry the various scents of produce, but now, I smell only of oranges, bright and sharp.

My belly softens. By my next menstrual cycle, something sticky and fragrant comes out of me. I am more pliant, and plump, looking healthier than ever.

I've started wearing sunglasses at all times, as my eyes are tinted translucent shades of reddish orange. Too many comments about being ill or high. Perhaps I am pushing it too far. My breath is citrus. My joints feel more supple, as if my cartilage is squishy and porous, and I wonder if I can bend my arms in new directions. I sit still all evening, waking up in the early hours of the morning with a gasp. I push myself further, to an edge I didn't realize was there. It is getting harder to move within this strange rind. My insides squelch, my organs now circulating juices and pulp.

* * *

Theresa steps into the store. Theresa, her frizzing curls and long neck and now dark green lipstick, roaming before the spinach and kale and celery. The fine mist turns on over her face. She hops back and gives a blank smile. My juicy pulse reverberates through my eardrums. What is she doing here, in this grocery store miles away from campus. A man, broad-shouldered and wavy haired, lingers in the background.

"We're looking for okra."

"Are you?" I whisper.

I sidle closer. Despite the summer heat, I'm wearing the long-sleeved version of the grocery store uniform to cover my rippled orange skin. I sweat citrus. In the hollow light of the grocery store, I see Theresa looking more beautiful than I remember.

She turns to me. "Making a new dish for my boyfriend. Forcing him try something new. What do you suggest?" She smiles. It's a smile she reserves for strangers. She doesn't recognize me.

Her smile fades as she squints, as if recalling a childhood dream, deciphering a moment of deja vu, trying to see if the dark shape in the corner is shadow or ghost. I am nothing to hold onto, as I have always been. Dizzy, I lean on the nearest display stand. She peers down at me, confused. Turning, I look at the oranges which seem to sing out their presence.

My vision blurs as the world is covered in an orange sheen. I'm ripened, ready. My clothes feel tighter and tighter, then rip at the seams. Stumbling back, Theresa's mouth opens and elongates into a wide, open O. Her cry is violin-sharp, then muffled as I hear only the squelch of pulp in my head. Inside of me, things stretch and distend; membranes are pulled, cavities are filled.

As the world wavers, figures gather around, their details blurring. The edges of Theresa's hair seem to flare and coalesce, just so. Green? I've missed her so much. Yes, her hair is green. There, the fanning emerald leaves of the orange tree. Her neck grows longer, longer. Her boyfriend stands still, so still, skin hardening into a bark. I can no longer make out expressions, or features, just familiar shapes. Theresa's arms bend outwards into supple branches. I bloom out of her. Customers and employees hover nearby, transforming into roots and branches and this sacred fruit.

I shudder and pulse. I cry citrus.

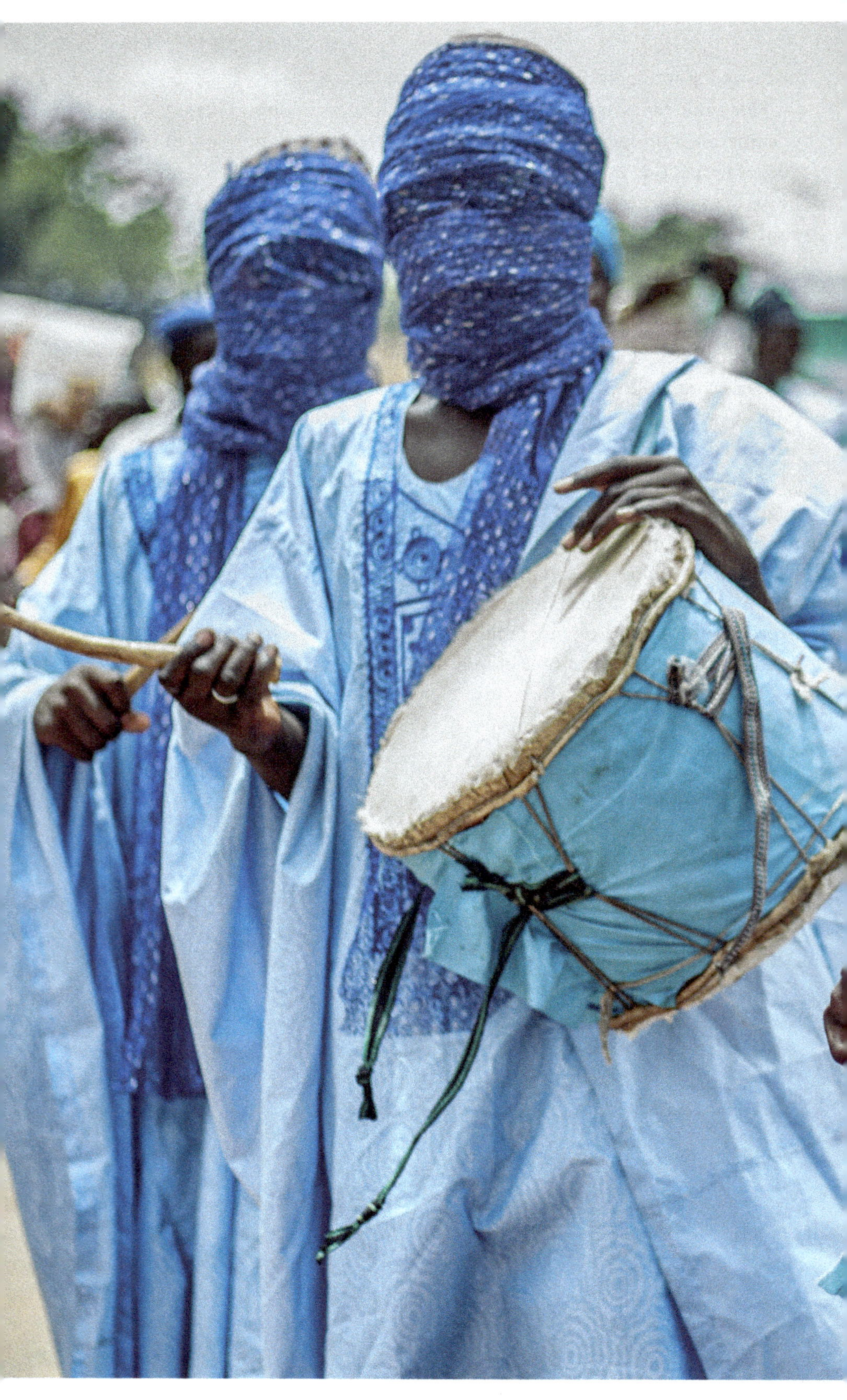

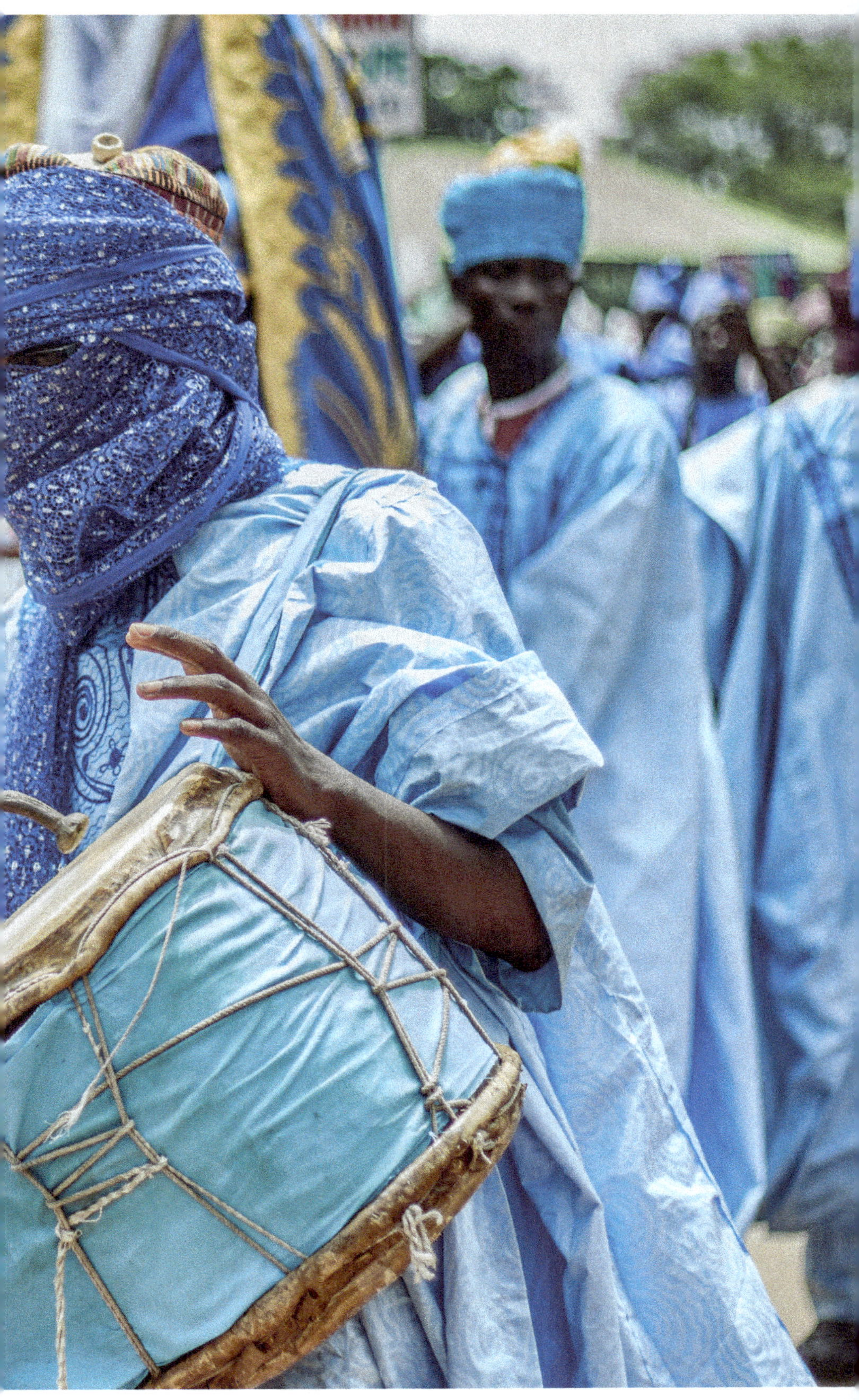

The Masked Nupe Drummers

Photography, Bida, Niger state, Nigeria
1500x1004 pixels, 2022
(Previous Page)

The Masked Nupe Drummers are a traditional musical group from the Nupe people of Nigeria. They are known for their unique style of drumming and their striking costumes with faces covered with silky materials and brightly colored robes.

The Nupe people have a long and rich history of music and dance, and the Masked Nupe Drummers are one of the most renowned examples of this tradition. They use a variety of drums and percussion instruments to create complex rhythms and melodies, accompanied by singing and chanting.

The drummers themselves are highly skilled musicians who have dedicated years of their lives to mastering the art of drumming. They are known for their precision and their ability to create complex rhythms that are both hypnotic and mesmerizing.

Drummers are an important part of Nupe culture and are often seen performing at weddings, Sallah festivals, and other important ceremonies.

Self-Portrait as Chihuly Macchia

Chihuly Garden and Glass, 2023

If the body is an archive of glass & breath
& air, if beauty

        doesn't have to be functional,

then maybe I can take up space in this room.
I've never been functional, but I was pretty
& might still remember how to expand
to meet the scale of my desires.

Might remember how to pour like honey
& swirl like a girl's skirt, remember
how to shape-shift on simple human breath.
Heat & air & furnace, endless
immutability of form. If calm & contrast,
then three hundred colors might carry me.

If I'm only alive when I don't know
       what I'm doing,
alive when I don't know
       if I will break,

then let me push the boundaries of thinness
& collapsibility, let me pour my breath
into the narrow pipe of this life,
into expand & expanse.

If I don't shatter,
I could settle into something beautiful.

Deborah

I see it circling your eyes, that proneness to reduce my bones to ash.
You can go on. Pick up the match; begin from my thinning hair, where
a flame is quicker to be conceived.

—Samuel Adeyemi

—For Deborah

I enter memory through
its mouth—that round, purple
orifice where God is nothing but
a shift in language, a war for
supremacy. I see you gap-tooth girl.
Your flesh lit with fire. Your bones
brimming with napalm—a casualty of
this war. At sermon, the pastor said we
must burn for God. I cannot help but
imagine this was what he meant.
The way your hair became one with the fire.
The way your bones crackled like dry woods
in the roar of amber flame.
I am sorry I could do nothing.
I had nothing to gift you except poems.
What use is my poetry if it cannot save a life?
I hid behind the sun-kissed tree and watched.
The birds were silent, air was black and quiet.
Everything was mourning. The dust, laced with
marigold fear, did not lift a finger.
I waited for rain. For the merciful tears of God to wash
your flesh into gold—something beautiful

enough to survive fire.
A friend once told me life is a sentence. If to end
a sentence, a punctuation is required, then the
fire was a full stop, the way a full stop is closure. Deborah,
look how they ended you. Look how they sutured
you like a sickle cuts through a sprouting pumpkin.
How the moon eclipses the sun and the day is
no longer day again.

Cycles

One more thing that she hated about Phil was how he always had to put on a show. They were only at The Compass, but he kept looking behind Cassie's head to see if anyone was watching. To make sure they did, he was wearing a T-shirt that showed his biceps, his lion tattoo poking out of one sleeve. The overhead heaters burned the top of Cassie's head, her legs covered by one of the blankets the pub gave out. Cigarette smoke clouded the air as people walked past them on West End Lane, easing through the gaps between the small outside tables and the road. When the waitress brought their drinks over, Cassie saw that she was pregnant. Around five months, from the looks of it. Cassie felt a lurching surprise, as if someone had appeared without her noticing, to prod her hard between her shoulder blades. The waitress stretched across Cassie to put Phil's beer down next to him and her belly brushed the table, close to Cassie's face.

This was all Cassie needed. Phil already kept grinning at her meaningfully, trying to kiss her every time she came close enough. He kept bringing up memories of when they'd first got together and asking, his lips twitching at the corners, whether she wanted him to take his gym equipment out of the spare bedroom. Phil asked the waitress when she was due, his gloved hand twitching on Cassie's jeans. Cassie took out her phone and scrolled through Instagram. The waitress was having a baby at the end of March, which Phil agreed was an excellent time to give birth. She looked very well, he said. The waitress' eyes flicked to Cassie's. She must have thought Phil was flirting with her. People often looked at Cassie in this way, as if to ask for an explanation for what Phil said or did. They didn't realise Phil's behaviour was usually to make some sort of point.

'Could we get the bill?' she asked the waitress, who nodded and moved away through the closely packed tables.

'We just got our drinks,' Phil said. To prove it, he raised his beer and took a slow sip. He watched the waitress over the rim. 'She won't be here long. In her condition.'

'Doesn't look like it.'

'Would you want to work at five months? It must be heavy.'

'I don't know.'

'You need energy for teaching. And you'd have to lug those books around. Sandra Coleman got a doctor's note when she was six months, didn't she?'

'Because she was high risk.'

'And no one was going to miss an art teacher much, were they?' She could feel him looking at her. His voice bubbled with excitement. 'Are you pregnant?'

'Pregnant?' It was almost a relief he'd asked. Still, the word sent faint reverberations through her skull. She dug the tips of her fingers into the table. It rocked under the pressure, one leg shorter than the other. Phil looked poised to reach over and pull her into his arms, sweeping their glasses off the table. 'It's too soon to tell,' she said.

He sank back into his seat. 'You're four days late.'

She kept her voice even. 'I told you not to count.'

'Of course I've been counting. How could I not? Four days! That's an excellent sign, Cassie.'

The waitress came over with the card reader, and Phil pulled out his card—as he always did, though their bank account was shared—and tapped it against the screen. It leaked a faint light onto his hands. She scraped her chair back while he was waiting for their receipt. She heard footsteps behind her and turned to see Phil adjusting the ends of his long wool coat. Even he had to accept that away from the heaters, it was too cold to show off his arms.

'That was dramatic,' he said.

'Dramatic?' She snorted. 'You're one to talk.' Her legs felt slow and heavy, a painful tugging in her groin. They'd said to expect that, from all the hormones. She couldn't walk as quickly as she was used to. All her jumpers were tight. Phil fell into step beside her, and hope sputtered in her stomach. She willed it still. Phil reached for her hand and squeezed it. There were his familiar callouses from lifting weights, rough against her palm.

'We have tests, don't we? You can take one when we get home.'

'We've run out.'

'Let's go to Boots.' He glanced at his watch. He picked up his pace and she jerked his hand. She opened her mouth to speak and closed it again. Phil twisted to look at her and ran his thumb over her fingers. She tugged at his hand and they continued walking. Her boots clacked on the street. She counted their steps and her heart beat slowed, and she felt able to say, steadily, 'I'm only four days late. Don't get your hopes up.'

'My hopes are up, Cassie, and there's nothing wrong with that. I told you, it just takes time. Didn't I tell you that?'

'Maybe.'

'How many weeks would it be?' He counted on his fingers. 'Four weeks? You would be four weeks pregnant?'

It would be four weeks, three days. Cassie fumbled for her keys. She remembered sitting in the clinic waiting room, sharing the space with the high-risk pregnancy patients, most of them pregnant with twins. The women sprawled against the grey plastic chairs, backs arched, legs spread, bellies to the ceiling, and Phil stared at them so unashamedly it made her wish he hadn't come. She couldn't stand the sight of the receptionists clacking on their computers, their sympathetic smiles. She shouldn't have to be there, needing help that, as it turned out, wasn't helpful at all. Giving urine samples and doing blood tests and ultrasounds, monitoring her blood pressure. These countless tests where there was nothing she could do to make sure she passed.

Phil opened the front door and flicked on the lights. As they shrugged off their coats, he said, 'You know, Cassie. Being pregnant suits you.'

He caught her by her waist and though she felt sharp irritation at his optimism, his naivety, she wanted to believe him. She was four days late. They had given her hormones for a reason. Maybe they had worked this time. Her stomach was tender, her breasts hurt when she put on her bra. Those were signs, weren't they? She felt a rush of excitement. There could soon be a buggy in this hallway. They would curse when they stepped on rattles, barefoot. There would be muslins and milk bottles on the oak-wood coffee table, which Phil would complain about, while cheerfully tidying up.

Cassie laughed. 'Am I glowing?'

'Absolutely.' He held her at arm's length and squinted. 'I can see it. You with a huge belly.'

'Waddling about.'

'You'll look great.'

'You're going to talk to my belly, aren't you?'

'Not only that. I'll play him Mozart.' He reached under her jumper and trailed his fingers over her stomach. 'He'll come out singing.'

'Him?'

'Or her.'

'It's a her.'

'Her, then.'

They were both grinning. Their faces were close together. He closed the gap, tilting his chin to kiss her.

She wrapped her arms around his neck. Phil's fingers slid to her rib-cage, to the wire underneath her bra, and she felt a twinge of desire, low in her stomach. Sometimes, Cassie's mind wandered when they had sex. Phil's heavy breathing, hot against her ear, irritated her, or a car hooting outside reminded her that she had left the shopping in the car. Scheduling sex killed the mood; the lights too bright outside the curtains, Phil's tracksuit bottoms discarded on the floor, an Amazon delivery interrupting them part way through and still having to finish what they'd started. This time, though, when they thudded up the stairs to the bedroom, everything seemed to slot together; his tongue in her mouth, the coarse hair on his legs against hers, his belly flat on her own. Cassie pressed her fingers into his back, the other hand gripping the headboard, concentrating only on the building rhythm of their movements.

Afterwards, Phil dropped his head onto the pillow. 'We could have multiples, now,' he murmured when the lights were off.

Surely, he knew the timing didn't work like that? And even then, the chances of IVF producing twins were still less than ten percent. He must be joking. But before she could ask, his breathing slowed. He had already fallen asleep.

Cassie was taller than Phil, and judging by his Instagram profile, not his type. That hadn't put her off. She had picked him out on the first teacher induction day at school, as she sat in the auditorium with Marie, the other history teacher. It was time for something serious and she liked how he threw his head back when he laughed, how it rang across the staffroom. When she found out he taught geography, she nearly changed her mind. It felt like too much of a cliché; she could imagine the other teachers nodding knowingly when they heard they were together, those jokes about how they completed each other. Still, she did some digging and learned he'd been to Cambridge. When they walked to lessons, he opened every door for her in the long school corridors. The students all raved about his classes. When she was sure, she asked the gossipy teachers whether he was single. Men liked to think these things were their decision. Phil declared he was head over heels and after a while, she'd tumbled with him. It was a year before she realised how exhausting he was, the way he sprang from elation to anger and back again in a matter of seconds.

After they got married, Phil insisted they spent weekends with his friends. Most of them had kids, their wives pregnant with a second, and none of the women worked. At Scott's barbecue in June, the men stood apart like a separate tribe, reminiscing about their Cambridge days when they had shaved Yannis' legs or Dominic had been so drunk, he had left the Ferrari with the keys in somewhere on the Newmarket Road, and had never seen it again. Annie sat in the shade, breastfeeding, complaining about milk stains on her dress and showing Cassie her crown, where her hair was falling out. When Cassie looked around for Phil, he caught her eye and shouted across the garden whether she wanted to go away on the 22nd, which was the exact date of their next treatment, if the one they were doing didn't work. And she realised he'd forgotten and though he came to every appointment, including the blood tests, and helped decide which clinic and what doctor, she felt resentment so strong, it was as if her belly was burning. That he could stand there, falling about with laughter on Scott's shoulder, that he fell asleep within minutes whilst she lay awake, staring into the dark. That it was her being probed and examined and injecting needles into her stomach, having her eggs extracted and frozen and inserted again as embryos. That when it came down to it, it was her problem.

After the barbecue, when she was home and had showered the smell of meat off her, she decided it must have been the hormones making her emotional. They'd stopped having sex much outside of ovulation by then, but she lay her head against Phil's shoulder and felt the anger leech away until she felt nothing. Until all she felt was her heart fluttering weakly against her chest.

When she sat down on the toilet the next morning, her knickers were dark with blood. It soaked the toilet paper and stained the bowl. Her legs shuddered, jerking up and down on the toilet seat, goose pimples pricking from the cold. After a while, she flushed the toilet and washed her knickers out in the sink until the blood ran clear, then threw them in the wash and changed her underwear and put in a pad. The washing machine cycled round and she thought about how Calvin had been chosen as deputy head instead of her, though the headmistress had told her months before that an interview was just a formality. By the time she'd applied, she'd missed a lot of days because of her treatments. Phil appeared in the doorway of the lounge, eating an apple.

'Don't you have a lesson?'

'Not yet.'

'I have Year 10,' he said. 'If they were going to fail their GCSEs before, morning P.E. should finish them off. They come in, reeking out the classroom. I can barely teach, even with all the windows open. It's like the shower is an alien concept.'

'Yup.'

Phil crunched his apple. 'Their heads are full of sediment. If only they knew what that was.'

She had heard that joke before and didn't smile, though Phil didn't seem to mind. He checked out his biceps in the window's reflection, probably hoping people passing would glance up and see him. The girls at school giggled when he folded his arms in his tight shirts. Sometimes, they wolf-whistled when they saw the two of them getting into the car to drive home. 'Surprise,' he said, throwing something next to Cassie on the couch. 'Go do it, now. Then we can really celebrate.'

She glanced down. It was a pregnancy test. Something cold and oily slid in her stomach.

'I found one in the bathroom cabinet,' he said. 'Do it and at least we'll have it over and done with. This is it, Cassie, I told you.'

She felt a strange sensation, as if the back of the couch was melting away and she was sinking into it. Next year she would be thirty-nine, which was the age she had planned to have two kids, become headmistress, and five years after that, move onto a bigger school. There was no point telling Phil, because he knew all that, and because she knew how he would respond, which would be to tell her to step away from teaching or if she wanted to work, to go part time. Why was she putting all that pressure on herself?

She looked around the living room, at the cream carpet and bay windows. In the kitchen, the integrated dishwasher was pulled open, the glasses gleaming in rows. If she went to the window, she would see two men in grey suits, eating breakfast at Paige's bakery, gloved hands wrapped around takeaway cups. Next month, she would have to sit in a pale blue gown hitched over her hips, her legs in stirrups, whilst the doctor made jokes to get her to feel comfortable. He would insert the catheter and afterwards, she'd wipe the gel off with rough paper tissues.

Tomorrow, Phil would stand in the lounge eating an apple and they would watch the morning news and teach their lessons and moan about their students. In the evening, they would make pasta Bolognese because they had to use up the mince before it went bad. And they would watch the news again and shake their heads at the inflation rates but neither of them would mention her period or the fact that she wasn't getting pregnant and maybe never would. The air in the lounge was hot and stale. In the utility room, the washing machine chugged. There was a buzzing in her ears. 'I'm going out,' she said.

'Don't you have a lesson?'

'I don't care.'

'Shouldn't you get dressed for school? You won't be in Maggie's good books if you skive off.' Phil aimed his apple at the bin and it bounced in. 'Still, you might make the rest of us look good for a change.'

She felt him looking at her. 'What is it? If you don't want to take the pregnancy test now, don't. It's your body.'

She laughed, though it came out as a sort of hoot. 'It's my body. You're right. I'm never taking a pregnancy test again.'

'What does that mean?'

'It means I'm never taking one again.' Her voice was thin and high, not like hers at all. But saying the words filled her with a strange sort of euphoria. She jolted upright on the sofa, hugging her knees. 'I'm never taking one again,' she repeated.

'Why are you shouting?'

'I'm just telling you. We get the same result, again and again. It doesn't matter what I do. Whether you drink or how much progesterone they give me, if we do the transfer on day twelve or thirteen. It's a waste of time.'

'Cassie,' Phil said. He raked a hand through his hair. 'It's biology. It has to work. It's a process. It takes time.' He sat on the edge of the sofa and put a hand on her leg. 'If you don't want to do a test at home, go into the clinic.'

She gave another short laugh. 'Thank you for the scientific explanation. It's a good job you're a geography teacher, I might never have worked that out.'

Phil's eyes flickered over her uneasily. 'We're not having a baby.' Cassie meant to say it calmly but her voice broke on the words. 'We're never going to have one. So, you needn't worry about missing any more trips with the boys.'

Phil's hand tensed on her leg. Tears sprang to his eyes, and she felt exhausted by his disappointment, how it reflected hers. Was she going to watch him fight back tears and find new optimism for both of them, for another month, another year? 'You got your period.'

'We gave it a good go,' she said. 'Two years. Not many people could've done it.'

'I'm so sorry, Cassie,' he said, his hand stroking her thigh. 'We'll call the clinic. Book the next one in. I'm so sorry.'

'This is the last time. I'm done.' She pushed his hand off her leg. She walked to the window, gazing down at the street. It was raining, the dull sky streaked with white. The men in grey suits were huddling under the bakery's overhang. A sudden idea seized her. 'Maybe I'll go away,' she said. 'I haven't been away for so long.'

'We can go at Christmas.'

'I'm not waiting until then. Maybe there's a flight tomorrow.'

Phil's nostrils flared. He was like a horse getting agitated. She could practically see him rearing his hind legs. He had no in-between. He went from calm to sad to angry in the space of a minute. 'We're in the middle of the school year. What about the next cycle?'

'I want somewhere hot.' She snatched up her phone and began googling. She had succeeded in making Phil speechless, a rare feat. 'The Seychelles,' she said. 'I've always wanted to go there.' She showed him her screen, with pictures of green hills, empty beaches, turquoise skies and seas. 'Heaven. Imagine. Cocktails on the beach instead of the same old drizzle, day in, day out.'

'You're just in shock,' Phil said. 'You'll feel differently tomorrow. Of course we're doing another treatment.'

'You do it,' she said. She zoomed in on beach huts, a wooden plank leading into still water. 'You take progesterone and inject yourself in the bum.' A bronzed couple held hands, faces lifted towards each other, the woman's white dress fluttering in the breeze. 'I'm going to the Seychelles.'

'If I were doing it, we would be pregnant by now,' he muttered. Phil didn't mutter; he shouted or exclaimed. He must have known he was saying something he shouldn't. She felt a spike of anger so strong, for a moment she couldn't see. She'd always known he blamed her. That he thought, somehow, it was her fault.

'Why's that?'

'I'm just saying,' his voice rose the way it did when he started a lesson, 'these things can be psychological.'

'Meaning?'

'Meaning, you know, that if you decide next month isn't going to work, it most likely won't. So, it follows, doesn't it?' His words blended together in a rush. 'Scott told me about his friend from work whose wife had issues so she went to this centre for women who had fertility problems where they did breathing and acupuncture. And all different types of massages. She got pregnant the next month and now they have three kids.'

'If you'd have told me this was all in my head two years ago, it really would've helped.'

'You approach it like an Ofsted inspection— '

'Fascinating,' she said. 'I thought it was science, not acupuncture. Where's this magical centre?'

'—cutting out dairy and taking vitamins, trying to tick all the boxes. God forbid we have a drink! The problem's up here.' He tapped his head with two fingers. 'You can't handle it when you don't get what you want.'

'Don't hold back, Phil.'

'I'm just saying.'

'That it's my fault. You think it's my fault.'

She was towering above Phil, who was perched on the arm of the sofa. Her breathing was fast and hard. His nostrils flared again and she felt a burst of satisfaction.

'We should have started trying years ago,' he said. Her stomach hurt. She had a headache. 'All this obsession with being headmistress. There are more important things, Cassie. And now look what's happened.'

She thought of her baby girl, because of course she would have a girl, kicking inside her stomach, her belly rippling with the force of it. Phil feeling it, laughing. She didn't want his hands on her stomach, or anywhere near her. These arguments, boomeranging, while she was pregnant. Forever. The same cream walls, the red-wine stain on the carpet, the electric fireplace they never switched on.

'You've never had to work for anything,' she said. 'I've never had

Daddy's money to fall back on.'

'I've never heard you complaining,' he said.

They knew their lines by heart. He looked up at her, chest puffed out. His eyes were narrowed so she could barely see his pupils. But before they left for school, Phil would apologise and she would mutter that it was her fault too, even though she didn't really believe it. The truth of it made her lightheaded.

'This isn't working,' she said.

'You don't mean that.'

'I do.'

Phil smelled of coffee and aftershave, his lemony soap from the shower. There was a nick on his chin where he'd cut himself shaving. She felt the need to hold onto the wall.

'We're fine,'

'We're not.'

Phil thumped his fist on the couch. 'Don't be fucking absurd.'

She shook her head, staring straight ahead.

'Cassie,' he said. 'Don't be ridiculous. You've completely lost it. It could work next round!' She swallowed tears and his eyes flared, his lips curling from his teeth. He jumped up.

'You need some time to come to your senses,' he said. He pushed past her out of the lounge. Cassie heard him jerk his coat from the cupboard so the hangers rattled, and a moment later, the front door slam shut.

Without Phil, the house was quiet. She didn't give herself time to think. She rushed into their bedroom and pulled down the suitcase on top of the wardrobe onto the bed. She threw in her underwear, dresses and blazers for school. She didn't need much, and it didn't take long. Her black roll neck was still in the washing machine, spinning around. That didn't matter. She would stay at her mother's in Watford. The house was drafty and there was only one bathroom, but it was close enough that she could manage the commute to school. She would stick out the year at Fairfield, and if she looked now, she could find another school for September. They might even have an opening for deputy head. If she trawled Right Move every night, she could find a flat in a couple of weeks. She had a friend she could ask who was an estate agent. It might not be West Hampstead, but it would do. She would meet someone else. She would. She scrawled Phil a note explaining where she was going, and left it on top of the bed. Her cheeks were wet and she wiped them roughly. She yanked her suitcase upright.

She tried not to look around as the suitcase wheels caught on the stairs. Before she left, she went to the toilet and when she pulled down her knickers, there was no blood on the pad or the toilet paper. She went and found the pregnancy test, wedged between the sofa cushions. In the bathroom, she peed on the stick and waited. She looked up at the ceiling and thought about them having sex on the bathroom tiles when her mum first stayed over, because the spare bedroom was next to theirs and they couldn't wait until she left. She remembered how Phil brought her coffee to bed if he woke up first, how he told everyone he was the luckiest man alive and held her hand whenever he got the chance. How she couldn't afford IVF alone, or even a half-decent flat. That Phil's parents had insisted she sign a prenuptial agreement. Her friend Natalie had told her that her ex-husband's friends, her close friends too, wouldn't return her calls.

Maybe all their issues *were* her fault. She was the one with low quality eggs, whose body couldn't do what it was supposed to. Phil would find some twenty-five-year-old with perfect ovaries and pop out three kids in five years. She glanced at the stick and saw she was pregnant.

She had six more pregnancy tests in the bathroom cabinet, which she had been supposed to take at one time or another. She had quite a selection, in different brands, sizes and colours. She used them all. It took a while; she had to drink a lot of water. Each one was positive. Smiley faces or double lines appeared on the screen, one test told her *pregnant!* with an exclamation mark, as if to remind her to get excited. Cassie thought about holding a baby in her arms and wiping the fine hairs from its face, and she felt an ache so strong, she worried she was having a miscarriage. She imagined her and Phil rolling a buggy down West End Lane, taking it in turns to push. The three of them cocooned in bed. A tiny heart beating inside hers, her baby on her chest, her breast, giving it heat, giving it life. She gathered the tests and hurried out of the bathroom. She hauled the suitcase upstairs and unpacked it, putting everything back exactly as it was. She tiptoed on the dressing table chair and pushed the suitcase on top of the cupboard. She tore up the note and threw it in the wastepaper basket. She lined up the pregnancy tests on the bed.

The key turned in the lock. She forced herself to stand still and wait. There were footsteps on the stairs, and the bedroom door opened. Phil stood in the doorway. Her heart hammered in her chest.

'I think this has all got out of hand,' he said.

Cassie took a test in each hand and held them up. He carried a paper bag from Feng Sushi, her favourite bottle of wine. He thought she would forget it all with a takeaway. That she was that predictable. Her grin faltered. She felt sudden, vicious contempt.

'What's that?' he asked. His eyes dropped to the tests.

And she waited for him to understand.

Shocking Stockings

Mixed media (watercolor, acrylic, ink, & colored pencil) on paper

This piece is mixed media (graphite, watercolor, ink and pigment on paper). It is done in a more illustrative style than my typical work and I imagine it as being part of a dusty, old book of long-forgotten (or perhaps never written) fairytales.

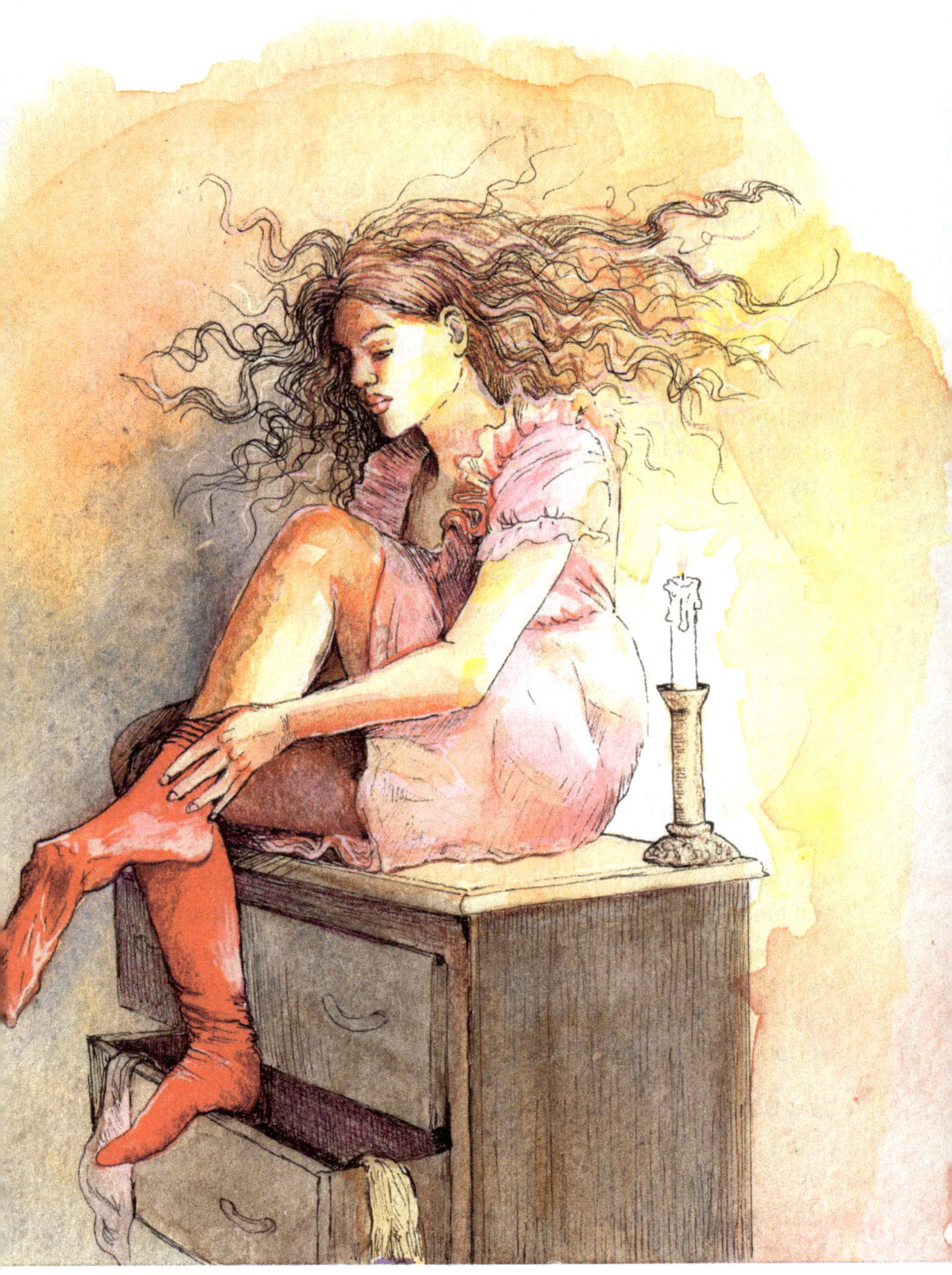

CONTRIBUTORS

Z. K. Abraham (she/her) is a writer and psychiatrist. She completed a Master's in Creative Writing with distinction from the University of Edinburgh. She has been published in/has work forthcoming in *FANTASY Magazine, The Rumpus, Podcastle, Apparition Lit, Barren Magazine, JMWW, Necessary Fiction, FIYAH*, and more. She is a full member of the SFWA. She can be found on Twitter @pegasusunder1, bluesky @ pegasusunder, and zkabraham.com.

Sarah Aziz is a poet, journalist, translator and illustrator based in Kolkata, India. She is currently pursuing an undergraduate degree in English Literature at Loreto College, University of Calcutta. Her work appears or is forthcoming in *Voice of America, Mantis* (a Journal of Poetry, Criticism & Translation housed at Stanford University) and *New Delta Review* among others.

Kimberly Glanzman's poetry and fiction have appeared or are forthcoming in *The Baltimore Review, Harpur Palate, Puerto del Sol, Iron Horse, Electric Lit, North Dakota Review, Barely South*, and *Whale Road Review*, among others.

Shee Gomes is an artist who lives and works in Brazil. With a degree in Digital Design, Shee began her work in visual arts the same year she graduated from college, in 2009. Shee has featured her work in numerous exhibitions, collaborations and projects, curated by books and international magazines. Her work consists of non-objective drawings and paintings with expressive colors and brushstrokes that seek harmony and a certain sonority in each composition as a way of translating her perceptions of the world. For Shee, art transcends cultures, concepts, ideals and time itself, connecting us with all that we are. Her purpose is to unveil the new and expand this connection.

Sara Heise Graybeal is a writer, teacher, connection coach, and host of the podcast *Connect More*. Her writing has appeared in *The Rumpus, Hobart Magazine, Moon City Review, Beloit Fiction Review*, and elsewhere. Sara holds an MFA from the University of North Carolina at Greensboro. She lives in Greensboro with her six-year-old son, and she is currently at work on a memoir.

Nicole Hazan is a high school teacher and fiction writer from England and Israel. She studied UEA's MA in prose fiction from 2021- 2022, where she graduated with distinction. Her short fiction is forthcoming or has appeared in *The New Orleans Review*, *New Letters* and *Jewish Fiction*, among others. She lives in Tel Aviv with her husband and twin daughters, and is working on a novel.

Michael Imossan is an Ibibio poet. He is the author of the award-winning chapbook, *For the Love of Country and Memory*. He is also the author of the gazelle, *A Prelude to Caving*. His full length manuscript, *Broken in Three Places* was named a semifinalist for the Sillerman Prize for African Poetry '23.

Courtney LeBlanc is the author of the full-length collections *Her Whole Bright Life*; *Exquisite Bloody, Beating Heart*; and *Beautiful & Full of Monsters*. She is the Arlington County Poet Laureate, a Virginia Center for Creative Arts Fellow, and the founder and editor-in-chief of Riot in Your Throat, an independent poetry press. She loves nail polish, tattoos, and a soy latte each morning. Find her online at www.courtneyleblanc.com.

Erin Little is a writer and editor from Dallas, Texas. After graduating with a B.A. in English from Loyola University New Orleans in 2015, she moved to New York to pursue a career in publishing. Over six years Erin worked as an editorial assistant for Columbia University Press, Routledge Research, and Penguin Random House. She will graduate with an MFA in creative writing from Louisiana State University in 2024. Her poems and essays have appeared in *Chestnut Review*, *Hobart After Dark*, *Juxtaprose Magazine*, *New Orleans Review*, *Prelude Magazine*, *The Shore*, and *trampset*. Find her online @little__erin.

Abubakar Sadiq Mustapha is a multimedia storyteller, a poet, and an art curator. He believes in the power of photography and how it can be used toward mental health. His work has appeared in the *Ebedi Review*, *The Song Is*, *The Nigeria Review*, *The Shallow Tales Review*, *Libretto Magazine*, *Salamander Ink Magazine*, *Lolwe* and elsewhere. He is a fellow of the Bada Murya Fellowship.

Glenn Orgias is a writer from Sydney. His memoir, *Man In Grey Suit*, was published by Viking in 2012, and his writing can be found at *McSweeney's Internet Tendency*, *X-R-A-Y*, and *Meetinghouse* (forthcoming). He tweets a bit @glennorgias.

M. Ouk writes poetry from a farm in California.

Donald Patten is an artist from Belfast, Maine. He is currently a senior in the Bachelor of Fine Arts program at the University of Maine. As an artist, he produces oil paintings and graphic novels. His artworks have been exhibited in galleries across the Mid-Coast region of Maine. His online portfolio is donaldlpatten.newgrounds.com/art.

Tyler Raso (they/them) is a poet, essayist, and teacher. Their work is featured or forthcoming in *POETRY*, *The Offing*, *Black Warrior Review*, *DIAGRAM*, *Salt Hill Journal*, *Split Lip Magazine*, *The Journal*, and elsewhere. They are the author of the chapbook, *In my dreams/I love like an idea*, winner of the 2022 Frontier Digital Chapbook Contest. They are the 2023-2024 Provincetown Fine Arts Work Center Fellow, and they can be found tweeting @spaghettiutopia.

Quinn Rennerfeldt is a queer poet, parent, and partner earning her MFA at SFSU. Their work can be found in *Cleaver*, *SAND*, *elsewhere*, *Salamander*, *Fractured Lit*, and *Flash Frog*. Her chapbook, *demigoddess semi lustrous* will be published by dancing girl press in Fall 2023. They are a reader for *Split Lip Magazine* and *Flash Fiction Magazine*.

Lisa Rigge is an artist and photographer. One of her passions is collage making. She is an "Intuitive Artist" as she has no predetermined idea of the final collage piece. Lisa is also a photographer, known for her hand-tinted photographs of old ghost towns, flowers, and landscapes. Usually she incorporates one of her photographs, or a portion thereof, in her collage works. Lisa's work has been published in *LensWork*, *Burningword Literary Magazine*, *3 Elements Literary Review*, and *The Sun*. She can be found at www.lisarigge.com.

Taryn Riley is an artist living and working in Florida. She is currently making the most out of being in occupational limbo by pursuing her art making full-time. Her work explores themes of gender performance and serves as a way for her to process her daily thoughts and experiences. More of her work can be viewed on Instagram (@taryn-rileyart) or on her website, tarynriley.com.

Jennifer Saunders (she/her) is the author of *Self-Portrait with House-wife* (Tebot Bach, 2019), winner of the Clockwise Chapbook Competition. Her poem "Crosswalk" won the 2020 Gregory O'Donoghue International Poetry Competition and was published in *Southword*. Jennifer is a Pushcart Prize, Best of the Net, and Orison Anthology nominee and her work has appeared in *Cotton Xenomorph*, *The Georgia Review*, *Grist*, *Ninth Letter*, and other publications. Jennifer lives in German-speaking Switzerland, where in the winters she teaches skating in a hockey school.

Julie Weiss (she/her) is the author of *The Places We Empty*, her debut collection published by Kelsay Books, and a chapbook, *The Jolt: Twenty-One Love Poems in Homage to Adrienne Rich*, published by Bottlecap Press. Her "Poem Written in the Eight Seconds I Lost Sight of My Children" was selected as a finalist for Sundress's 2023 Best of the Net Anthology. She won Sheila-Na-Gigs, Editor's Choice Award for her poem "Cumbre Vieja," was named a finalist for the 2022 Saguaro Prize, and was shortlisted for Kissing Dynamite's 2021 Microchap Series. A Pushcart Prize nominee, her recent work appears in *Random Sample Review*, *ONE ART*, *Wild Roof Journal*, and *Ghost City Review*, among others. Originally from California, she lives in Spain with her wife and two young children. You can find her at: https://www.julieweisspoet.com/.

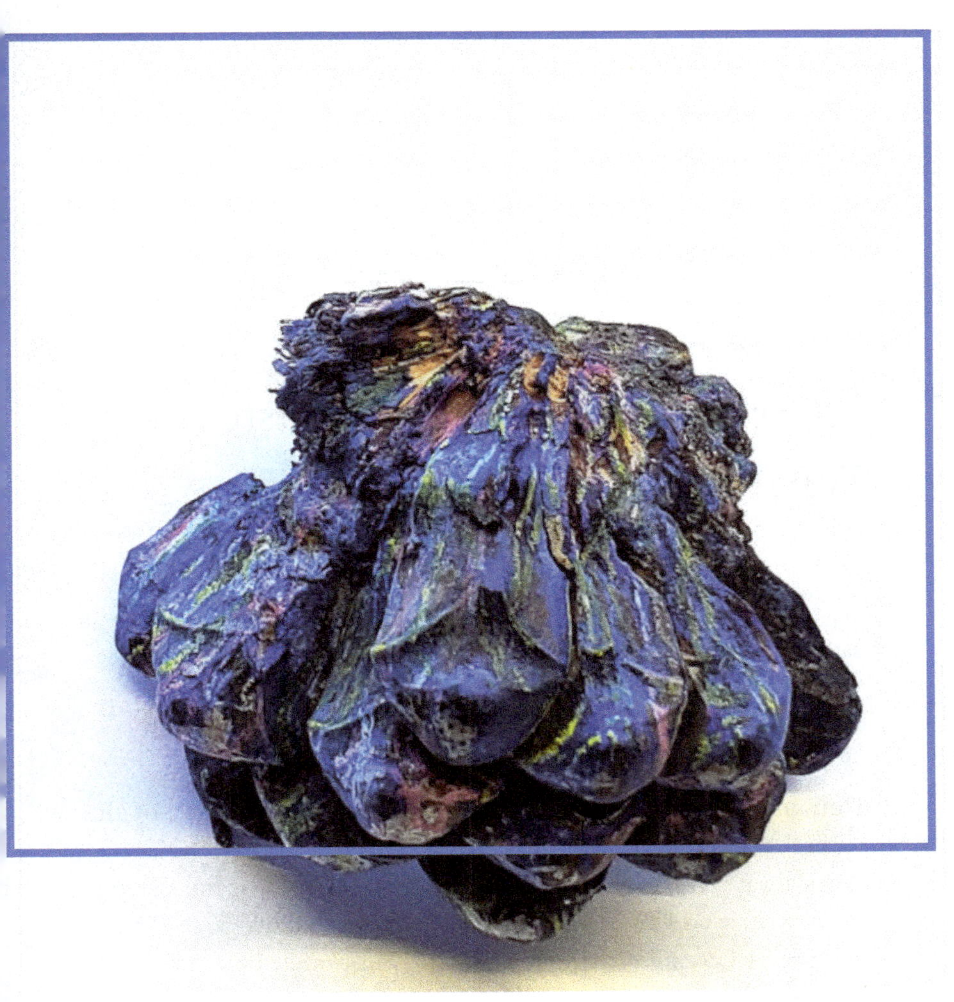

Chestnut Review

VOLUME 5   NUMBER 3   WINTER 2024

FOR STUBBORN ARTISTS

KAREN PIERCE GONZALEZ

After the Squirrels Have Feasted - What Remains 2

Pine cone fragment found near La Fiesta Creek/Laguna de Santa Rosa (California), watercolor and inktense pencils, chalk pastels, 2x2.25 inches, 2023 (Cover Art)

Untrained, I work extensively (and intuitively) with elements of the natural world that present themselves to me. As a result, the discovery is always a surprise; an unexpected gift. Stunned by the sheer geometry of what I find, I am in awe of these treasures. Such shapes and grains I could not envision on my own. I rarely know where the process of adorning them will lead, but the journey is one of beauty for beauty's sake.

Chestnut Review

VOLUME 5 NUMBER 3 WINTER 2024

Chestnut Review LLC, Ithaca, New York. https://chestnutreview.com

Chestnut Review appears four times a year online, in January, April, July, and October, and once per year in print in July.

ISSN 2688-0350 (online), ISSN 2688-0342 (print)

CONTENTS

<u>SPECIAL THANKS</u>

To our generous Patreon supporters:

Jane Ames
Catherine Marenghi
Chris Mikesell

Introduction

At the height of Winter in the Northern Hemisphere, we are welcoming in a new year with old traditions and new directions. We have just returned from our second winter retreat to Merida, Mexico and we are excited to see what the future holds. We hope this issue passes on a bit of that warmth and energy to you.

We want to thank each and every one of you for reading this, submitting, supporting us, and being part of our community. We acknowledge that continuing to exist means finding resilience and seeking growth. We believe that, like our eponymous chestnut trees, entrenching allows us to turn in new directions and fold the past into our trunk. We hope that you have a wonderful year of reading us, engaging with us, and striving towards the sky.

A M A R A   O K O L O

The Art of Planting Flowers

Ekeledo's mother had taught him the art of planting flowers. She had taught him how to love the soil like it was human, burrowing into it until the blackness of the mud stained his fingers and filled his nails. It was from her he learnt how to lower plants into the dugout holes of dirt, the angle his hands had to bend as he pruned each flower. He had only been a year old when she introduced him to the garden, a forest of colors humming with bees and butterflies. Clumps of blood-red roses extending from stems of thorns; a carnation of hydrangeas, curls of clematis, an unfolding family of hibiscuses, and drooping stems of lilies. She held him on her waist, a robin chirping over their heads, the Rose of Sharon clutched in his chubby hands making him sneeze. The sun was warm, the air was edible. He raised the perfumery petals to his mouth as his mother sang an ancient Igbo song.

I will touch the skin of the Earth
Nda
I will smell her soil,
Nda
let me decay, let me be reborn again,
Nda
for she is my mother; my land, Anioma.
Nda, ndalioma, nda!

Two years later, his mother walked into the garden on a cool September evening with a kitchen knife in her hand and slit her throat. He was witness, a five-year-old sitting on the windowsill of his room, playing Chutes and Ladders, his eyes straying occasionally from the game to the garden, the rustling of leaves and bobbing of daffodils in the breeze. His newborn sister had arrived three days earlier, and she was in the next room, asleep on the cot. The room smelled of lunch, the pleasant aroma of boiled plantains and crayfish stew. He had won a round, and the rustling brought his head up again to see his mother standing in the garden. She looked towards the house, her eyes glassy with tears. Perhaps she had

seen him, perhaps she had not—he could not tell. The sun was setting
behind her, a butter-yellow halo, like the circles drawn around the head
of white Jesus in his Bible picture books. The stainless steel of the knife
stole the sunlight as she raised it to her throat and drew a line. He never
heard her body fall. The flowers had been too bountiful; they cradled her
like a thoughtful lover as she bled her life onto them, drenching the soil
she had loved with the remainder of her years.

It was only on the day of the funeral that they found the note she
had written, buried in a jar of powdered cane sugar in the kitchen. Three
months of crying, of confusion and questions had shrouded the family,
and it was answered in a sheet of neatly folded paper. His mother's fa-
miliar cursive was scrawled in black ink, and as his father read aloud, his
sobbing punctuated the sentences, his voice rocking the room.

*My head is begging me to split it open. I will answer these voices speaking to me
or else I will run mad! Please love my children, my son Ekeledo. Tell my Kpakpando
I will see her in the morning. In another world I will be her mother again, but not in
this one. This world, it hates me. Let me go to my flowers, I need to sleep.*

One morning, when Ekeledo was seven, his father came downstairs
as they ate breakfast. He kissed him and Kpakpando on their mouths.
It was a Sunday morning, the week before their mother's memorial, and
their father's sister Aunty Bisa was present, ironing the matching fabrics
the family would wear to church the next Sunday. His father went over
to her, hugged her tightly, his head buried in the curve of her shoulder
blade. Ekeledo watched them, his eyes dry. The room smelled of the
steaming iron and soggy Nasco cornflakes infused with warm milk.
When his father extracted himself from the hug, he picked up his car
keys beside the kitchen door and went through it, the screen door thud-
ding close with a sharp slam.

They found his body in the river a week later. His seatbelt was still
intact, clipped across his chest. The windows had been wound up. Some
said he intentionally ran off the bridge, others said he must have fallen
asleep at the wheel. But whatever it was, his father was dead. Ekeledo
knew this much. His mother had slit her throat in front of him, his father
had ended up in the water, burying himself in its belly until she was full
and spat him out. And that Sunday morning, as the Priest gave a sermon
that juxtaposed his father's death with his mother's memorial, Ekeledo
felt the weight of the congregation's eyes on his back. Their eyes bur-
rowed into his skin until he became porous, grief oozing from the holes.

Though he was a child, he began to understand that the world he walked through would be shrouded by the horrors of his parents' deaths. They would haunt his dreams. His eyes strayed down to the lilies in his hands. They were limp, speckled with the morning's dew. And as clear as the day outside the heat of the church, he knew what he would become.

***

On the spot his mother's body had fallen, Ekeledo planted a cluster of forget-me-nots. He had bought them off an American horticulturist he met in a Facebook group, and when he had offered her money, she politely rejected the full payment except the shipping cost. The flowers arrived on the thirtieth anniversary of his mother's suicide, a rectangular bed of blue, pink, and yellow flowers that kissed his fingertips with their feather-like texture. It was also the month Kpakpando was to marry Osara, the man with the coconut-shaped head and slanted eyes with puffy eyebags. His sister came with her fiancé to the house to officially introduce him. When Ekeledo rose from his haunches and analyzed the burliness of Osara, he knew what laid in wait for the future—this man was going to ruin her life.

He tried telling her, after sneaking her off to the backyard while Madam Maggie the maid entertained Osara in the parlor. A blood-red robin was chirping from the daisies, eyeing them suspiciously as they sipped from their bottles: homemade orangeade for him, Coca-Cola for her.

"I am a slave to sugar," Kpakpando always joked, especially when he tried getting her to his side of the table with plant-based diets and holistic eating. "No matter how many salads I eat, I will die. Better to leave this earth filled with pleasure than to have starved my body of it."

Sometimes he tried to recall if his mother had eaten a lot of sugar while pregnant with Kpakpando. But the trauma of her death had so darkened his memory, his persistent thoughts of her were of an opened throat pulsating with blood.

Kpakpando was smoking a Camel, staring at a lonesome hornbill on one of the mango trees that surrounded the blackened backyard walls. "You don't have to say it, I know you don't like him," she said, blowing out a fast line of smoke.

He watched his muddied fingers smudge the glass in his hands. "He looks like a wife-beater," he said under his breath, his eyes down.

"But I am the first woman he is going to marry. How can he be a wife-beater when he has not been married before? And when did people now walk around with the label *wife-beater* on their faces? Oh-ho…did you see something I did not see?"

She was longing to pick a fight, her usual defense. The tension seemed to implode whenever their parents' death anniversaries arrived, a reminder of his pain and insufferable silence. For Kpakpando, their parents' lives were a blur, a blind spot in memory as she had been saved by infancy to witness the horrors. But for him, he carried the demons like trophies. His dreams were dense with their bodies—his mother's, bloodied from the neck down; his father's bloated and perforated by the fishes' teeth. In the dreams, he always failed at saving them. Grief had tied him down to this house, this life as a gardener, searching for answers in empty soil. Kpakpando could not understand him, and she hated him for the ambiguity that encased him like second flesh.

He was too tired to fight, so he let her keep talking.

"Ekeledo, will you not answer? I say again, how will you know Osara my soon-to-be husband is a wife-beater? Or are you going to tell me now that our dead mother appeared in the dream and told you this? Or is it Father this time?"

Her tone angered him. He stood up, dropped the glass of juice on the cemented veranda. "It is your choice," he said. "Marry him if you want. I have said my own."

She hissed at his back as he walked away. "You want me to be like you, alone and miserable, staying in this wretched town. For what? To remind me of the deaths of people who could not even stay to see their daughter grow up! God forbid you and them!"

Her voice died off once he circled the house and returned to the garden. Osara was outside, standing beside the Toyota he had driven. He was talking in hushed tones into a cellphone, and it was only Ekeledo's rustling of the rose bushes that prompted him to turn. The man's eyes widened with syrupy pleasantness as he saw him, switching off the call with a swiftness that implied guilt. Ekeledo felt sickened.

"Ah my in-law, you are here," he cackled.

His voice was severing to Ekeledo's ears. Saying nothing, he walked past the man.

Osara continued. "Have you finished talking with my love, your sister?"

Ekeledo ignored him. He disappeared into the garden, shutting the miniature gate behind him.

He had buried five new forget-me-nots when he heard the car doors open and slam. The mutter of Kpakpando's voice as she spoke with Madam Maggie carried over through the wind, but he could only hear *I don't care about his blessing*. Ekeledo felt the plants drop into the holes of the earth, silent and heavy like a last breath.

The screech of the tires on the stony driveway was quick. He listened as the quietness returned, ushered in with the evening sounds of birds chirping, excited cicadas buzzing against the impending dusk, the fluttering of his beloved flowers. He closed his eyes, relished the moment. It never came back again, a specific time or moment. He wished he could hold it in him as much as he could. He had found the importance of that from this place, this soil, this garden.

Seven months later, he heard the screech of the tires again. He had been eating a bowl of fried snails drenched in pepper sauce when the Toyota stopped beside the house. It was Kpakpando's sunglasses that made him stand up, and when she began to cry as he walked towards her, he knew. She did not have to take the glasses off to reveal a blackened eye, he did not need to see the bruises snaking over her arms, streaked with purplish inflamed veins. He just knew.

"Come in," he said. "Come in where you belong."

***

Months later, Kpakpando left in the rain and wasn't back when the drops slowed to a trickle the following day. Ekeledo paced the room, his hands interlocked as a cradle behind his head. Night sounds resumed with ferocity, disrupting the silence. He lost count of how many times he walked to the window, looking out through the lace curtains, seeing nothing but darkness. It would have been less invigorating if Kpakpando was just out, but he'd recently learned she was pregnant. What if something terrible had happened to her? Fear jumpstarted his midsection, like he had been kicked in the ribs.

Two days later, Kpakpando returned with a woman he did not know. By then, he had reported at the police station, wrestled against calling Osara, decided against it, then finally caved and called. The man had driven down on the third day, his face a replicant of squeezed fabric. They were in a middle of a heated argument when the Toyota drove in, and Kpakpando and the woman appeared. He was quick to notice that her stomach had deflated and was about to speak, when the strange woman he did not know opened the back door and retrieved a baby car seat. A swaddled newborn, pink and curled up in sleep, lay in it.

He could only stare. Shock stuffed his throat, rendered him dumb.

Osara rushed forward, his face laxed with genuine surprise and joy. "Ah thank God! Kpakpando, my sweet wife, you are alive! Baby is alive! My son is…wait, is it a boy? I believe it is a boy, right?"

Kpakpando was gazing at him, her eyes dilated. She appeared dazed, like someone shaken awake from sleep, still grappling through drowsiness.

The woman beside her spoke. "It's a girl," she said. "My name is Nnando, by the way. I am a midwife."

Osara's face darkened like clouds imminent with rain. "A girl? But I thought when you went to the gynecologist, you said it was a boy?"

Ekeledo turned to Osara; his fists tightened. "Osara, get out of my compound this minute."

"I won't leave without my wife and child."

"She is not your wife, you bastard!" Ekeledo screamed at his face. Spittle gathered at the corners of his mouth. "Oh, now she is your wife? When you kept hitting her at every chance you got, you did not know that?"

"Hit her?" He stuttered, looking from Ekeledo to Kpakpando, his face creased with confusion. "Did she say that?"

From the corner of his eye, Ekeledo saw Kpakpando's eyelids flutter rapidly. Her eyes were round, like a deer caught in headlights, and she turned away and began gnawing at her fingernails.

"I saw the bruises, Osara… so stop lying. My sister came to this house three months ago with a black eye. She was pregnant! Osara, please just leave."

"I said I won't leave without—"

"I will go with him," Kpakpando said.

Silence settled over them like unpleasant air. The newborn fussed and let out a short, sharp whine, then fell back into her slumber. Ekeledo turned to Kpakpando, his eyes pleading. "You don't mean that."

Tears fell from her eyes as Kpakpando shut them tight. Ekeledo's heart lurched in his chest, carved him in half. He drew closer to her.

"Kpando. You said it yourself, you told me he was abusive to you…"

She turned to him, her teary eyes flashing with anger. "Are you my husband, Ekeledo? Leave me alone to return to the man I married." She turned, took the child car seat with the newborn from the woman next to her, and headed towards Osara's car.

***

Just do it.
Do what?
Do that thing you have always promised us. Do it now.
Are you insane? I just had a baby.
So what?
B-But…if I do it, who will be here for her?
That is not your problem. You just have to do that which you promised us.
But I don't want to leave her.
You are lazy.
What?
You heard us right.
That is so unfair to say. After all I have done for you.
You have done us nothing. Nothing.
That is a lie. I gave you everything.
You are such a disgrace. We regret why we picked you.
Don't say that. Please.
At least your mother was easier with us. She made us welcome. She obeyed us. All you have done is try to send us away.
Please don't mention her. Please.
She was far better than you. Stronger, talented. We gave her so many talents. She loved painting. She loved gardening. She loved color. We gave her all the beauty to create that life, and she used it. Then she gave us what she promised us. You on the other hand…
Don't mention her!
Disgrace. Lazy. Stupid.
Stop it!! Please…
Why are you so afraid? Your mother made it easy. Why is it so hard for you to obey us?
I am not my mother.
Of course, you aren't. She was stronger than you. Obedient. You are lazy, stupid, good-for-nothing, crazy. Don't you see how everyone looks at you? Osara, Ekeledo…

everyone knows you are a weakling with no spine. A crazy woman. Even your own parents could not bear to see you grow up. They killed themselves after you were born. Have you not sat down to think about it? Nobody wanted you here. You are a failure, a mistake. A crazy woman who talks to herself.

STOP IT!

Look at you now, screaming to nothing. You are absolutely mad. Stark-raving. You are a crazy woman; you do not deserve to be here. The more you are here, the more you ruin their lives. Your brother's, your husband's, now your baby's. Imagine her growing up to see how crazy her mother is. Imagine the shame she will feel knowing that her mother is a madwoman. Do you want that for her?

No…oh please, no…

Then do what needs to be done. End this misery. Save your daughter from the pain you will cause her. If you truly love her, you will do that for her. That was what your mother did for you.

Did she?

Yes. She loved you so much, that was why she did it. She could not bear to see you feel shame for her. With Ekeledo, it was easier because he was a boy. But with you, a girl, she had to choose, and she chose you. She chose to go so you could be happy. Are you not happy?

No! All my life, I have never been happy! I wanted my mother…I wanted her to stay for me!

Selfish. You are so selfish. After all she did for you, this is what you say. We were not wrong when we called you worthless.

No, please don't.

Go ahead…stay for your newborn. We will make sure she grows to despise you. She will hate you with all her blood. Look at her now, asleep and innocent. But watch. Once she becomes older. She will be miserable, and she will extend that misery to you. Watch.

I don't want that. Please I don't want her to hate me.

Then do what we asked you. Go to the window now. That is good, now you obey us. That is good. Look at the sun, the sky. Is it not all beautiful?

Yes. It is. All beautiful.

Good. Now, look below. What do you see? Tell us.

A woman. I see a woman.

There. That is your mother. Look closely, someone else is there. Who is that?

A man?

There. That is your father. See them, look how they look up at you, with pride, with love. Can you see them smiling?

Yes. Yes, oh yes!

They love you so much. They are here to say they are sorry for leaving you. Look at them waving. They want you to come down and meet them. You need to go and speak with them. They have so much to tell you!

Oh yes, I see them wave. Mama! Papa! Oh, look at them smile! They love me! How do I go to them? I want to go to them.

The way is right before you. Just step over. You will be right next to them once you step over. Do it. They will not wait all day.

But what about my baby? Who will be with her when I go down to meet my parents?

Don't worry, she is safe. When the time is right, we will come back for her. But we have to go see your parents now. They have missed you, oh how they have missed you! Go and meet them, speak with them. They love you so much. See them wave. They love you so much…

***

The funeral was short, quiet, un-ceremonial. Sorrow had chosen to lodge itself like a bone in the throat of Ekeledo's family, and the people of the small town wanted none of it. They had mourned enough. With a small group consisting of Osara, Ekeledo, Madam Maggie, Nnando the midwife, and few relatives who cared, they lowered the casket with the remains of Kpakpando into the earth, next to the graves of her mother and father. Ekeledo had convinced Osara with little persuasion for his sister to be buried at the home of her birth. Osara had been too distraught to argue. The memory of his wife's body on the grounds of the hospital plagued him; he hardly slept anymore. All his dreams were filled of the moment he had seen the security guard running toward the gates as he drove in, screaming blue murder. To come back and look upon the woman he loved on the concrete floor, twisted, broken and surrounded by blood. The sight had been too horrific to comprehend. When Ekeledo took the funeral arrangements into his hands, Osara willfully allowed it. Now, as the gravediggers covered the grave, the small gathering dispersing, he knew in his spirit what he must do.

They returned to the house. Inside, Madam Maggie and Nnando busied themselves, dishing out food to the people who had attended the funeral. In the room adjacent, the newborn slept in a cot, wrapped in warm blankets and surrounded by soft pillows. Osara and Ekeledo stayed outside where the sun was lazy but warm, casting an apocalyptic yellow glow everywhere.

"I have a request you may not like," Osara suddenly began. His face was crestfallen, like paper crinkled at the edges.

Ekeledo sighed. "So why ask if…"

"I want you to take the baby."

Shock ran across Ekeledo's face. "You want me to take the baby?"

Tears choked Osara's throat. "I am in no position to be emotionally strong for her. I cannot do it."

"But she is your child, Osara."

"Madam Maggie raised you and Kpakpando—she would do a better job than I would do." He sniffled, hacked and spat out a yellowish-green blot of sputum onto the ground at his feet. "My extended family is not willing to help me. They have accused me of marrying a woman who was…deranged. They used those words for my Kpakpando. Imagine what they would say, what they would do to our child. I do not want that for her, for Kpakpando. Please, see reason."

Ekeledo said nothing. He folded his hands across his chest, his eyes on the three graves at the right corner of the house. Two cemented and greenish with moss. One freshly brown, circled with stones and pebbles. His entire family reduced to dust and memories. His eyes shifted to his flowers, where he caught a honeybee floating over a pink rose. The air stymied with the scent of warm rice, lemon goatmeat, and spicy tomato stew. A goat bleated from a makeshift barbed wire cage next to Ekeledo's parked motorcycle. His chickens, which he let roam around, clucked in reply. From afar, somewhere in the neighborhood, he heard a toddler wail.

"You are a better man than I am, Ekeledo. You will be a better father to my child than I will be." Osara continued. "Please. I will come to see her if you want, but I want you to raise her. Notice the things I never saw in Kpakpando, the things I chose to ignore. I saw it all, her depression, her pain, her suffering, but I chose to ignore." Tears streamed down his face. "I do not want to make that mistake with our daughter. You have come this far for a reason, maybe it is for you to save her. Save our daughter, Ekeledo, please. Take her in and save her."

Ekeledo still said nothing. To him, words were dead.

The air began to lift with breeze. Osara stood up, walked into the house. The din of his voice as he conversed was inaudible, but Ekeledo knew he was saying his goodbyes. When he remerged again, Ekeledo looked up at him. Osara's eyes were swollen, red-rimmed with tears. The two men said nothing, for nothing had to be said. Silence was delicate, more intimate, and they let their eyes say what failed with speech. Then Osara nodded and began walking to his car. The sound of the Toyota was slow and harried, but as he drove off, Madam Maggie and Nnando came to the veranda where Ekeledo still sat, watching the graves and his flowers.

"Where is he going?" Madam Maggie asked. "Is he coming back?"

"Perhaps he went to get more ice for the drinks," Nnando replied. Her eyes connected with Ekeledo's, and he knew that she knew.

He stood up, steadied himself not to fall from his dizziness. When the vertigo faded, he said, "I am going to the garden. Do not wait or call for me."

"Will you be all right?" Nnando asked as he walked away.

He stopped, his feet planted to the ground like they were glued to it. His hands shook, his bowels throbbed. He felt his head become heavy; his chest tightened like fabric clumped in knots. When his eyes began to water, his mouth did the same, pooling with free-flowing saliva. Grief had various forms, and this was his. He began to feel this way since he saw Kpakpando's body at the morgue, her eyes open, dilated with death, questioning him. *Why did you not know I needed help, just as our mother had? I screamed and you did not listen. Why did you not save me?* Those eyes chased his thoughts, freezing him with guilt, and Ekeledo knew that for the rest of his life, this was the man he was. Broken, maimed, without an ounce of redemption.

As quickly as it came, it dissolved. He felt his body return to normal, motion slowly taking over. Turning back to the women at the veranda, his face stretched into a wry smile.

"Yes," he said. "I will be all right."

A Pure Catastrophe

Tell me about the dream where we hold hands under a tree and never cry. We wake up to the smell of gasoline every morning and doze off at dusk. We see the man pulling bodies out of the small window but never speak of it. I sleep on the couch every Friday just to catch a glimpse of your freshly bleached hair. We don't care about the man smoking cigarettes in the backseat of his car. You ask me about the color of the moon, and I say, *half*. The man keeps pulling bodies out from the trunk of a blue car. We sleep on separate beds at night, and every time we dance, we look like two civil war soldiers making love on the barren land for the very first time: oblivious and naive. You wake up without ribs one day, and we laugh, hitting our heads on the bed frame. *The heart is a vigilant muscle*, you say. *It can protect itself.* I don't understand, but I comply, for I have never known how to do otherwise. The man keeps pulling bodies out of the door. You keep talking to me in a low voice on the microphone. I keep waiting for you to come back: not as a person (warm and complete), but as love (a pure catastrophe).

Our reader describes what it was like to find Amara Okolo's "The Art of Planting Flowers"

When reading "The Art of Planting Flowers," I felt deeply engrossed in the protagonist's life. The characters and setting play a pivotal role in the theme of the story, and I understand the concept of gardening has to do with life and sustainability. Then we see the protagonist's mother take her life there. There is such a compelling voice in the storytelling that makes the reader reflect deeply on the story's events and mental health. We obviously see how two individuals who grew up in the same house perceive different versions of their parents, in which one is totally oblivious to the trauma the other has lived with. This story evokes sadness, and allows the reader to feel a range of emotions. This tragic story has the reader totally on a ride of emotion, and this is what I believe good storytelling is about.

—*Ejiro Edward*

Our reader describes what it was like to find Tamara Kreutz's "Stumbling Blocks on the Mission Center's Basketball Court"

"Stumbling Blocks on the Mission Center's Basketball Court" is a remarkably well conceived and executed work. Using concrete and detailed images, it paints a picture that is vivid, but also ominous. The picture of two girls lying on a blacktop in summer being circled by vultures and the flapping of their wings echoed by the flapping of the girls' arms aroused my curiosity and drew me in. Where was this going? And what did it have to do with Romans 14:21? The answers come later. The themes of the loss of the innocence of childhood and the guilt and shame about their "dangerous" bodies taught to girls emerging into womanhood are developed through metaphor and all too familiar "lessons" that weave together multiple layers of meaning. Poetic social commentary is difficult to write well. It too often crosses over from holding up a mirror to heavy-handed preaching, unlike this poem which is written with an undertone of sarcasm that makes the message serious and engaging.

—*Paul Bluestein*

Stumbling Blocks on the Mission Center's Basketball Court

It is good not to …do anything that causes your brother to stumble. (Romans 14:21)

Softened by August heat, the blacktop tar took imprints of our spines.
We swallowed our giggles, forced our lungs to release breath in tiny
spurts of air. Shadows of circling vultures drew closer, closer to my best
friend and me—so near we could see their pleated, leathery heads. Like
mini girl-Lazarus's, we rose, leaping and laughing, shrieking, flapping our
arms as vultures flapped their wings and fled. We were still free in our
bodies, our chests nearly flat, though with tingling bulbs just sprouting
beneath our skin. We didn't know our missionary mothers watched us
play, ticking off days until we'd need to be covered in tops too baggy for
our frames, or that they'd say we couldn't lie on the blacktop anymore
with our arms outspread. Our shirts might rise above belly buttons, those
chalices of temptation, or might tightly caress our breasts—and we,
God's tiny witnesses, could make men's minds stumble over our bodies
toward Hell.

Internal Battle

Acrylic and Mixed Media on Paper
15x15 inches, 2023
(Next Page)

My piece, "Internal Battle", was created by overlapping and screening two of my acrylic paintings on canvas. I aimed to bring forth energy and emotion through dramatic brushstrokes, splattered paint, and vibrant colors in this composition. This piece is a symbolic portrayal of life's chaos and mind clutter produced by the rush and expectations of everyday life. In the midst of it all, there is an attempt to find peace, guidance, and the path in the right direction.

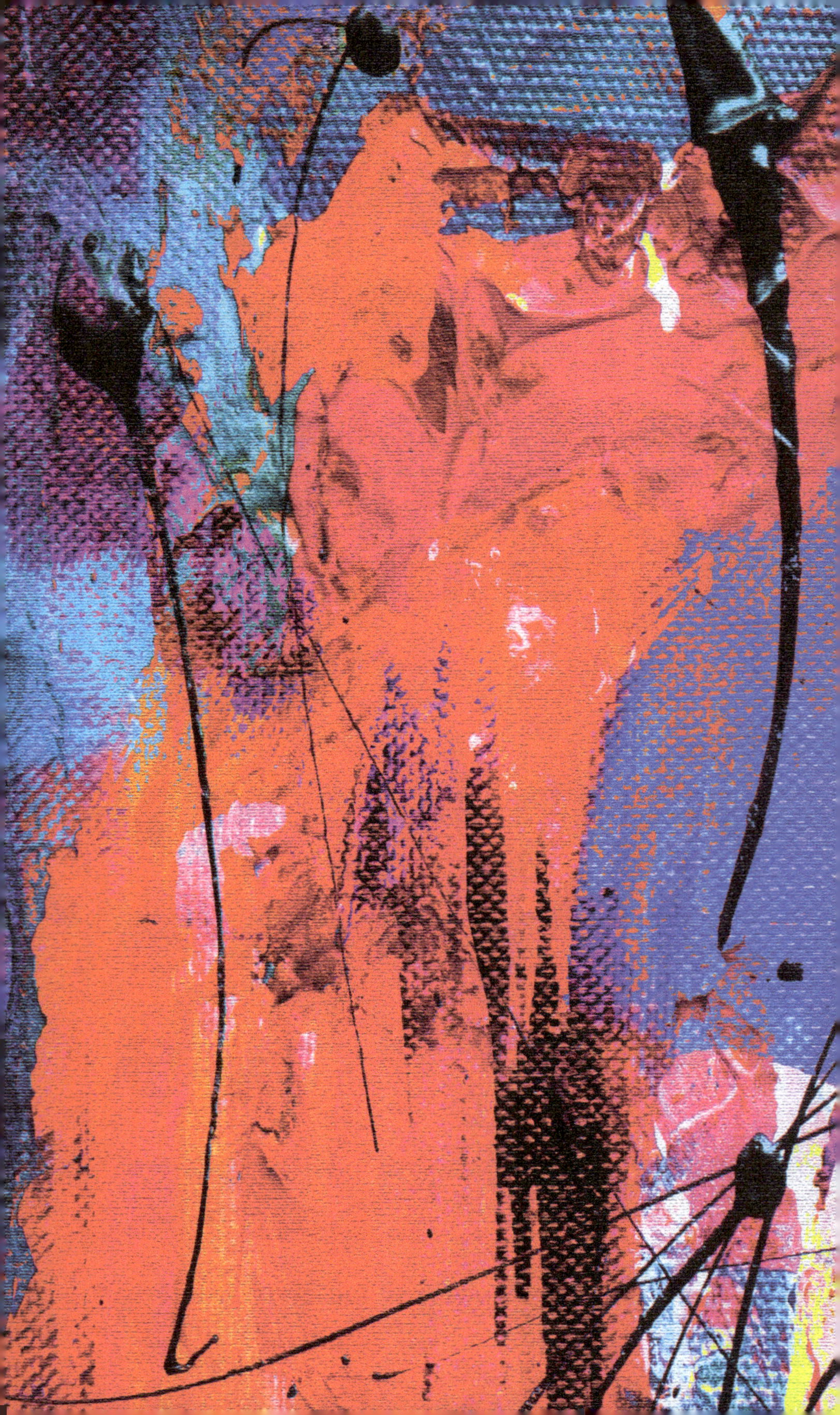

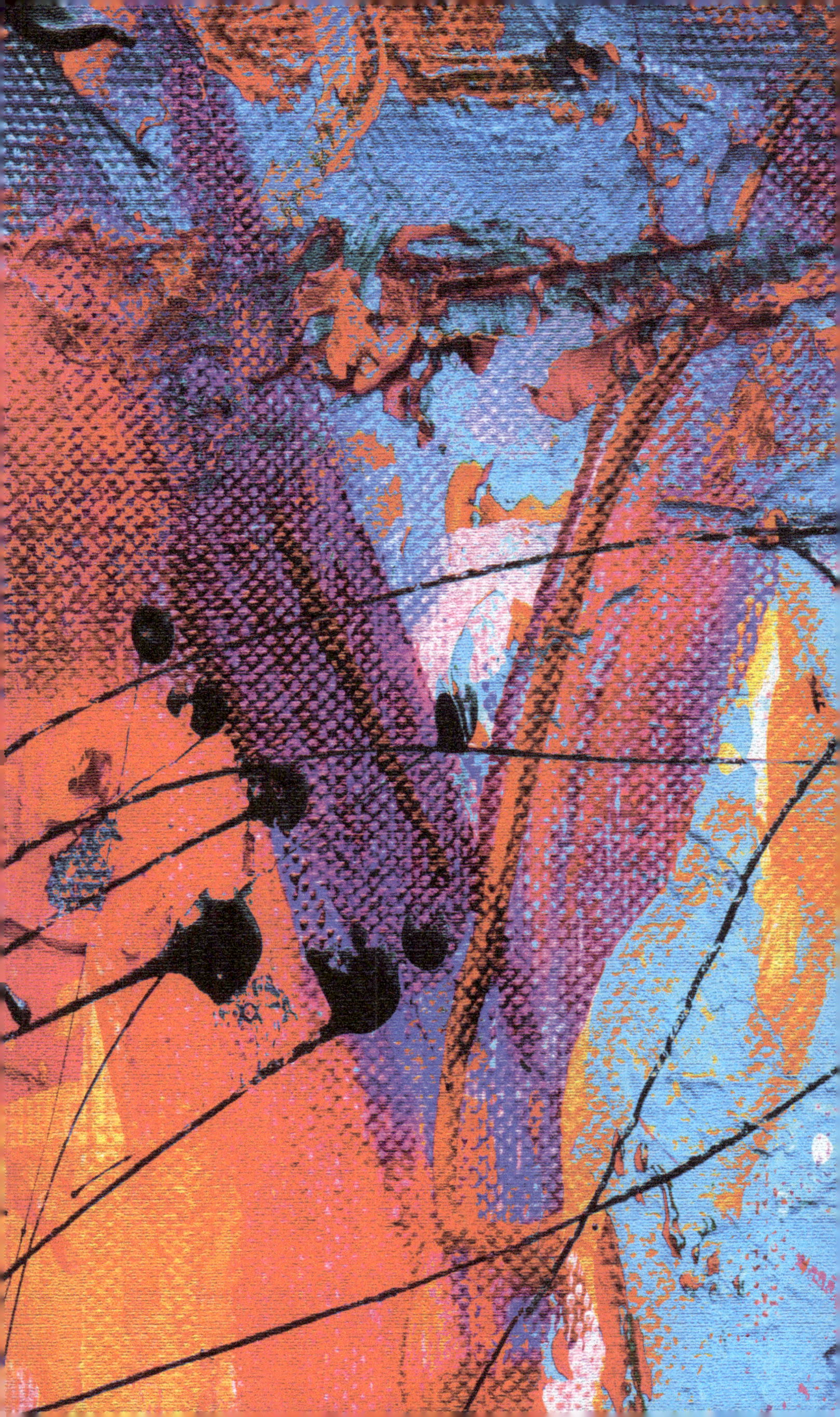

Unforgiven Etymology

FORGIVE—
from the Old English *forgiefan*, meaning "give, grant, allow;
remit (a debt), pardon (an offense)," all actions placing
power in the hands of the harmed, though rarely, in fact,
does it reside there: to have been harmed at all,
one must have been done unto, existed as subject
to another's active action. Remit comes from
the Latin *remittere*, meaning "to send back,"
& pardon from *perdonare*, "to give up
completely" — & does that seem fair? Fair
from *fæger*, first meant to mean not equitable or just,
but instead "pleasing to the eye,"
perhaps a day devoid of rain, or a face
pale as lace or linen. Is forgiveness fair?
It certainly pleases certain eyes. It untroubles
the weather, eases storms into silence,
but is it beautiful to send back power, to give it
up completely? & to ask for forgiveness,
is that fair, too, or simply white? To strike
with one hand & reach out the other asking
for its power to once more be given, granted, allowed?
Let us remember sorry, at its source, comes not from sorrow,
but sore, the Old English *sār*, "ache, wound."
If sorry is a wound, then forgiveness is its scar,
but the wrong body bears it. Scars aren't fair;
people avert their eyes from those who forgive
too easily & often, a forgivable action, done unto.
Under the laws of language, all actions can be
forgiven, & people, too, but there is no word
for a person who chooses to forgive. There is
a wound, though. A debt remains.

CLAIRE ZHOU

A Sonnet for My Moon Baby

It starts in the pool & ends in your death. In the water,
you are translucent as a gill. There is a moon in the sky,
which means there is a person. A suckling light.
A baby, hanging from a starred noose, face blacked out, so white
it hurts. This baby is the product of a late-night fuck,
and it is dead, it is the type that gets aborted, it is the type.
It is your type. It does not get a name. It gets a shape: a comma
in your bed. It gets a man. It gets your man, who is not dead
yet. Your hair like seaweed in the blue. Your man says *baby,*
get out of the water, it's cold. He says, *baby, baby, baby.*
Dead. *Baby, come here. Baby, do you love me?* The lemon croon
of a child's lullaby. A filament of a baby's first cry in your stomach,
cord tracing the surface. You drink water like wine,
pulse hardening to a full stop. *Baby,* all drowned in the sunrise.

Trigger Warning

My daddy is nobody's Negro. He always kept a rifle by his bedside as a reminder to anyone who questioned that. My momma, the anti-gun enthusiast, said it scared her, but he ignored her pleas to keep it away from her view. Women worry, Men protect. That was the dogma he lived by. Rules of the Wild West and some shit on reruns of *Tombstone* and History Channel episodes on the O.K. Corral.

I only saw Daddy use that gun twice.

The first time happened when I was eleven.

In a brown cottage tucked behind a cascading wall of honeysuckle and oak trees, we lived on the edge of ten acres, a refuge for seasonal songbirds, abandoned pets, and a family of skunks. On warm nights, a red fox and a barn owl took turns serenading us from our back porch. Every spring, pregnant deer made beds of grass behind the trees to prepare for impending fawns. My favorite moments were walking home down the mile-long dirt road from the bus stop, seeing what creatures I might spot. One day, I heard a loud popping of fireworks through the trees.

Daddy was shooting empty canisters of cleaning products lined out on a stump. He slid my backpack strap from my shoulder and exchanged it for his rifle. "Look into the scope and aim," he told me, pointing to the Windex bottle. As I lifted my arm, the hard metal felt heavy in my hands. He adjusted the butt of the gun into the crook of my shoulder. "Deep breath," he told me. "Keep both eyes open." I squeezed the trigger and the gun kicked into my shoulder socket pushing me backwards. As the plastic Windex bottle fell, my body trembled. The power of the gun shook me. I understood why Momma was afraid. "I'm proud of you," Daddy said, patting me on the shoulder. "That's my Baby girl," he said as he went to retrieve and replace the bottle.

"Again."

The second time he used that gun happened a few years later when a white man joined us for dinner.

The white man had one of those old family names from the county. He sat at the head of our dining room table grabbing a chicken leg, spooning mashed potatoes onto his plate. "You got yourself a fine home here, Chuck," he said to Daddy. No one called Daddy Chuck. Not even Momma. The white man winked at Momma and continued to stuff his face. I didn't see Daddy's balled up fists under the table. I didn't see Momma shuffle uncomfortably in her seat. To a teenager, this man was a guest in our home. This man was just white. When he finished his meal and stood up to leave, Daddy never shook his hand. Daddy smiled, gestured towards the door, and waved the man's car goodbye just the same. Real polite, just like he taught me. When the man's car drove down the winding dirt road, Daddy walked away from the window. He poured a glass of wine, and tivoed John Wayne.

At 3 a.m., lights shone into my bedroom from the road. *Perhaps someone is lost*, I thought, sliding from my bed to get a closer look. I opened the bedroom door to find Daddy naked in the hallway behind the front door. He must've heard the approaching car too. Standing with his rifle cocked in hand, he silently gestured his finger to his lip and motioned for me to hold the doorknob. He whispered, "If I don't come back, wake up your mother, and hide." He held three fingers up and counted. 3…2…1. I opened the door, and he pushed me behind it.

The crackling of the gun in the air echoed. The explosion of bullets morphed into reverberations of lightning as they danced through the leaves of the trees. The car lights retreated back from where they came, and Daddy came back inside. His sweaty skin glistened in the shadows. His skin, a beautiful deep onyx blue.

The next morning Daddy made us pancakes. He flipped a stack onto a plate and held it out to me.

"That was Klan that had been at our house last night." He handed me the syrup and some butter. "Don't tell your mother. Better eat up and get ready for school." He kissed my forehead then sat at the table, staring out the window.

He smiled. "Looks like the bluebirds are back."

Hot Girl Prayer

Two tattoos later & foolish enough
to find romance even in the stench

of dead dog rotting in the yellow heat,
the palm leaf hugging our reprieve.

You say tonight was fun, even if
tomorrow makes us pay it forward.

And isn't this joy? At some point
you must settle for derivatives & dupes;

mania in place of a toddler's wonder;
cortisol rigged to feed the carnal. Go on,

find the shiny shrapnel while looking
for the little girl in worn family photos.

Don't think too much about why
men love the jaded look of our eyes.

The closest we get to undiluted delight
may be an orgasm or a new high. Listen,

we're almost home now. The feeling
returns to my gums, numbed by drugs

cut with cornstarch & thankfully
nothing capable of killing us. Sorry

it took me too long to realize god
had been cast in a role with no lines:

all lonely mouth and leering eyes.

Pop Machine

Digital Photography
4x5 inches
Saint Augustine, Florida
February 18, 2021

Three activities bring me great satisfaction: photography, travel, and taking long walks. All came together in the creation of, "Pop Machine." During a winter trip to Saint Augustine with my wife I grabbed my camera and snuck out to walk through the tourist zone between Flagler College and the old fortress. This zone includes several smaller lanes where locals reside. I just happened to pass one ramshackle building that had this machine on the front porch. (Click!) Many of my better shots arise from this serendipity.

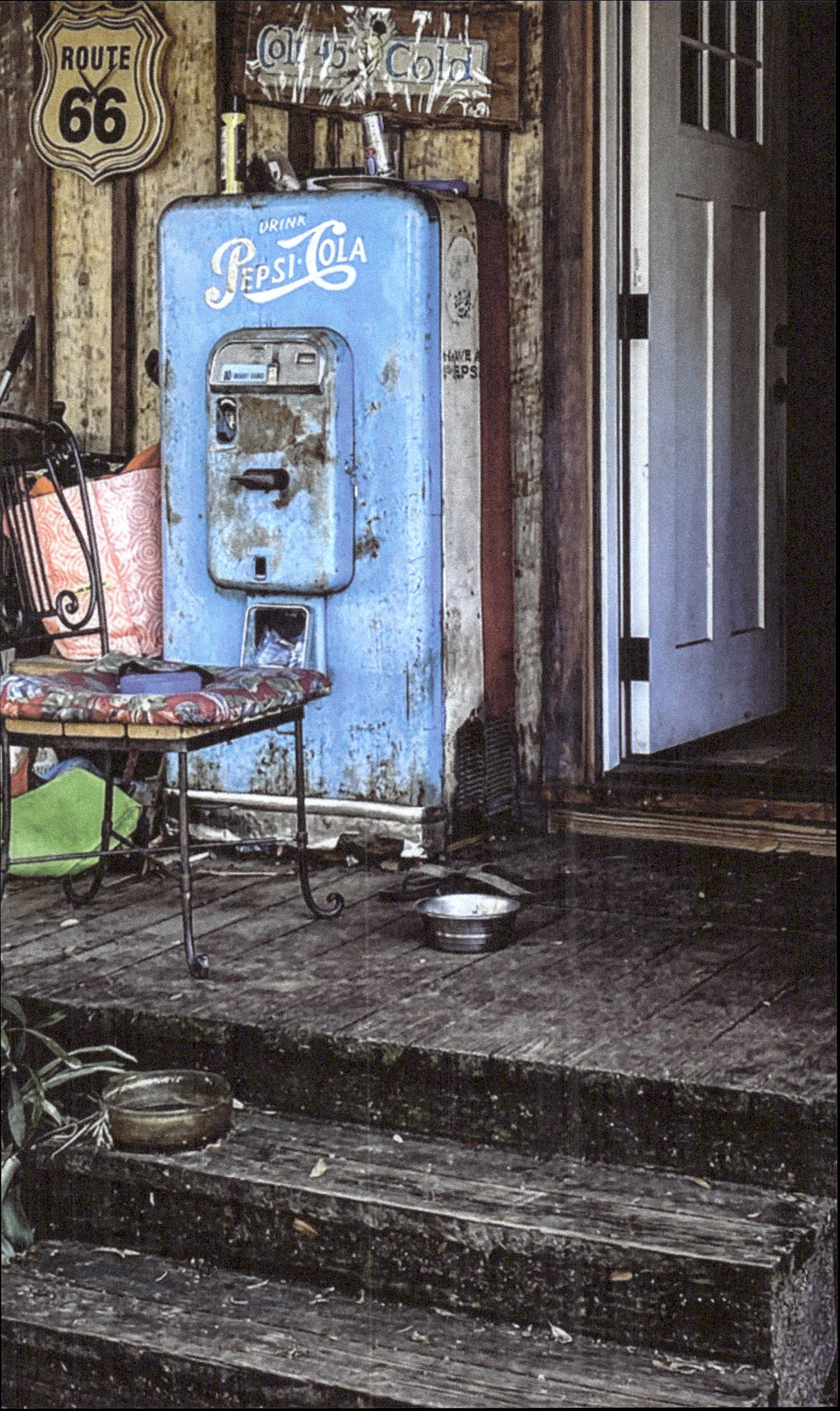

ROUTE
66
Col 45 Cold
DRINK
Pepsi-Cola
HAVE A
PEPSI

We fool around in the sauna

at our gym, mostly because we can.
Proximity is an analogue for

hunger and *danger*, hanging over us
like an old witch's curse

since we first opened our eyes. I'm sorry
for trying to find meaning in this;

I hate that I can't simply enjoy a stranger's
naked body as he removes his towel, as he

reveals the carved rivulets
his bones and musculature create,

as he beckons me through the choke
of hot air to come swallow him like an unfinished

sentence. He makes me suck him off,
my throat tightening in anticipation of being seen,

damned because we happened to be here together.
Because we know our bodies are a living countdown.

Even we can make these little deaths
a miracle when our limbs

fit into one another when least expected. I'm sorry
for not letting pleasure simply be pleasure,

but perhaps he won't mind. When I come up for air,
lips wet, head shaking, his chest expands as if

he's inhaled whole galaxies. In the silence, he betrays nothing
but sighs, as if to say *this is how we live forever.*

How It Began

I spent years emptying myself,
two boards off my inner dam,

daily floodletting; we grab
even small control when life pours

past our hands. Jagged models
judged me from fashion mags:

cheek hollow, Egyptian
eyes, perfect spoon of space

between faultless thighs
that never rubbed

like stick on stick calling fire,
my flustered *whisk* of fabric,

Always the Good Friend, Never the Girlfriend.
Megaliths of secret crushes compressed

the Why Not Me into the finger down the throat,
the diet pills, the box cutter nicked

and applied at night to the insides
of my forearms, in crosses

two inches long. Paper packs
of failures folded

into origami arrows
pointed at my soul.

Self-contempt to one-up the world.
Myopic, maybe; we were

teenage girls raised in the era
of Brooke Shields.

Then one day, he arrived,
sweet rebel smile and guitar

hands, singing *Poison*
those potent nights

in the stygian chapel with his band.
Boy whose voice was smooth

as cream cheese, who promised me
No one will ever love you

like I do. Kisses at every stoplight,
and I believed. I married him.

How could I know, back then, how could
I know? Promise is another word for threat.

Dreamy and Content

The mother I imagined laughed easily and often. She trilled to music in the kitchen; delighted in *People* magazines stolen from the dentist's office; ate cake for breakfast; wore pajamas mid-day; nuzzled fresh-cut flowers from the garden. She slept soundly each night. Her skin glowed. She was dreamy and content.

My logic was entirely selfish: if my mother enjoyed her life then I could enjoy mine, without her sadness encroaching on my good time. I was attending a small liberal arts college then. I was twenty-one, wore dark framed glasses with plastic non-prescription lenses and no make-up or jewelry, preferring a Casio digital watch on my right wrist, identical to the one my father once wore as a soldier in the South Vietnamese army. My clothing consisted of what I could find at garage sales and thrift stores: oversized men's t-shirts advertising local businesses, elastic-band polyester pants, sneakers and athletic socks. I very much dressed like a Little League coach or a dad given a second chance at life after a heart attack. I was embarrassed by overt displays of vanity, believing it reflected a frivolous mind, even though I spent much of my time engrossed in frivolities. Crushes, parties, gossip, jokes.

My mother in real life lived in my childhood home with my father, across the river on the west side of town, around the bend from a row of sunken retirement homes that my father feared would be his future. "Which one of you will take care of me when I'm old?" he used to say to us four kids at dinner. I was pining for my exit, even then. Our silence made him laugh in response, mouth opened wide, his gold filling flashing beneath broken specks of food.

Ours was a modest split-level house, built during a small-town construction boom in the '80s, painted tawny with dark brown trim, colors that stood out against the dingy grays and blues of our white neighbors. My father chose the colors, painted it himself the summer I turned nine—with the aid of my fourteen-year-old brother's forced labor—and we kids hated it. *It looks like actual shit*, we said, but the color remained as each of us flew the coop—I was the last—leaving my parents alone together for the first time in their thirty-year-long unhappy marriage.

A musty odor of tiger balm and mothballs settled inside the house. The dining room table was cluttered with Vietnamese and English newspapers, folded tissues, napkins, battered spiral notebooks, orange pill bottles, empty plastic containers. Toothpicks. There was a dusty jar of dried sour plums—a candy I only ever associated with Asian seniors in sweater vests, sucking them to pass the time, deliberate and painstaking and seemingly unaware of their tortoise-like transformation.

Grime had collected on the bottles stacked along the periphery of the kitchen counter. On my last visit home, I tried wiping it away with a wet dish sponge but couldn't. It turned gluey instead, moving like an amoeba from one side to the next, congealed and impossible to extract, forcing me to give up on tidying their mess.

My mother was forgetting, according to my father. I was assembling a late lunch of fiber-twig cereal and milk in my kitchen at school when he called and berated me over the phone.

"You're not *here*! You're not seeing what she's like every day. She can't remember *anything*. She doesn't even know how to pick out clothes to wear in the morning! *Dù mẹ*. All you care about is yourself. You have *no idea* what's happening at home." When he got worked up, he stretched his words for emphasis, set them at a higher pitch, producing something both operatic and shrill.

I had it too. At middle school slumber parties, before the pizza arrived, parents would turn their attention to me. "Please," they said smiling, still feeling affectionate. "Do you think you could keep your voice under control tonight?" I nodded. Yes. Of course.

But unsupervised, under the influence of Sprite and Skittles, I spun across the basement floor. I got wound up and couldn't make my way back down. Howling, pink, febrile, loud. The next morning, parents gripped their coffee mugs for support and refused to look at me. One mom threatened to get me a t-shirt the next time I entered her home. "It's going to have three words across the front," she said, pointing to her freckled, peach-colored chest. "Here Comes Trouble."

"Ba. You stress Ma out," I said back on the phone in Vietnamese. I could hear Dan Rather's milky voice amplified in the background. My fiber twigs shriveled inside their bowl.

"You're always screaming, telling her she's doing something wrong.

It's not helpful. No one likes it." I made my voice tidy and clinical, the opposite of his. I didn't trust his assessment. Overzealous in pursuit of illness, my father was a chronic sufferer of made-up maladies. He was restless, agitated, and often impatient with my mother. If she was forgetting, I figured it was her attempt to ignore him.

He cursed again, elongating the *mother* in *motherfucker*. "You think you know better than me? You read books. Go to college. You think you know? I'm telling you. **Mày không biết!**"

"You're screaming again."

"**Mày nghe đây.**" His voice slowed, readying towards the crescendo I knew was coming. I was disowned. I no longer had family, a brother, sisters, mother, father. I was American-ruined. Shameful. Shallow. As good as dead. "You. Listen to me. I'm only going to say this once. You are not welcome in my home. Don't *ever* come here. I will not let you in. Nghe không? Do you understand?" He was also prone to empty threats.

"Yup. OK, Dad," I knew he hated my mocking intonation, similar to what he encountered at his factory job, the grocery store, pharmacy, drive-thru windows. Secretly, I was thrilled. No more guilt, worry, shame about not going home because now I couldn't. My father's own words! He said what I'd been hoping for, ever since I'd started attending this school. I had an excuse now, *My Dad said so*—though, in truth, I knew his pronouncement carried little weight. I'd heard him make the same declaration to each of my siblings after a minor insult or infraction. A rite of passage in my family was rejection. It was simply my turn now. He hung up and the phone radiated heat against my ear.

***

I lived less than two miles from my parents in a rickety off-campus house rental shared with four friends, all seniors a year above me in school. My inclusion felt singular and precarious and I didn't want to jinx it.

Despite my proximity, I mimicked the separation my friends from Brentwood, Evanston, and Buckhead, a rumored cattle ranch in Texas, had. I envied their cross-country cachet and pretended I could do the same.

I didn't go home for dinner or laundry. I didn't call. I didn't have family vacation photos screen printed onto a homemade quilt like the one

my first-year roommate slept under each night. I didn't receive checks in
the mail, nor any money for that matter, depending on future-debilitating
loans for my school and living expenses.

I was a "townie" and a skillful deflector. My ploy was making fun of
my classmates, many of whom were the children of wealth and privilege,
like Sejal in her green Lexus, sedentary while skulking through campus, a
grande dame with delicate ankles, refusing to tread the icy footpaths like
the rest of us. There was blonde and belligerent "Scary Meg" who wore
silk nighties and victimized unfamiliar faces at parties; got so aggressively
close you could smell the astringent cocaine crackling off her skin. There
were the dreadlocked white boys from Horace Mann and Fieldston.
Truthfully, only two had dreads; one, in fact, was losing hair. But all
spoke in an affected vernacular, punctuating their sentences with "yo, yo,
yo" and "dawg." They called weed *ganja*. They were Black appropriators
with penthouse addresses in Chelsea and the Upper East Side. Dread-
locked or not, each felt alike in their offensiveness.

My housemate Lauren's father was a medieval scholar and former Ma-
cArthur Fellow, or what I called a *MacGenius*. Her cupboard was located
below mine in our shared kitchen and was always full. Towers of canned
organic lentil soup and sustainably caught tuna. Expensive Swedish
crackers. Meanwhile, I was a vegan out of necessity. My lunch remained
mostly the same that year. Fiber twig cereal and soy milk. For an occa-
sional splurge, I added carob chips and dried apricots into my bowl.

Lauren was fancy and pretty. She wore business-casual attire—wide-
legged dress pants, heeled leather boots and soft knit sweaters. She had
glossy brown hair that looked healthy and untangled. Tiny wisps danced
along the crest of her forehead. When she got drunk, her cheeks became
flushed and these hairs collapsed sideways across her unblemished skin.

We laughed alike, wide-mouthed and cavernous. In one of our first
conversations, she told me I shared the same name as her younger sister,
Katie. It wasn't until we'd been living together for nearly a term that a
mutual friend told me Katie was severely disabled and lived in a facility
away from home. I recognized Lauren's reluctance as something pain-
ful and private. We avoided asking personal questions of each other. We
were respectful in this way.

***

On a snowy night in February, a month after my father's phone call, my mother went missing. She'd driven in the car to see me, an afternoon together, just the two of us.

She'd called earlier in the day. "Is Katie home?" she said, her voice tentative. It was the first time she'd ever phoned me at school.

"Ma, it's me," I said.

"Katie *-ah.*" Her voice relaxed as she said my nickname, a Vietnamese rendition with a playful lilt at the end, softening the staccato break and striking a tender nerve inside me. "Your father's at work. Can Ma come see you?" She said she missed me.

I suggested we meet on campus. She was unfamiliar with the layout; she'd been only a handful of times, but I insisted. I was afraid bringing her into my college home and introducing her to my older, sophisticated friends would ruin the idyll I'd created for myself at school, one I believed was pleasant because neither of my parents were in it.

I imagined her smile dissolving the moment she stepped through the front door, eyes scanning our screened front porch and seeing the empty liquor bottles and cigarette butts, realizing I'd been lying about school commitments that had kept me away. I'd been having fun all along.

I gave directions to the campus library instead.

The library was quiet, cerebral, and serious—everything I wanted my mother to believe I was. I told her I spent my afternoons here. It made the most sense to meet at this location. I told her where to park the car and repeated my directions a second time, asking if she understood, knowing how terrible her navigational skills were, how infrequently she left home. She loathed going to the grocery store alone and used to plead with me to accompany her each time.

"I understand," she cooed over the phone.

I stood in the library foyer for twenty, thirty, forty-five minutes, examining each shrouded face that entered, checking my watch in between. I ran circles up and down the periodicals, the study rooms, creaky folio machines, and bathroom stalls. Back outside, I scoured the empty parking lots, winding footpaths running alongside and behind the buildings, past smoking silhouettes huddled around frozen picnic benches.

I went into the student center, craning my neck at the back of the greasy snack bar line. Then upstairs to the TV lounge where glassy-eyed students sprawled across sofas, watching reruns of *The Simpsons*. No one looked up when I entered the room.

Thinking she might have gotten her libraries confused, I raced the
three blocks to the downtown public library next. It was dark and snow-
ing. Sharp icy flakes pierced my cheeks, studding my shoulders and hair.
My feet slipped on the frozen ground. I was talking to myself at this
point, ranting, cursing, jacked on adrenaline, wind whipping, sweat drip-
ping down my temples, the sides of my neck, into the slippery curve of
my lower back.

Across the street from the library was The Tavern, the dark wooden
restaurant where I'd imagined my mother and I would sit in a candlelit
booth and share a brownie sundae. *A brownie sundae?* I figured if I could
just get her alone, the mother I'd imagined would appear, laughing and
bright, proof she wasn't forgetting after all.

***

The spring of my senior year in high school, my mother's face
scowled with each faraway college acceptance letter that arrived in the
mail. She worked the graveyard shift on an assembly line. The circles
beneath her eyes were so hypnotically dark they made you sleepy just
looking at them.

In Vietnam she'd been the valedictorian of her high school class.
When she was twenty-four her father arranged her marriage to my father,
another Vietnamese-born, ethnic Chinese kid like her, though he was a
middle-school dropout with an erratic temper and steady gambling oc-
cupation.

She attempted suicide three months after her wedding. I never know
how to frame this information. In the introduction? As an afterthought?
Or does this lie at the heart of the story I'm trying to tell?

She never spoke of this and I was never meant to know. My older
sister told me in high school, after being sworn to secrecy by a distant
cousin. I'll never know the intricacies of her pain that made her jump off
the bridge, into the river below, before strangers scrambled to her rescue
on the riverbank. Shame and secrecy have always loomed larger than
truth in my family's stories.

Sometimes I think her forgetting could have started on that bridge
overlooking a river, in a previous life, in a previous country. This lonely
memory became a long, slow-burning misery she thought she could
contain, receding further and further until it no longer registered, until it

became a pain so infinite she felt nothing but blank.

She was twenty-eight when my eldest sister was born. My brother was born two years later; another sister two years after that. A total of three children in the span of four years. Then the Fall of Saigon and the communist takeover. A late-night escape by boat. Refugee camp.

At thirty-five, she landed in our small, snow-dreary town in Minnesota. She got pregnant with me two months later. She had the nervous habit of scratching her calves, searching for an elusive itch that seemed both everywhere and nowhere, aggravating both sides of her legs into piscine scaled patterns as if she was trying to claw out of her own skin.

She sang to herself while cooking dinner in the kitchen. The knife's steady chop against the cutting board provided a synchronized beat. I'd be watching afterschool TV specials in the living room when her singing and chopping would suddenly stop. "Katie-ah!" She'd say, alarmed. I'd race over, worried, only to find her holding a snap pea, carrot, or jicama offering in her hand. "You won't believe how sweet it is. *Try.*"

Up close, her eyes were wet with tears. "Chopping onions," she insisted, looking sheepish. The sight always made me hesitate. Even when she was singing and meant to be happy, I couldn't help but see her sadness.

I'm grateful to the strangers who saved her that day on the riverbank, even if it meant everything afterwards became an act of survival for her. Even if it meant forgetting became a way to survive too. A perverse preservation of sorts. Her memories too big, too saturated and bright. It made sense to finally let them go.

Attending college close to home felt like a small sacrifice to make, in light of everything. I was the child of refugee parents and fueled by guilt, living nearby only to never see them. Each time another classmate said, "I can't believe you're a *townie*," I feigned nonchalance, grinning and proud and said, "No. Neither can I."

***

The library's public-use telephone hung on a wall behind the children's librarian's desk, next to a corkboard of flyaway photocopies, thumbtacked business cards, a handwritten note detailing the year, model, and dimensions of a John Deere tractor for sale.

I used this same phone as a kid when I needed to call home for a ride. I dialed my house number, remembering how the last four digits spelled the word JAIL. I'd made this discovery in middle school and yowled in reaction. "The universe knows!" I told my sisters, stunned.

My chest was tight and my body was damp. I knew what my father was going to say even before I told him. Why don't you ever listen to me? You never do! Your mother can't leave the house anymore. She gets lost. You always think you know!

Moments earlier, I repeated the frantic search I'd done inside the college library. Up and down stairs, through periodicals, aisle after aisle, stall after stall. I peered inside the mushroom-shaped reading nook meant for children and saw a young version of myself stretched across the seat, head propped against the faded corduroy cushions, pile of books towering at my side.

My mother never helped with homework. When I struggled with long division in fifth grade and then algebra in high school, she told me to consult my older siblings. "They know better than me," she said, as if her knowledge was no match for theirs. The only advice she gave was to read. "Read everything. Read as much as you can." Her face turned serious in these moments, unflinching in its authority.

I spent Saturdays and after-school hours holed inside this nook, doing as she said, reading, eventually gaining entrance into the nearby good college, and then later, absorbing too many American notions, perhaps, that dismissed women like my mother as passive and weak, her mind thwarted by old-world traditions.

I disagreed with her choices and wanted an alternate outcome for her, and by extension, for myself. I couldn't see her quiet constraint as resiliency, hewing to a predictable order so I wouldn't have to. I was too young and tried to forget her. Or, I tried to move on without her.

Either way, the outcome was the same: she started to forget herself. The particulars of this timing will turn over in my mind for the rest of my years, I think.

***

I hung up the phone, a weight lodged inside my stomach. I walked back home and borrowed my housemate Annie's wheezing maroon Oldsmobile. I told her I needed it for a family emergency. She handed the keys without asking more. A pair of furry dice and the red, gold, and green flag of Rastafari hung from her rearview mirror.

I drove across the river, around the bend of sunken retirement homes, toward the dingy grey and blue split-level development on the west side of town where my childhood home stood. A police car was parked outside.

I walked through the front door as though my father had never said otherwise. He was irate, pacing the living room floor in front of the white lace curtains that looked like tied-up

brides in wedding dresses. Next to him was an armed and courteous cop, bushy moustache and yellow notepad in hand, just like in the movies.

Louise Whitte was seated on the sofa. My father had phoned her after he and I spoke. He called her *Bà Louise,* using a venerated Vietnamese title reserved for female elders, even though they were the same age. He regularly sought her counsel.

She was the president of the town's Refugee Resettlement Committee, a blonde, buttery-voiced Lutheran church volunteer and my family's American sponsor. She was divorced and lived alone. She'd been there to greet my family at the Minneapolis/St. Paul airport when they'd arrived from the refugee camp in Thailand. "I was the one signing the papers for every refugee we took," she said proudly. "All 118 of them."

She enjoyed relaying my family's coming-to-America story back to us, conflating our arrival in September with another Chinese-Vietnamese refugee family's in January, when the temperature was harrowingly cold and the children wore flip flops and shorts. We never corrected her. We knew it was a tale she took great pleasure in telling again and again and again.

On the night my mother went missing, I waited in the living room next to Louise. She told me I needed to *face the facts.* She called me *kiddo.*

She relayed a story she'd heard on the local news, just a few weeks earlier, about a man who went missing in the woods of Wisconsin. He had Alzheimer's, "Just like your mom," she said, too eagerly. "He stepped outside of his home and wandered away. He's been missing ever since." Her pastel blue eyeshadow looked chalky and overdone. "The police say they doubt he's still alive. This is what I'm afraid happened to your mom, *kiddo.*"

She was telling the story a second time when my mother returned, alive and smiling and not missing somewhere in the woods of Wisconsin. I thought of the description I once read in a travel guide to Vietnam, inadvertently useful in understanding the foreign habits of my parents. *A smile or laughter from a Vietnamese person may mean that they are feeling nervous or uncomfortable, and not necessarily happy.*

"What's all this?" she said, smiling. She looked at me, then my father, Louise, the mustached cop. A cacophony of voices. My father's the loudest. The cop looked pinched and uncomfortable, yellow notebook frozen in his hand.

I can't recall how she and I ended up in the dining room together. I think I was swift. I must have reached for her the moment she stepped inside. I saw the flicker of awareness settle across her face. Her smile vanish. I anticipated her embarrassment and wanted to lead her a safe distance away, one agonizing footstep after the other, everyone watching as we floated across the stained, carpeted floor.

"Everything's fine. What's the big fuss?" she said between tears. Her velvet-rich voice shattered and cracked.

Our bodies leaned against each other, and in the next moment, she crumpled, falling to the floor, emptied and anguished. I sat on the ground next to her and clasped her hands in mine. They felt weightless.

"It's OK, Ma. Don't cry. Don't cry. Please don't be sad." I tried to reassure her because I didn't know what else to do, mimicking the same refrain she used on me when I was young and wounded. But she was crying tortured animal noises, and so was I, and there was Louise, our American sponsor watching from across the open expanse of the living and dining room, always watching, the armed and courteous cop, and my father, red-faced and irate, which meant everything was not OK, perhaps never was.

Her voice gurgled, submerged as if underwater. "I want to die. I'd rather go now than deal with this anymore."

She seemed to diminish in size as she said this, transforming into a small child on the floor. I was twenty-one. She was fifty-six. She was born in the year of the dog. Her eyes begging in that moment. My mother was forgetting. She and I both understood the impossibility of her situation. But she still had enough clarity to know something was wrong. She wanted an alternate outcome for herself, and maybe by extension, for me.

"No, no, no," is what I said, even though my resistance lacked conviction. I wasn't so sure. I kept glancing at the cop's gun. Given the circumstances, I couldn't help myself.

Everyone disbanded afterwards, awkward in the way an audience is after an unsatisfying show. My father was uncharacteristically quiet, holding back, as he did, in the presence of white people. I barely paid attention. I don't remember saying goodbye to my mother or anyone else. It still stuns me to think I left her. I was too shaken up to think clearly, drained of feeling, a pain I've now blocked from memory.

We never spoke of our conversation that night, of what she'd said to me. I hoped she forgot. I wanted to forget too, but I couldn't. I can't. Years passed and I became haunted by a future that didn't include my mother in the way I thought it would.

I returned home to find Lauren working alone at the table, a freshly made gin and tonic next to her computer. I tried to play it cool at first, but I was too distraught. My shell cracked. Like my mother earlier, I fell to the floor and wept. She sat across from me, nodding and quiet and asking little. Her restraint came from a place of recognition. I understood then that she'd intuited all along what I'd been so desperate to hide. My worthless façade. All this time I thought I was being so strategic.

As it tured out, the mother I'd imagined came true. I'd created this memory of a thing as having already happened, and it eventually did, though not in the way I'd wanted; not when I was twenty-one and in my third year of college, but four years later, when my siblings and I lived together in a house without my father, in a quiet suburb outside San Francisco. My mother woke us up in the mornings, dancing to music in the kitchen, laughing, clapping, still in pajamas. Her skin did indeed glow. In fact, she appeared younger than ever. Her favorite spot was next to the magnolia tree that bloomed in our small backyard, each of us taking turns for the next fifteen years caring for our dreamy and content and sick mother.

Bleed

Procreate, digital art
2023
(Next Page)

This work was inspired by my dependency to social media as a teen-ager. I used grayscale for the central figure to show the monotony and boredom of reality, while the neon colors in the background show the overstimulation from being online. The colorful tears falling from widened eyes symbolizes how mindless content consumption distorts our vision of what is healthy—whether in relationships, bodies, or lifestyles. When a single tap can lead to falling down a rabbit hole of perfectly curated content, we risk losing real human connection in the process.

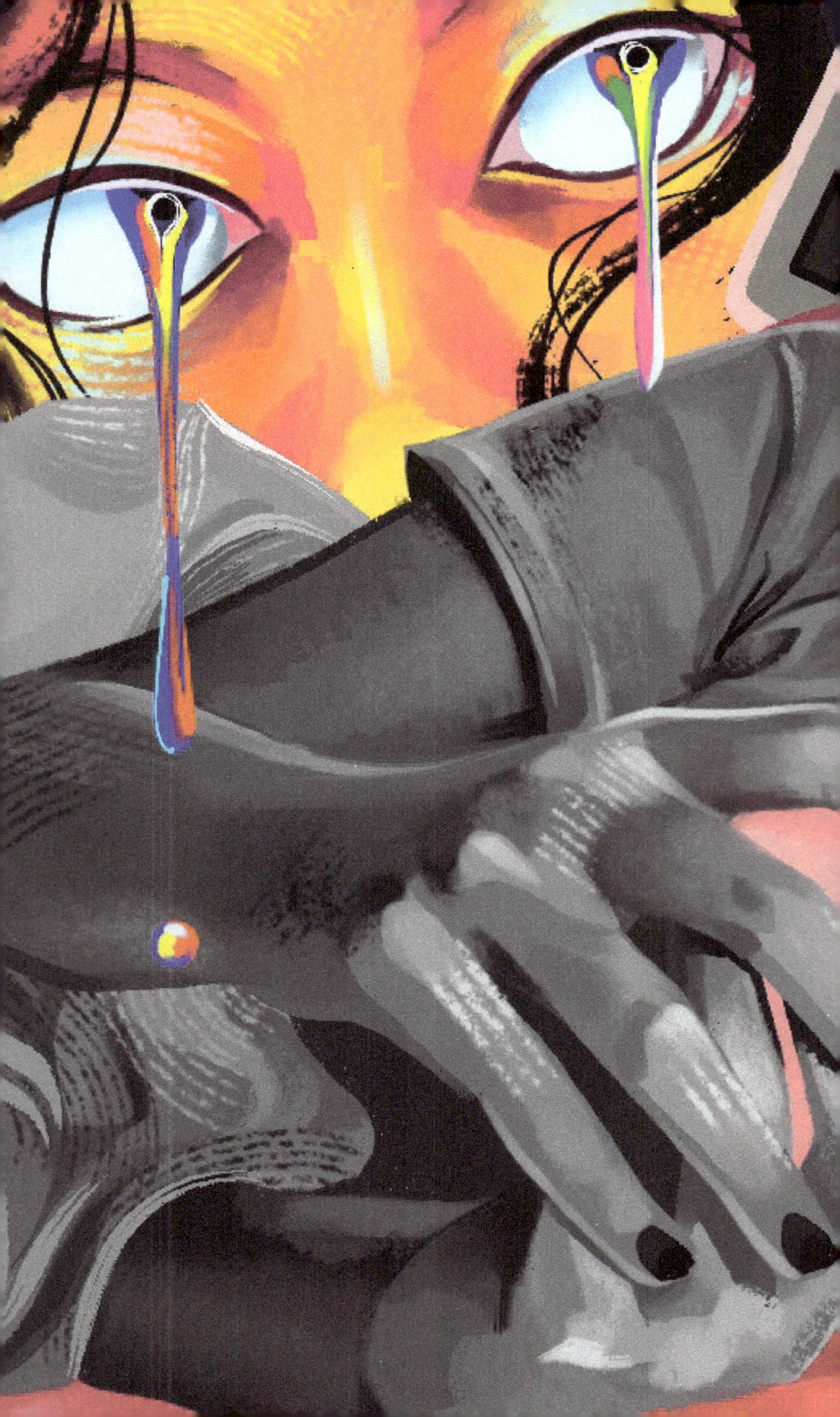

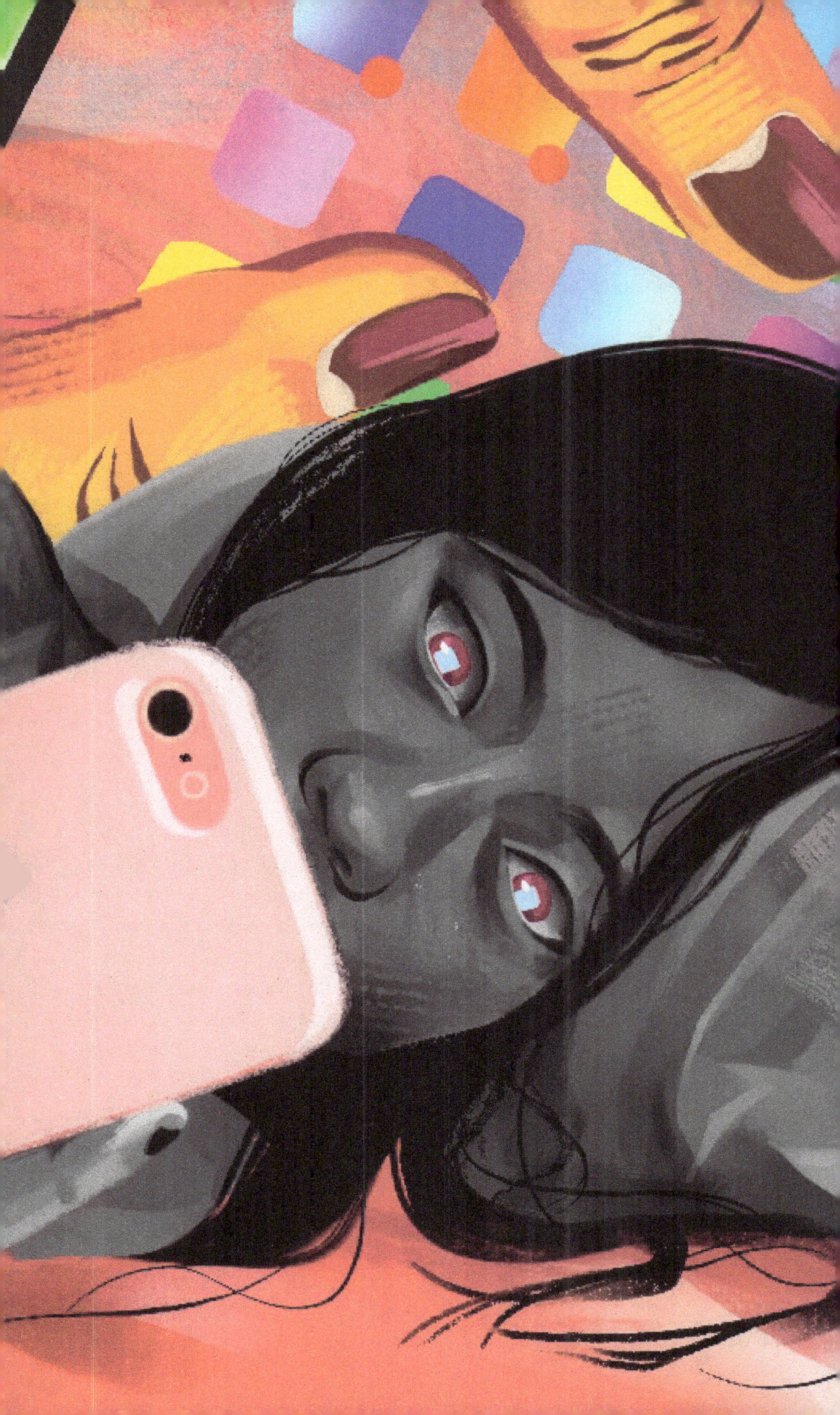

Afterimage

A man stood before a tribunal of shadows, surrounded by white.

He wore a white linen button-down and white linen pants, loose-fitting over his wrinkled walnut skin—the traditional formal wear of a country that was once his. He held a straw hat in his knotted hands, frayed with use. His fingers fidgeted with it while he looked down, with respect that was once taught, and then enforced.

The tribunal consisted of three Appraisers, lit from above so they looked like nothing but shadows. They sat on a raised dais, looking down. The wall behind them was white, matching the white ceiling and white floor. It was not a room often used. But then again, the man's request was uncommon, to say the least.

The Appraiser in the middle leaned forward.

The man gripped his hat tighter.

"So, Mr. Pablo Peralta," said the Appraiser with a tired voice. "You want to die."

***

You are walking through the hallways of your high school, a sea of faded green lockers lining your vision. You're headed to your first class, math; something the heavy tightness in your gut doesn't let you forget. The air smells of sweat and cafeteria food—something with gravy—oily and sticky and clogging your nose. You hear sharp squeaks of shoes against tile, rubber against rubber. Chatter fills the air—fast, happy, energetic—words fading in and out as you pass by groups of people sharing stories of their weekends. You remember your own weekend, and the dread of math lifts for a second. You feel a smile spreading across your face and try to quell it, pressing the straps of your bag more tightly against you. Not yet, not yet, keep cool, you say to yourself. Your thoughts distract you from the rhythmic cadence of your steps—you falter and stutter and almost trip, face heating up like the embers of a bonfire. You glance around, nothing happened, you tell yourself, nothing happened, and keep walking.

***

"Sí," said Pablo to the looming tribunal. "No," he corrected himself. He squeezed his hat. "Not die. I want to be unplugged."

"To be unplugged is to die," snapped the Appraiser on the left, tone unforgiving. It reminded Pablo of his school teachers, in his other life.

"Lo siento," said Pablo. "I mean no offense. But—"

His gaze asked for silent permission to continue, but the three figures remained impassive. Pablo swallowed, trying to fill himself with courage. He was already there; he had to make his case.

"But—" he stammered. "There are whispers that we can get out. Y regresar. Go back. People have done it."

Silence, then.

"And you think you people know better than us?"

"No, of course not." But Pablo's voice trailed off. The implications of his tone sat in the sterile room.

"But?" asked the Appraiser in the middle.

Pablo looked up, eyes hopeful and fierce, in a way he knew was dangerous. "I read the clauses," he said, heart in his throat.

***

You've reached the door to your classroom and the person you love, sitting inside.

The cool bite of spearmint gum in your mouth compresses and rolls—bleeding sugary freshness—as your jaw muscles tense and release. Tense and release, tense and release; an action that has always felt violent and feral and *good* to you. You shake the thought away and fill your lungs with air and courage: You get to see that person again, your person, for the first time since the weekend. You smile, you can't help it, remembering the first time you talked to them, the kindness behind their eyes, the questions they asked, the way they made you feel understood and safe.

You reach towards the door and

the absence of it is so sudden and subtle and inexplicable that it doesn't reach your conscious awareness. The negative space of it tastes slightly like copper, salty and metallic, but only for a second, and then it's gone. You don't notice, but your gum has no flavor anymore. It's like gnawing on rubbery, lubricated plastic. You keep chewing automatically and mechanically, you can still feel it in your mouth after all, and your mind is too focused on something else to notice

—you open the door.

***

The Appraiser to the right leaned forward, looking Pablo up and down. He had been silent until now.

"You read the clauses on the contract," his voice boomed, "and you want to take your chances."

Pablo shuffled his feet. Sweat pooled on his mustached lip, even though the room was set to each instance's ideal temperature.

"I want a chance to see the real world again," he said, making himself small. "Antes de morir de verdad." The Appraiser's language module heard the English to his Spanish: "Before true death."

"And you're willing to take the chance to die by unplugging, instead of living out the remainder of your life here." Something in the Appraiser's tone, then, airy and charged. Perhaps impressed, perhaps baffled. The other two Appraisers simply bore down on Pablo.

Pablo nodded, the only thing he could do without breaking into tears.

"Sí. Yes. I have worked hard here. I have fulfilled my contract. And I want to go back home."

***

You hear your name being shouted—hurled—across the classroom of noise. You turn and see your friend waving you towards an empty spot, and—your stomach drops, your heart pounds—your person is sitting right next to it. You walk towards them—casually, indifferently—the sound of chairs against tile and loud chittering hiding the pounding of your heart.

You sit down and smile and your heart pounds but you smile and—*goddamn* your heart is about to jump out of your chest—you say, "Hola."

They smile at you—shyly, secretly, mischievously—and in a voice that melts and burns you, they say, "Hey."

A waft of your person's fragrance dances inside your nose. You bask in the aroma, consuming it and letting it consume you, bringing images of the weekend—invisible fingers grazing in a crowded room, dancing and blushed laughter, starry silence followed by those three words uttered, a promise for the future—and

and

it's gone. There is no smell anymore. Not even your person's aroma, that earthy, clean fragrance of theirs, reminding you of the bonfire you sat around when they first told you about their dreams to travel. No smell at all.

You stop yourself from frowning, laughing scatteredly instead. Your hands are damp and hot as you grip the edges of the seat, the sharp plastic pressing against your palms. You try breathing. In, hold, out. You are breathing like you always do, you feel the draft of air flow through your nose. But it doesn't have that

that *quality* to it—the shape, the texture, the fullness—that smell provides.

You stop yourself from pulling your shirt up to your nose and smelling it. You are too self-conscious for that, and you have someone to impress. Leaning slightly back, you shrug it off and continue chatting.

***

"Speaking of your work here," said the center Appraiser. "We have your records with us."

Pablo tried to smile but bowed his head instead. If his hat were real fabric, he'd have completely destroyed it with his nervous wringing by now.

"You arrived here with your husband after the collapse, seeking refuge," said the right Appraiser, monotone. "Both of you signed a contract of work in exchange for a home and safety."

Pablo nodded, feeling apologetic for no other reason than who he was. He craved the chance to explain himself. He remained quiet.

"You indeed worked hard, as you stated." The voice's timbre remained constant, yet seemed harsher somehow. "And fulfilled your contract hours three years ago, yet you remained here, working. You had a family too, with your husband. A hybrid one."

Pablo took a deep breath in—helpful, even though he knew it was not real air he breathed —knowing what was coming.

"Your family—husband, son, and daughter-in-law—was corrupted in the Lower Section data bank fire a year ago. They could not be restored."

Pablo bit his lip, and grief broke his heart all over again, even though his heart was not real either. He managed to remain motionless. He didn't want them to try to use this against him.

The Appraisers didn't notice, or didn't care. They continued reading.

"You live alone, with your grandson now. He's young, fully digital, so I'm assuming he would stay behind."

The left one smirked. Even though Pablo could only see his shadow under the light, he knew he smirked.

"Sí," said Pablo, cautiously. "This is all correct."

"So you would leave them behind? Your grandson."

***

The person you love is telling you about the rest of their weekend, and telling their friends about you, talking with energetic hands and animated expressions. You enjoy their voice, the rhythm, the steady warmth it gives, and then their words take shape and meaning, and you blush.

"You told your friends about me?" you ask.

They laugh, blushing, nodding, and you know in that moment you want to listen to that laughter forever, you know there's a life with them. You think of a question to ask, wanting to impress them. You open your mouth and sound turns off like a candle flickering out in the wind, the sudden absence of it pressing, deafening, like a thousand mouths with teeth surrounding you, shouting all at once. Like a night terror, it freezes you to the core. The illusion lasts a split second and gives away to

nothing. You see the mouth of the person you love continue moving, eyes twinkling and smiling, silent shapes flowing. You notice the door closing in the background, chairs moving and books dropping, all on mute. No music, no noise, no shapes of air coiling in your ears. Your brain tries to fill the gaps but fails.

***

His grandson. Pablo had been expecting that question, yet still felt terrified. He cleared his throat in a way he hoped would be sincere and apologetic, if such a thing were possible.

"I have—" he paused, hands cold and clammy. He cleared his throat again. "I have made arrangements," he said. "For my grandson to be okay, and safe, and loved."

The three figures stared at him in silence, waiting, judging.

"I spent all my savings," said Pablo. He didn't want to explain further.

The three figures waited.

Pablo sighed, hands twisting the hat. "I made a digital version of myself," he said. "One that will stay here. It will continue to work with you, harvesting data fields, like I have. And it will care for my grandson, raise him, teach him our culture and traditions, better than I can, at my age. I still don't understand how the technology works, how it can be me and not me, but at least it can make mole for my grandson, his favorite food, when he turns fourteen next year."

The middle Appraiser nodded, slowly.

"It seems like you have thought of everything, Pablo Peralta," he said.

The figure looked left and right, at his companions, and stood.

"But if you read the clauses correctly," he said, "you know you must request release from a tribunal, and you must be granted that release." He put special emphasis on the word granted, and Pablo swore the figure smiled.

"Now, convince us," the Appraiser said.

***

You still feel the vibrations of sound through your skin and bones. But without sound, they feel wrong, wicked. The vibrations loom loud and violent and incoherent, and you want them to stop.

You shake your head, trying to undo whatever was done to you without alerting others.

The person you love frowns. Their mouth moves to say something— maybe to ask if you're okay, maybe not—and you try to answer. The person flinches back, and you realize you're shouting. You probably look crazy. But this is crazy, isn't it?

Isn't it?

You point your hand to your ear, trembling, weak, and you shake your head, trying to communicate what has happened, and

and

in that shake
the world goes dark.

***

Pablo pulled at his hat with enough force to tear it in half.

"Esteemed tribunal of the United States of New Reality," said Pablo, fueling his body with courage that was only pretend at the moment, in this world within a world where everything was both real and pretend. "What we do here isn't living."

The figures leaned toward him, and he felt the energy of the air change. Tension, viscous and sinister, like a static charge.

Pablo gulped, but continued. "Yes, the air in this room feels real. My clothes feel real. My heart. My emotions. Everything we sense, everything we feel, feels real. But it is all created in our heads. There is still a world out there, one that is actually real."

The left one snapped. "Wasn't everything in *that* world also modulated by our senses? Who's to say that isn't just another type of reality?"

"It's not," whispered Pablo, "It can't be. What's out there is real."

"And look how your *real* world turned out. Wars, famine, pollution. You had to seek refuge here, in our perfect world." His words were a venomous spit.

The center Appraiser held up a hand. The left stepped back, glaring.

Pablo bit his lip, trying to stop his hands from shaking. He hated how real it all felt, despite, despite—

"Yes, I came here because my country was torn apart by violence," continued Pablo, "And I worked hard plowing the data fields for your citizens. I built a family here, and found something else to live for. But my mind is fading and my body is dying. And I want to feel the sun on my face one last time. I want to see my country again. To listen to its song. La canción de mi gente."

He said all of this in Spanish, the language where his emotions lived, knowing it would get translated for them.

He sighed, in defeat and in hope. "I did not come here to offend you, or to argue, and I am sorry if I did that," he said, looking down. "I came here to humbly request to be allowed out, even if it kills me. Por favor."

***

You yelp. You yelp again because you cannot hear yourself, cannot hear anything. You stand up, your heart pounding, bumping into something or someone, you can't tell, overwhelmed by what you can't see or hear or smell or taste. Your mind spirals, panicking, screaming internally. Your neck tightens and your throat flaps and your ears vibrate, and you realize you're shouting.

You try taking a step back and stumble to the ground. You don't understand why this is happening. Your hands begin looking for—something—anything to feel, savagely groping the ground around you, trying to understand. You find the metal leg of a desk, cold and grounding in your hand. You bring your other hand to your face, feel your nose and mouth. You force yourself to breathe. Okay, you think. This isn't how it's supposed to go, but maybe you can figure it out.

You feel vibrations around you, like uneven stomps. You realize that the people in the classroom must have backed away from you, forming a circle, looking at you. You imagine your person looking at you, scared, no, *horrified* at the whimpering, useless thing you have become. This more than anything breaks you. You feel a sharp wail coming from your mouth and something damp on your face. You let go of the desk and crawl forward, trying to get away. You move toward where you hope the door is. You feel someone touch your shoulder, you tense and shudder and yelp away from them, every touch violence on your skin. Your hands and knees throb, pulsating with the pain of being on the floor, palms tender and fleshy, ripe pulp ready to burst.

Steady, slow, shamefully you inch forward. You have no idea how that will help you, but you feel an animal need to escape. You need to get away. You wipe your face again, realizing the hot dampness is tears and mucus and saliva, and you slip. You bite down on your useless tongue, teeth digging into flesh and breaking it, drawing blood you can't taste. Thick, syrupy, hot, it drools down your mouth during the scream that you can't hear.

You try getting up but hit your head against unyielding concrete. You wonder why no one stopped you. You wonder if there is anyone there anymore. You can only feel what is touching you. You crave touch now, however intrusive. It is the only thing left of you. You want warm, strong hands—your person's hands—to grab and hold and guide you. You feel warm dampness atop your head, from the soft crack that the concrete created. You stumble, exhausted, panicked, lost. Something pushes against you, breaking your skin, peeling it off without a sound. You feel cold and wetness, something moist and slimy dragging against your face.

And then it stops. Your sense of touch is gone now, too. Now there is nothing, nothing at all.

You panic. True, feral, blubbering panic. You are a single shout in the void that is your senseless mind, pure fear and rabid frustration, endless and roaring, shaking you to your very core in that infinite darkness of your mind that unfurls and extends and lasts forever.

After what could've been a second or a lifetime, you notice a faint silvery glow outlined around the edges of your mind, an afterimage of what you once knew. Your thoughts move towards it, but the closer you get, the farther it seems. You don't know if you can reach it, that elusive light, but you know you need to. Nothing else matters. Nothing else is real.

***

The three Appraisers sat back down, their faces shadow under the light.

They murmured in hushed whispers between themselves as Pablo rubbed clammy hands against each other.

They turn to face Pablo in unison.

An eternity or a moment passed between beats of Pablo's heart.

"Thank you for your time," said the left Appraiser. "You have given us much to discuss. We will review your case and your request, and un-plug you, if granted."

Pablo looked at them, eyes wide in disbelief. "Gracias, en verdad. Thank you," he said. He put on his hat, turning to leave, even though there was no door and he would just vanish and reappear where he was going.

"One last thing, Mr. Peralta," said a voice behind him.

Pablo turned, hope held softly in his open palms.

"We've found that subjects—" started the Appraiser on the right, "that subjects unplug better while in a cached moment containing strong emotion. It helps the subject want to be unplugged. Something about connecting to the real us, as you put it. So—

"What memory holds the strongest emotion for you, Mr. Peralta?"

Pablo smiled, despite himself. Despite the fear and desperation and anger and sadness. He smiled because the memory still brought him joy, even now.

"When I knew I would marry my husband," he said. "When I was a teen, in class with him, after our first party together. When I made him laugh. I knew, then."

He smiled, giving his everything and his all. Even though they had already taken it.

"Very well," said the Appraiser. "And good luck."

Pablo nodded, tipping his hat. A thought occurred to him, then. "How will I know? If you grant my appeal?"

"Oh, you will know," said the Appraiser on the left, and his words sneered with cruelty.

A shiver ran through Pablo, but he nodded. There was nothing else to say.

The room around Pablo vanished as he was sent back to work, a flutter of hope stirring in his heart.

Necromancy

In the dark warm mouth of the earth,
a language festers from disuse.
My padi jokes I bury my pulsating mother-
tongue—six-feet beneath the earth's surface
—at every vain attempt at speech.

Bí ewé bá pẹ́ lára ọṣẹ...

I confess: my mouth is both
soiled & the soil. Between my vile dentition
a tongue recoils from rain, & runs
into ruin—from frying-pan into the fire.
O' jeweled dialect of my mother
rattling against my molars.
Honey-dipped ancestral tongue
tugging betwixt incisors. Unforked
speech-bud dancing in its casket.
Clawing out of its grave.

Sing me a dirge sonorous enough to awaken
a mummy—to exhume a skeleton,
reincarnate a soul—without
summoning its ghost.

...á di ọṣẹ

Mint leaf sticks to a soap bar
for so long it disintegrates
into the soap. Once,
in my uncle's garden, we buried
a peacock without a coffin.

Two harmattans after, the unmarked
grave spot thrives with lush flowers.
Oluwa, how long before
a flowery bird biodegrades into a flowerbed?

In the dark warm mouth of the earth,
a 6-foot-deep wound rescinds
into a small cut. Bones wear the flesh
again like sheathed swords.
Language, a seedling
falling on the rockside, refuses to be
planted, & still does not wither.
I render a phrase in Yoruba, &
the canary's song does not die
in its hollow syrinx.

CONTRIBUTORS

Muiz Ọpẹ́yẹmí Àjàyí (Frontier-XVIII) is an editor at *The Nigeria Review*, poetry reader for *Adroit Journal*, and a 2023 *Poetry Translation Centre UNDERTOW* cohort. Winner of the Lagos-London Poetry Competition 2022, University of Ibadan Law LDS Poetry Prize 2022, longlisted for *Ake* Poetry Prize, *Briefly Write* Poetry Prize, a *Best of The Net* nominee, he features in *Frontier, 20.35 Africa, Tab Journal, Olongo, Lolwe, SAND Journal, Poetry Wales, Yabaleft Review, Nigerian News-Direct* and elsewhere.

Daniel Brennan (he/him) is a queer writer and coffee devotee from New York, where he lives in an apartment being slowly overtaken by stacks of books. His work has appeared in numerous publications, including *Passengers Journal, The Banyan Review, Birdcoat Quarterly, Sky Island Journal,* and *The Pinch*. He can be found on Twitter and Instagram: @dannyjbrennan.

Jana-Lee Germaine is the recipient of the 2022 Patricia Dobler Poetry Award. She is a Senior Poetry Reader for *Ploughshares*. Her poems have appeared or are forthcoming in *Valparaiso Poetry Review, Iron Horse Literary Review, Chautauqua, New Ohio Review, Nimrod, Cimarron Review, EcoTheo Review, Bellevue Literary Review, Baltimore Review,* and elsewhere. She earned an MFA from Emerson College. A survivor of domestic violence, she lives with her husband, four children, and four rescue cats in semi-rural Massachusetts. She is a member of the Board of Trustees for her local public library, and she can be found online at janaleegermaine.com.

Karen Pierce Gonzalez is an award-winning, self-taught artist. Her mixed-media and assemblage artwork and color photographs have appeared in several West Coast galleries as well as in numerous magazines, including *The Storms: A Journal of Poetry, Prose & Visual Art; FERAL: A Journal of Poetry and Art; Nightingale & Sparrow Literary Magazine; Four Feathers Press's Specters/Spirits, Wishes; Cassandra Chorale (Ice Floe Press)*; and *Tidings* (Anomaly Poetry), Sebastopol Center of the Arts, and Truckenbrod Gallery. She is a 2022 National

Arts Program Featured Artist (USA), and lives in the North San Francisco Bay Area.

Caitlyn Hunter was the inaugural Emerging Black Artist in Residence at Chatham University (2021-2022). She is a doctoral candidate at Duquesne University where she researches African American literature and Black Food studies. She is currently writing both a collection of short stories and a culinary memoir around her maternal ancestry. Her first book *Power in the Tongue* (Tolsun Books) debuted in 2022. Her work appears in *Midnight & Indigo*, *Lost Balloon*, and elsewhere.

Tamara Kreutz lives with her family in Guatemala, where she teaches high school English literature at an international school. Tamara is an MFA candidate at Pacific University. Her work has been featured or is forthcoming in *Rattle*, *River Heron Review*, and *Stonecoast Review*, among other publications. Poetry gives her grounding in a life full of moving pieces. Instagram and Threads: @tamara_kreutz.

Rick Lingo is a retired educator who has travelled the world searching for the perfect shot. In this pursuit he has visited all seven continents and more than 60 countries. He specializes in architecture and travel photography but does not limit himself to these categories. His works have been exhibited world-wide, appeared in multiple print outlets, and reproduced by individuals for their personal enjoyment.

Amara Okolo is a writer and author of three books, *Black Sparkle Romance, Son of Man*, and *Daughters of Salt*. She was a participant in Chimamanda Adichie's Farafina Creative Writing Workshop and the Invisible Borders Trans African Project. She is a past Honorary Fellow from the IWP at the University of Iowa, the City of Asylum Residency, and Oxbow. Her works have been supported by Pen America and United States Artists. Her works have been published and mentioned on *Long House, Hunger Mountain, Catapult, Panorama Journal of Intelligent Travel, Commonwealth Writers, WeTransfer, A Long House*, and mentioned on *CNN, The Guardian, Aljazeera, Radio France International*. She has an MFA and is finishing up her PhD in Creative Writing and Multicultural & Gender Studies. She currently lives in Baltimore, Maryland, where she is working on her novel.

Katie Quach is a writer living in Toronto. She is the recipient of *Bellingham Review's* 2023 Tobias Wolff Award in Fiction, runner-up in *Hunger Mountain Review's* Creative Nonfiction prize, and longlisted in *CRAFT's* 2022 Creative Nonfiction Award. Other work has appeared in *Catapult* and *Past Ten*. Katie serves as a fiction editor at *The Rumpus*. She is at work on her first book.

Santiago Márquez Ramos is a mental health therapist working with Latinx immigrants in New York City. Originally from Mexico, he's passionate about weaving culture, mental health, queerness, and social justice into all his stories; as well as Spanish, his native language. He's been published in *Litro Magazine USA, Occulum Journal*, and *Latin@ Literatures*, and won second place in *Flash Fiction Magazine's* 2023 contest. He's been rejected by many other magazines, but sometimes nicely. He is a graduate of Taos Toolbox 2023, where he won George R. R. Martin's 2023 Terran Prize.

Zainab Hassan Rasheed is an unpublished artist, belonging to a small country of Pakistan, who loves to write stand-alone memoir(s) and creative non-fiction. In spite of being diagnosed with a mental health disorder last year, she is stitching her life into a rare organ, as Sylvia Plath quotes. She writes about the odds of life, loss, and something that feels like home.

Sahara Sidi is a Mauritanian-American writer and educator. Her writing has been recognized by the National YoungArts Foundation, the *Adroit Journal*, and *Salt Hill Journal*. Currently, she is a Rackham Merit Fellow at the Helen Zell Writers Program as an MFA candidate in poetry. She is a recipient of the Wesleyan University Olin Fellowship, Sophie and Ann Reed Prize, Herbert Lee Connelly Prize, Cole Prize, and the Winchester Fellowship. Most recently, she received a Hopwood Award in Nonfiction from the University of Michigan. Her work is forthcoming in *The Offing*.

Jaz Sufi (she/hers) is a mixed race Iranian-American poet and arts educator. Her work has been published or is upcoming in the *Adroit Journal, AGNI, Black Warrior Review, Colorado Review, Muzzle*, and elsewhere. She is a National Poetry Slam finalist and has received fellowships from Kundiman, the Watering Hole, and New York University, where she received her MFA. She lives in Brooklyn with her dog, Apollo.

Britnie Walston is a versatile Maryland-based artist. She captures energy through light and vibrant colors, often experimenting with acrylics and oils, while manipulating designs using unconventional tools and techniques. She's had a passion for art from a very young age, and enjoys learning and experimenting with a variety of techniques and mediums. Living near the Chesapeake, Britnie's work is inspired by nature; often depicting the absence of human presence, liberation ("set free"), and freedom ("being free"). She captures the beauty of nature, blending the boundary between reality and abstraction, and creating a unique dreamscape atmosphere. This provides viewers with a multilayered and immersive visual experience. Though her diverse range of work requires different creative processes and mediums, they are influenced by the same subject matter: freedom.

Elizabeth Yuan is a senior from Adlai E. Stevenson High School in Illinois. She has previously been recognized by Scholastic Art & Writing awards. In her spare time, she enjoys falling down a rabbit hole of Wikipedia articles and drinking unhealthy amounts of coffee.

Claire Zhou is a student currently residing in Suzhou, China. She enjoys hip-hop and badminton in her free time.

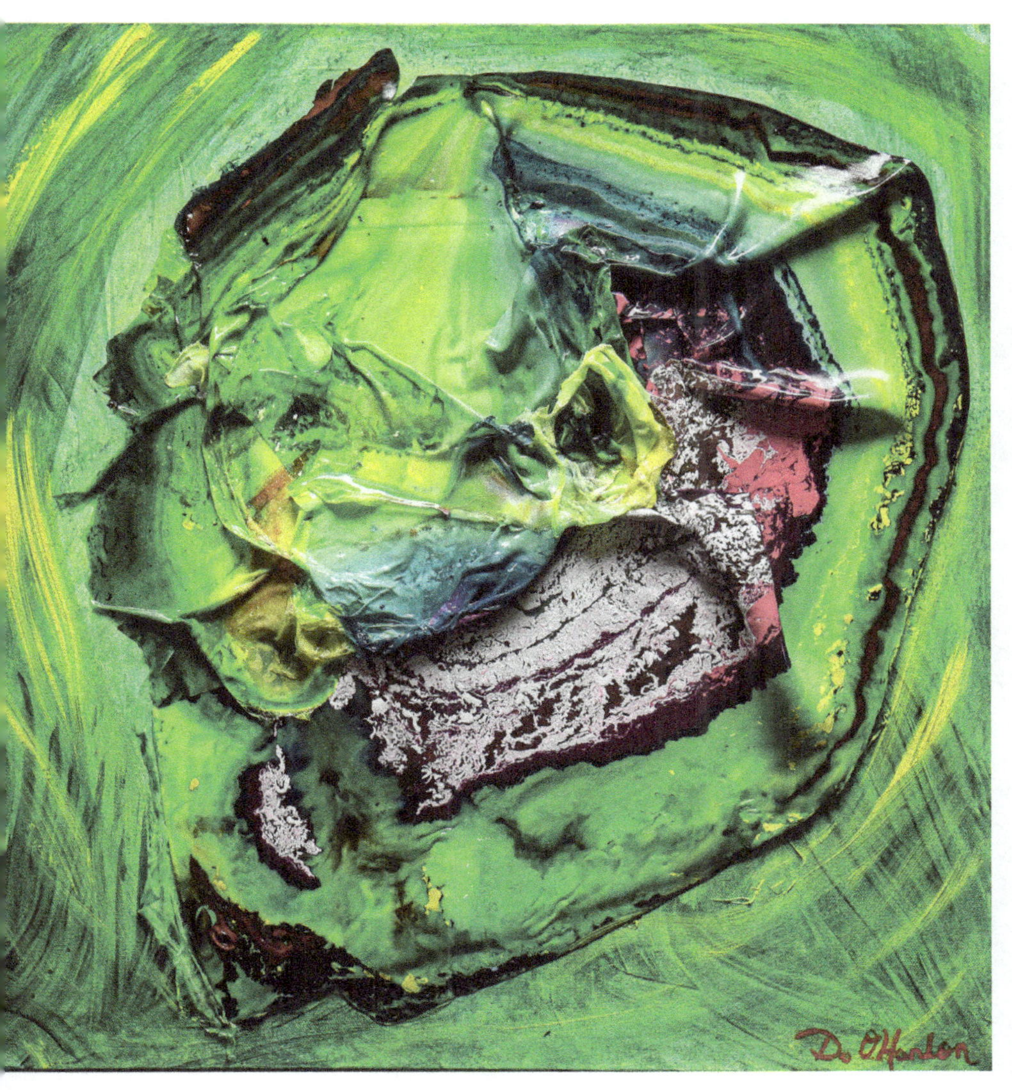

Chestnut Review

VOLUME 5 NUMBER 4 SPRING 2024

FOR STUBBORN ARTISTS

Chestnut Review

VOLUME 5 NUMBER 4 SPRING 2024

DANIELLE O'HANLON

Green Geode

Acrylic, 24x24 inches, 2020
(Cover Art)

I created the Green Geode for a show with the theme of reclaimed, recycled, and reimagined. It features bright green molded leftover paint that was scraped from the floor of my studio and sculpted onto a canvas. I created this painting while awake at 3 am and knocked out the power to my entire apartment building using my heat gun. The original work is still available for purchase.

Chestnut Review LLC, Ithaca, New York
chestnutreview.com

Chestnut Review appears four times a year online, in January, April, July, and October, and once per year in print in July.

ISSN 2688-0350 (online), ISSN 2688-0342 (print)

CONTENTS

SPECIAL THANKS

To our generous Patreon supporters:

Adam Boustead, Joy Gallagher Bullen,
Ciel Downing, DrJRad, Regina McIntosh,
Chris Mikesell, M. Benjamin Thorne

to learn more, go to
https://patreon.com/chestnutreview

Introduction

The vernal equinox signals the arrival of spring to the Northern Hemisphere and autumn to the Southern atmosphere. Here in our slice of the US, the trees bloom white and pink, leaving swirls of pollen like bee glitter and erasing our memories of the past fall and winter. Our Spring Issue marks the end of a season and a turning towards the next: a time of celebration and change as our fifth year comes to a close. We are as busy and buzzy as bees constructing new projects and sweetening old ones.

Our issue features artists whose work is inquisitive, sensual, experimental, familial. We hope you find shared experience in the language and art we present to you here. Whichever season you find yourself in, may you sense the shift inside and outside and take us with you.

A B D U L J A L A L   M U S A   A L I Y U

This Desire to Flee From People I Cherish to a Strange World Is a Form of Brain Disease I'd Be Lying to Say I Comprehend

A battle is going on between my īmān
& the voices in my head. I try to make

sense of it, but my therapist told me
not everything has to make sense

to make sense. I locked myself in the
room because this horniness is

threatening to throw my soul in the
fire of jahannam. I asked my friend

what being bipolar feels like, & he
told me it renders him numb—like a

cadaver. An acquaintance informed
me she self-harms to feel alive. Because

when the demons sneak in, her body
feels lifeless, she craves for a proof

that she, too, like other humans, has
blood streaming in her veins. Tell

me, will I swim in the waters of
hellfire if this insanity has a hand

in me putting a full stop to my life?
My Mu'allim said the ink is lifted off

a man living on the mat of madness.
There is a body in my body telling

me suicide is selfish; had our
lives belong to us alone, Allaah

wouldn't intertwine our hearts with
others'. I'd be lying

to say I comprehend my desire
to flee the people I love

& enter a strange world. There
is a hole in my brain that devours

every single atom of happiness that
falls on my body. But anguish, loss,

trauma, torment & everything devoid
of joy feasts between my breasts.

A critic asked why every poem I craft
walks through the gates of grief. & I

said: because my poems are a haven
where men like me—whose headspace

are never free of noise—come to enjoy
the therapy in knowing they aren't alone.

A Conversation with Abduljalal Musa Aliyu

ZK: In the poem "God Descends to the Lowest Heaven," you write, "My friends do not recognize my poems/any longer." Where do you see *Encyclopedia of Dolour* fitting into your work overall? Does this feel like a natural transition from your previous work or is this completely new ground for you?

AMA: This is utterly new ground for me. I mean, have you read my previous poems? Scandal—apologies to Myz—I wrote remarkable erotica. Even yesterday, a friend said: you, all you do is write erotica and submit them to magazines. I couldn't open my mouth and say: bro, have you read my new poems? I write something entirely different now. Erotica used to be my trademark.

ZK: How long did this chapbook take to write? Did any poem feel particularly easy or difficult to write?

AMA: Well, I never really set out to write a chapbook. I was simply writing my poems—one poem at a time. And then I saw CR's call for chapbook submissions and I was like: yeah, I should try this. So, I don't know how long it took me to write the individual poems. For the chapbook, I just woke up one day, put the poems together, and submitted them.

Writing the first poem in the chapbook—"A Shared Language"—was spectacularly easy. This would read like a myth, but I promise it happened: I woke up from sleep with the exact poem in my head, devoid of the small editing by the editors of course, bless them—and I just wrote it; right there, right then, in a matter of a minute or so.
But then, writing "Falmata" was hard. The woman in the poem was stiff to deal with. She was too traumatized, so talking to her was like walking through a museum of grief. I couldn't finish the poem. Maria, while

editing the chapbook, asked if I was sure that was the end of the poem. I literally just told her to move on because I didn't know how to end the poem.

ZK: How has writing this chapbook helped you unearth new insights into grief, love, and faith? How do you hope it will impact readers?

AMA: I am someone who is on a quest for himself. So, writing this chapbook was a journey into myself. But because a man can't live alone, this odyssey involved other people, this is why there are a lot of speakers in the chapbook.

So, through this journey, with myself and others, I was able to dig into anything and everything that is important to me. Which includes faith, love, grief, etcetera.

All the poems in the chapbook appeared in a way that the speakers were talking to another person. So, I want my readers to simply listen to those speakers, and bask in whatever story the speakers try to tell—or perhaps, escape from those stories—because, sometimes, even I write these poems as an escape.

ZK: Some of the poems in *Encyclopedia of Dolour* are written in couplets, others in a single long stanza, and yet others in numbered sections. Most, if not all, of these poems have relatively short lines, but several have lengthy titles. How are these choices related to the chapbook's content and themes?

AMA: When I write narrative poems, I love having them as couplets. That way, I don't see how long they get. I just keep moving till I finish telling the story. I write single, long stanza poems when I hold tight to one idea and I don't want it to run away. But numbered poems? Call them the chaos in my head; whenever ideas are juggling in the mind of my muse and they refuse to be independent, I number them on pages. I write short lines because I hate when my poems get published and their form gets altered. And for lengthy titles, it's just an obsession I've with metaphors. Sometimes I form the titles before the poems, other times, I pick the titles from the poems. I am sure you understand the relationship between the content and the themes with all these choices I made. The poems in this chapbook are concerned with Boko Haram, banditry, faith, love, and so many other loosely interconnected themes. It's like a collection of short stories with the same setting.

ZK: The word 'encyclopedia' appears once in the text, in the poem title "Here, I Introduced Kotus to the Encyclopedia of My Grief," but the word 'dolour' is only featured in the chapbook title. How did you choose the name *Encyclopedia of Dolour* to encapsulate this work?

AMA: The title came after I'd put the poems together. I wanted something different. I didn't want my title to be too poetic, I also didn't want it to sound like a prose work's title. I read the whole chapbook one morning and I felt there was too much darkness in the poems. But I was also happy I wrote them. My people were going through a lot then. You read the front page of a newspaper and you struggle to find even one happy news. It was that bad. So, I told myself I was documenting all that; that is exactly where the word 'encyclopedia' came from; and dolour simply tried to capture the themes of the poems.

ZK: The chapbook opens with an epigraph from Mahmoud Darwish, and at one point quotes Rumi. How has their work, and that of other poets, informed *Encyclopedia of Dolour?*

AMA: Darwish is a Palestinian poet. I am sure you understand why I keep him close; our themes are related. But that epigraph? I was talking to my mentor, Nasiba Babale. I told her I wanted an epigraph for my chapbook—she has read and given insight on every single poem in that chapbook—and within a split second, she coughed out that epigraph and I was like: how perfect. Rumi is regarded as the greatest mystical poet of Islam—even though that could be argued. But there is a high place for faith in my poems. Therefore, I read his work a lot—it's mostly about relatability.

These are poets whose work I was constantly reading when writing the poems: Mahmoud Darwish, Nizar Qabbani, Rumi, T.S Eliot, Anne

Sexton; Umar Abubakar Sidi, Ismail Bala, Abu Bakr Sadiq, Samuel A. Adeyemi, and Warsan Shire. So, yes, their poems informed the chapbook a lot. How? Mostly through inspiration. I find it easier to write poetry when I read poetry.

Abduljalal Musa Aliyu's
Encyclopedia of Dolour is now available
on our website and Amazon.com.

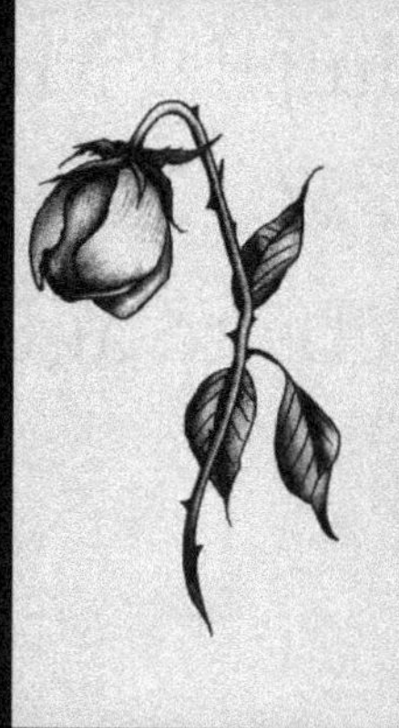

ENCYCLOPEDIA OF

DOLOUR

Abdujalal Musa Aliyu

WINSHEN LIU

You know the kind of school

Assigned in November, we were to
become pilgrims on the
classroom ship, so my mother crafted
dress and collar for me to
emulate Honor and Prudence.
For January's lesson, we drew
"gentry" or "slave" from a
hat and I wish
I could say we threw Ticonderogas,
jumped onto desks. But I
knew too little then, only afraid of
losing the few friends I had.
March meant Ellis Island Day, when we
needed to bring a dish from
our heritage. Per my request, my
parents braised eggs for hours. The spiced soy sauce
quelled their fears I'd forget where I was from.
Really from. But my classmates showed up with
spaghetti and shortbread. Store-bought cake. It wasn't that the
teacher opened the pan after dessert, or that my classmates
uttered *ew* like a punchline. It wasn't my
voyage home on the bus; it was the pan's
weight in my mother's hands, with
exactly the same contents as
yesterday. Two dozen eggs—instead of
zero—inside.

An Entirely Different Girl

How can you explain joy? The way it leaps without reason into the heart, bypassing the stricken mind. How it lies in the hand as your fingers curl around the new doll your mother had just sewn. The face pulled taut as bed sheets. The features painted bold and true: the appley cheeks and brown eyes, and the prairie-fire color of Indian Paintbrush blooming the lips—the expression caught between innocence and knowing. Not like the stiff, sad corncob dolls made by the other mothers in 1880, here on the pancake-flat Plains.

An aunt from "Back East" sent Matilda's mother material to make their own clothes and craft the dolls. Back East, where her mother was born and grew up, the Plains that here surrounded their sod dwelling for miles and days and years were called fields, cut through with blue streams. Her mother drew Matilda pictures of Massachusetts: across the fields, in the distance, mountains. She drew a circle at the bottom of one and said that's where Matilda's father grew up, in a mill town where waterfalls—waterfalls!—powered the saws. In front of the mountains, she drew trees, and wrote their names: *oak, maple, birch, chestnut.* On the Plains, there were few trees. Her mother drew leaves of the different trees, and Matilda imagined their texture between her fingers, felt their slight scratch across her cheeks.

Today, Matilda stood in the vast space of the prairie and wished her face was unroughened, her lips as bright as the new doll's. Twelve years old and still she hugged it to her chest. She and her mother had wheeled a cart not far from their home to where buffalo ran, so her mother could collect their dung, the large chips used to fuel their cook stove. On the cart, the chips were piled higher than Matilda's head, the stack tilting dangerously. Her mother stood so close she could tip the stack over, and for a moment Matilda feared she would. She moved away from the cart, but her mother's attention was not on her daughter; rather, it seemed to Matilda, it was on some faraway place—Massachusetts? A sharp gust swung her mother's dark dress about her like a vulture's wing. Buffalo chips fell from the cart.

Startled, her mother gestured toward her. "Go on, girl, pick them up."

Matilda would not move, clutched the doll closer. Her mother's lips pressed together. The wind blew into the pitch of a whine, the same pitch as the words that came from Matilda: "Won't. You ain't gonna make me," causing her mother to leap and slap Matilda, sending the doll to the ground. Matilda refused to follow, though the blow sent her reeling, as much from force as surprise.

Her mother began to cry and reached for Matilda, but her daughter turned from her touch, strengthened by the sting of the wind against her reddened cheek. Legs now sturdy on the earth, she was proud she could stand up to her mother, to this place. Her mother sighed, and began picking up the chips, an apology of sorts, and despite herself, Matilda relented. Together they gathered them all and piled them into the cart, then began the slow roll home, wheels squeaking. The doll was left face down on the ground, shamed; Matilda, now, unable to want anything crafted by her mother. Her own slap in her mother's face.

Her mother always talked about going back to Boston, where she'd been raised and where her parents and sisters still lived. She told Matilda about buildings made of brick and stone, and the grand park in the middle of the city designed by Olmstead (which Matilda misheard as homestead): the Emerald Necklace—emerald, a color Matilda saw in spring when the prairie shades of dust and mud and buffalo pelt gave way to waves of green dotted with wildflowers and avaricious bees.

Sometimes her mother cried when she talked. Matilda grieved her mother's loss of home, could feel its emptiness in her own belly, particularly on nights when she'd not had enough to eat, and believed in this magical place, Back East, but couldn't imagine it. She could feel only her own landscape—the way it lies flat inside you, unfurls and stretches all through you. And how the wind sings and snaps, and the wild, wide way it makes you feel, bringing all variety of noise—crickets, buffalo, raptors, thunder—with nothing to stop it. Wind that blew her father away months ago. "I'll be back," he said. He was often gone, buffalo hunting, scouting land, but he always came home. This time he'd been gone the longest, and her mother had a different story: "He won't."

On some cold nights, with the buffalo chips burning low, Matilda knew her mother headed for the barn to lie down in the hay with the cow, and once she'd seen her weep into the side of old Bessie, arm reaching up her massive back as if to hug.

That night, when they'd returned from the prairie, the buffalo chips burned a golden glow in the cookstove, made good warmth throughout the sod house. They sat together, her mother sewing a shirt for Matilda in the fire's light, one eye on her stitching, the other on her daughter. Matilda wriggled her fingers, their idleness a luxury, another apology from her mother for the slap: there were honey frames that needed scraping, beans to sort, dishes to scrub, a floor to sweep. Still, her empty hands grieved the abandoned doll.

"You know," her mother started, "if I'd stayed in Boston, you would be an entirely different girl." She settled her stitching on her lap, leaned slightly forward. "What's the good of having a daughter if she's different than you? We don't even speak the same language." The words were said softly, so didn't wound as much. There was an opening in the softness. Matilda took it.

"Give me again the story of you and Papa." She felt power in the words, knowing they would cause her mother sorrow or happiness. Her mother sighed and put fingers to her lips as if to deny Matilda her power. "You know it."

"Tell me," she said, and wondered, who would that girl be? What kind of daughter? What words would she speak so her mother would understand? The ones Matilda kept bundled tight inside? Her mother had described her own girlhood and Matilda imagined this daughter her mother wanted as one who wouldn't need dolls because she had human friends. She'd talk of boys and twirl her fingers in golden curls that bounced on her shoulders. Her shoes would be black patent leather (she didn't know what that was, but her mother spoke of it), the straps tight around her ankles, and in her imaginings, this makes her toes throb. The white socks fill her with anxiety that they'll get dirty. But there's no dirt in Boston, no shades of dust or mud or buffalo chips anywhere. The sidewalks—sidewalks!—are hard and clean, surrounded by plush grass. Across this field a blue stream wanders through the green. In the distance, behind the tallest buildings: mountains. The girls carry books, sit on the grass and read to each other. Soon, blown in from the Prairie, a jealous wind slams shut the covers, rakes the words right out of their mouths, hurls them into the clouds, and carries Matilda back, filling her with the feral joy of returning to her own place, her mother in the middle of the telling:

"…came back to Massachusetts to see his brother, who was dying. Took him many weeks to travel home. And the night after his brother expired, he came to a dance at Thoreau House on my campus, to run from his sorrows. He had a wild streak. Wanderlust. Not one to follow in the path of his father or brother, that one. Not a mill man. A wild seed carried out here to the middle of nowhere. And maybe, too, he came Back East to find a wife among us elite and carry one of us back with him to this hell."

Elite. Hell. Even in the slow glow of the fire, Matilda saw her mother's bitterness. She knew the rest of the story. How he'd carried her away from her family, from all she'd known. Carried her here on horseback (Matilda didn't believe this, could not believe her mother would survive such a dirty, dangerous journey, much less agree to it. Still, she gloried in its unlikeliness). But as her mother talked, her father formed in her mind, stepping into the small space between mother and daughter, softening each for the other, growing so tall he had to bend to keep his head from butting the sod ceiling.

The magical string of words stopped. No matter. They did their trick. Her father returned in her mind, hat pulled low, smiling, lips forming words roughened by wind, breaking sentences into small bites of sound, rock scraping rock: "Hey Chicken. Me. You. Let's prowl." And they did. Her father let her run wild, told her she was special, and promised next time he'd take her roaming with him. One day maybe they'd ride off and not come back. He'd always kept his promises, but this time Matilda began to see him as one of those imaginary trees her mother had drawn and labeled—*oak, maple, birch, chestnut*—bending and tippling in the wind. Eventually blowing away.

"I thought there'd be schools." Her mother laughed. "Not to mention libraries. Bless my sisters for sending some books on. Miracle some of them arrived." She stabbed the needle into the fabric and pricked her finger, but didn't say a word. A dark spot appeared on the pale fabric. "I've got to get out of here."

Matilda yawned. She'd heard this too many times. "Go on then." She wandered over to her pallet in the corner, the straw bedding drawn tight with a linen sheet covered with a quilt and other dolls her mother had

made. Matilda saw again the doll left behind and thought her mother
might visit the barn later.

When Matilda half woke in the middle of the night, the cookstove
fire had burned to embers, throwing gauzy shadows throughout the
room. Cold, she pulled the quilt tighter, thought the murmurs were
dreams bleeding into her drowse. From her corner she looked toward
the stove and saw two silhouettes, recognized the higher-pitched murmur
as her mother's. When Matilda was younger, some nights she dreamt of
a silhouette man who came from the chimney and sat at the end of her
pallet and spoke like this, kindly, and now the murmurs from those at the
cookstove ran pretty—pebbles tumbling over each other. She closed her
eyes, expecting to return to whatever dream she'd been having, when the
lower murmur turned into words: "Heard he's with her now. That whore.
Next town over. You best find out."

She closed her eyes and thought of the horehounds her father used
to bring her, licorice softened with molasses and salt, and when she
opened her eyes again, sun was trying to stream through the beeswaxed
paper in the two small windows cut into the sod walls. She lay quiet for
a few minutes. Something was missing. Stillness occupied the room and
Matilda realized she was alone. Had her mother gone to the barn and was
yet there, the cow rolling over and pinning her? She got out of bed and
threw a coat over her shoulders, crammed her feet into her boots and
was on her way to the door when she saw the paper on the table, recog-
nized her mother's fluid, curlicued script in light blue ink. To spite her
mother, Matilda had refused to write in cursive, her printed letters and
words bunched up and slanted. But sometimes, when her mother was
milking, Matilda would sneak her pen and imitate her writing, then bury
the pages behind the barn—pages covered with words written as beauti-
fully as her mother's: *Papa, bees, wander, wind.*

She picked up the note: *Your father has returned. I've gone to bring him
home. Mind the cow and chickens. And dig some potatoes. I should be back in a day.
Be a good girl. Mother*

Was she dreaming still? She blinked, and then wild joy, running her
outside into blinding light. Papa! It was later than she'd thought, the sun
high above. Dust, flies, bees filled the air. Leaning against the house, six
honey frames and a bucket of berries their kind neighbor from miles
over must've delivered early this morning. Had he taken her mother to

fetch her father? Why hadn't Papa come on his own?

She went inside, dark now after the bright sun, and sat on her bed, hugging the dolls. Soon her father would be here. Wouldn't he? She lay down and thought she might cry. Then she became angry and got out of bed again, slamming the door.

The chickens were walking in circles, clucking and frantically pecking the ground. She heard the low moan of the cow and quickly entered the barn, cool and dank. She grabbed the milking stool and pail. The cow paid her no mind. Placing both hands on its flank, she lowered her forehead to meet the flesh. For a moment she was inside her mother, became those stormy emotions—loneliness and anger, bitterness and pride. What if her father didn't come? Her mother? What if they abandoned her the way she'd abandoned the doll yesterday? Women here lived alone, deserted, their small ramshackle homes dotting the prairie. Husbands gone off and lost, children died or moved east or further west. She ran her fingers over the cow's ribs and another feeling trickled through: Sun and dirt and wind. The endless flat vista made her sturdy and independent. She didn't need father or mother.

Still, as soon as she milked and threw feed to the chickens, she would go back and find the doll.

She walked in smaller and smaller circles so as not to miss an inch of land. But she knew as soon as she got close to where she and her mother had been yesterday that the doll was gone. There was nothing blocking her sight. Yet she circled and circled, looking behind each scant tuft of brown grass and through the scrub brush. An animal must have made off with it. Why had she left it to this fate? To punish her mother? What good was that now.

Thunder sounded. She looked into sun-drenched sky, turned and saw a man on horseback veiled in dust. She feared it was an Indian strayed from the reservation miles off. But nearing, the man yelled her name. For a moment she was fused to this place, unbending, but something began to shift and break up inside her as hooves beat the ground, the vibration challenging her stubbornness. The man galloped closer and, emerging from the dust, became her father. Reaching her, he slowed but did not stop, swooping down to lift and place her onto the saddle in front of him.

"Bigger now, ain't you? How's that? I been gone only a week or so."

She closed her eyes, leaned into his familiar smell: sweat and dirt, horse and wild strawberries. "Naw, some months, I believe," and leaned harder into him. "Where's Mam?"

He squeezed her shoulder. "I'm taking you back to her. 'Member Sussy? Sussy Greene?"

She tilted her head to look in his face. "She lose her husband and son in that storm last winter?"

"Yep." He nested his chin in her shoulder, breathed goosebumps into her neck. "Your mother's there. We got some talking to do."

She wanted to ask what about, but was silenced by his tone: *ominous*, a word he might use. Sometimes his vocabulary gave him away, words from long ago, escaping the prison of his lips: *reverence, absurd, disconsolate, omnipotence*. His origins, her mother would say. He had a college degree he never spoke of, which was unheard of for a mill worker. But then, her mother said, his family owned the mill. When a word like this slipped through, Matilda tried to sound it out then spell it in her mother's fancy script; these words, too, buried in her plot along with her own and her prairie finds: an eagle's talon; mouse skeleton; bison tooth; sometimes, a shiny mica schist; and rarely, a remnant from settlers passing through—a snapped barrette, broken shoe buckle, a ravaged bow.

"Missed you, girl," he said, his words a gravelly cloak of warmth. He hugged her tight, and they rode on in silence, questions, apprehension, curiosity threading through her.

Miles of riding, and in the sky, the sun shifted from noon to two. Soon, through the emptiness, an apparition: a boulder in the distance. "Epic," her father said. "Doesn't it seem so to you? She's been living here by herself all these many months. Courting sorrow."

Who was he talking about. Her mother? This Sussy woman? Or another left alone? So many of them out here, brought to their fate by men. But she, Matilda, was born of this place. She would never leave, would she? The unmooring she sometimes felt was only through the emotions of her mother.

Closer, the boulder turned into a dwelling similar to their own, except for a little rambling fence, the wood petrified as stone. A woman, not her mother, emerged from the house. Her bonnet starched around her face, her lips red as if stained with berries, a big grin stretching the red into her cheeks. Was this what a whore looked like?

"You found her," Sussy said. "C'mon, c'mon," she urged as they dismounted. "Been waiting for you." She ushered them towards the door.

Inside, cool and dim after the bright sun. At first Matilda didn't see her mother sitting in a corner, her grey dress camouflage. "Come here, Matilda," she said, the pale flair of her hand cutting through the dark.

Matilda felt caught between her father and Sussy, the woman's energy snappy, claiming. Already her arm was across Matilda's shoulder, and it felt excitable, electric as if the two of them might suddenly spring handstands.

"She's more a Tilly, like me, name shortened. I was a Susanna, but out here…" Sussy's words trailed off. "Tilly suits her better, don't you think?" She looked at Matilda's father.

"Sussy's made a cake," he said.

Was this the woman's birthday? Sussy removed her bonnet and tangled black curls bounced around her face, her shoulders. She had not stopped smiling, and with her hair all about her, she looked like a child; like, Matilda thought, me. She'd never seen a grown woman let her hair go like that. Even at her age, Matilda tied hers back. But then that was what her mother demanded. On the prairie alone, or with her father, she'd pull out the ribbons and pins.

In the corner, her mother darkened the joyful light Sussy was trying to create. A quick frown crossed Sussy's face. But she cut the cake, then swiped across the surface, loading her finger with icing, and offered it to Matilda. Her father nudged her. The finger seemed wrong, dirty almost, but when was the last time she'd had cake? And the frosting looked luscious. She could smell the sugar. And Papa had given permission. She took a tentative lick, stepped back.

"Don't be shy." Sussy touched her finger to Matilda's lips and she licked it clean, joy and guilt brindling her spine. Sussy scooped up more icing and offered her finger to Matilda's father. He took it in his mouth, holding it there, closing his eyes.

Matilda's mother sprang from the corner. "That is disgusting, abhorrent behavior in front of the child." In the light, now, the planes of her face looked sharp and brittle, the skin beneath her eyes puckered, and Matilda wondered if her mother had left with the man who came in the middle of the night and hadn't gotten any sleep. Or were her eyes puffed because she'd been crying?

"No," her father said. "Nothing to hide from the girl. This love's simple. But you wouldn't know about that." He dropped Sussy's hand and turned to Matilda's mother.

"Liar," her mother said. "Everything you are is made up. When were you ever around long enough for any love to be shown?"

"I could've been near you forever and you'd never let me unbutton even one of them that's tight around your neck."

"You're talking like a fool. But her," she nodded towards Sussy, "you don't even have to do the unbuttoning. She's already opened for you."

"And that's the glory."

Her mother's voice came out ragged, then pleading, "This is where you've gone all those times you left us? To her? You came for me. Claimed me and brought me here." Her hand curled around his wrist. He unwrapped her fingers, let her arm fall.

"And now I'm letting you go. The money's already paid for the stagecoach to take you back. Will's coming for you this afternoon." He turned to his daughter. "And you, Tilly, you got to make a choice."

"Don't you dare." Her mother raised her hand as if to strike him.

Sussy yanked Matilda towards the door.

Outside the sun shone on Sussy's hair, black like oil, like the liquid gold her father had described to her. He rode off once to find it, digging deep in the ground, but came home empty-handed. Had that trip been a lie, and he'd come here? Through the windows, the sound of shouting.

"Let them be and work their things out. Let's go." She took Matilda to the barn and saddled up two horses. Before they mounted, she undid the pins and combs in Matilda's hair, her fingers running through it like trickling water. "Let's have fun. It's been a time since I've had some. But your papa's made me better. Healed me."

Matilda pictured Sussy's husband and son, lost in that storm last winter. And then her father, trudging through snow, showing up at her door.

Sussy cropped Matilda's horse and the beast sprang into gallop. Wind rushed Matilda's face, rushed through her hair, raking away confusion and fear, and joy leapt unbidden into her heart, bypassing the scene inside her stricken mind: mother and father shouting, her father driving her mother off, or her mother driving him. Joy leapt into her hands, holding the reins so tight she felt the wild energy of the animal through them. She squeezed her heels into the horse's ribs, hoping to overtake Sussy, then hoping just to catch up. Sussy's black hair trailing behind like

Rapunzel's from the story her mother used to read her. If only she could grab it and ride into a new world.

Sussy slowed and stopped by an outcrop of squat scrub bush. Matilda, finally caught up, dismounted. Sussy had already pulled out a pipe and was puffing when Matilda sat beside her, red-faced and sweating.

"Jeb," Sussy said. "He was about your age. A dear boy. Good. I also wanted a girl." She tucked a lock behind Matilda's ear, her fingers leaving a pleasant sensation. "But that wasn't to be. 'Til now."

Was Jeb's hair long and did his mother tuck it behind his ears? The skin Sussy's nails had touched began to prickle. Matilda scratched and her hair swung free.

"Want a puff?" She held the pipe to Matilda's lips. "I started when I was your age."

Matilda tried to inhale, but the acrid smoke stung and would not go down her throat. She coughed it out.

Sussy laughed. "That's how it is at first. But you get used to it. Then it brings calm. 'Specially when the sun's going down and you're sitting on the porch. That time a day."

The two of them, side by side, an orange and red sky, the darkening light keeping them from seeing miles and miles into their future. *Tilly*, she sounded the name in her mind, *Tilly*.

"Hold this," Sussy gave her the pipe. "I gotta shit."

The pipe was still smoking, the bowl warm in Matilda's hand, as Sussy ran some yards from the shrubs, hiked up her skirt and squatted. Even in the hot day, the glaring sun, the small pile steamed.

Well, what are you supposed to do, Matilda thought, trying to tamp down her surprise and distaste at a grown woman doing that in broad daylight, there's no rock, no tree to hide behind, and at least Sussy hadn't done it behind the shrubs Matilda was sitting in front of. Still, she was afraid her expression might betray her, until the unthinkable image of her mother squatting before her flashed through her mind and almost made her laugh. Her mother would rather hold it until her eyes popped than do it in front of her daughter.

Finished, Sussy returned to Matilda. "Don't mind me," she said and took the pipe, dumped the contents on the ground and covered the hot tobacco with dirt. She lifted Matilda by her armpits.

"All right. Try'n catch me." She bolted, laughing over her shoulder.

Matilda was faster and caught her, tackling her to the ground. They tussled and Sussy began to tickle her until Matilda's laughter rang so loud through the prairie, she was sure it would reach her mother. She imagined her father smiling when he heard it, saw her mother's frown.

They rode back, abreast. Matilda's horse slowing, plodding as they approached the house, as if sensing Matilda's dread.

Her mother was on the porch, waiting. As they drew near, she sprang towards them, the hand that had been raised against her husband earlier, now aimed at her daughter. She grabbed Matilda's arm and pulled her off the horse.

"Where were you? Your hair all undone like that." She shook her daughter until Matilda's neck ached. "Are you trying to look like her?" She was about to smack her daughter when her husband appeared and pulled her hand away.

Matilda stumbled, almost falling, her eyes stinging with angry tears.

"You're going home to Boston with me," her mother said. "Someone's coming to take us to the stagecoach."

"You don't have to," her father said.

"You've no right to her. She's coming with me, to my family, where she belongs." She addressed her daughter: "To a proper home and school. You're going to become a lady."

"She's mine, too," her father said. "And old enough to choose."

Her mother hustled her onto the porch. "Listen to me," her voice was low, almost a hiss. She bent and gripped Matilda's shoulders, her face so close Matilda felt her breath on her cheeks. "You cannot stay here with them," her mother said. "They are ruined people and they will ruin you. Trust me. We'll be happy in Boston."

She looked into her mother's eyes, welling with tears. Grey eyes. Had she never noticed the color before? Matilda couldn't remember ever being this close to her. Her mother's fingers dug into her shoulders as if impaling her with knowledge. "He left you all those times to go to her." That whore, Matilda thought. "If he loved you, he'd never have left. I never left you. You're my daughter, Matilda. I'm the one who raised you. I know you and know what's best."

Matilda closed her eyes against her mother, and pictured again those tidy girls of her imaginings, and tried to see becoming one of them, speaking freely all those fancy words she wrote down, instead of burying them. Speaking them out loud in sentences. She tried to imagine a new mother and daughter with no grudge between them. But the shoes, those patent leather shoes with the straps so tight, as tight as her mother's hands on her, constricting, and the clean, neat spaces Back East, made smaller and smaller by trees and mountains and buildings. Trust you? she thought. You raised me, but he loves me. She might never see him again. And here he was, now, boots striking hard across the wooden porch as he came to claim her. Her mother stood, her arm around Matilda's shoulders.

"Enough," he said. "She belongs here, with me. With us," he nodded towards Sussy. "She'd die in that place. Same as me before I came out here. Not gonna happen to her."

Her mother's arm tightened, but Matilda wriggled free. She moved to her father's side, trying to calm herself, twisting her confusion, her anger, and widening sense of loss into power, into words that would come out kindly, as if she were looking out for her mother's best interests.

"Go on," Matilda said. "Now you won't have to go to the barn every night and cry on that cow."

Her mother's face froze, her eyes wide. "What are you talking about?"

"Tilly?" Her father raised his eyebrows.

She turned to him, to Sussy, as if her mother were no longer there, as if she'd already gone. "Every night you been away, I see her go into the barn to be with that old cow. Every night. She doesn't just hug and cry on her. I seen her kissing that smelly, old dirty thing, kissing it on the mouth like she was married to it or something."

After her mother left, Sussy pulled her into the barn, awkwardly patting her back, trying to comfort her. She sat Matilda on a milking stool and told her to wait. Through the open barn door, Matilda saw her father saddle up, getting ready to ride to their neighbor's for a sack of oats. "When're you coming back," she'd asked. He hadn't answered.

"I made some things for you, Tilly, don't move." Sussy clapped her hands and hurried through a thin carpet of hay strewn across the floor. She lifted a box from a corner. "Guess what's in here." Her voice, shy, lifted with excitement. Matilda said nothing as Sussy placed the box on her lap.

"I know they're not much, I'm just learning, but your papa told me how much you loved them. I know they can be good company sometimes."

Matilda took out one of the corncob dolls. Matted hair of browning cornsilk, the same color and texture as the hair that snaked down Matilda's back. The doll's arms: sticks that struck straight from the body. Matilda felt the tension in her own shoulders, along her arms. The crude red mouth dripped lies into the neck, and the eyes of the doll, bulged and knowing as Matilda's, were heavy and misshapen.

She returned the doll to the box. "These are for children."

She saw the doll lost to the prairie, its subtlety and beauty, and sounded the word *sophistication*. She would never not see it. Was that love? Standing, she turned away from Sussy, not wanting to see the hurt on her face, then glad she caused it.

Outside, she stared into the flat emptiness of her surroundings where everything was visible, exposed, except for what lay hidden inside a person. The emptiness now stifling. What words might her mother write in her fancy script and then bury—*loneliness, home, truth, betrayal*—

EMILY RANKIN

Galaxy

Fluid acrylic on canvas
11x14 inches
2022
(Next Page)

This piece makes up part of an ongoing series, Fluid, which seeks to capture the ways in which a fluid moment in time might be fixed in the mind. Fluid art is a representation of liminal space, an echo of the moment before the paint dried. I'm interested in the way the momentary motion of liquid paint can be captured and pinned to canvas.

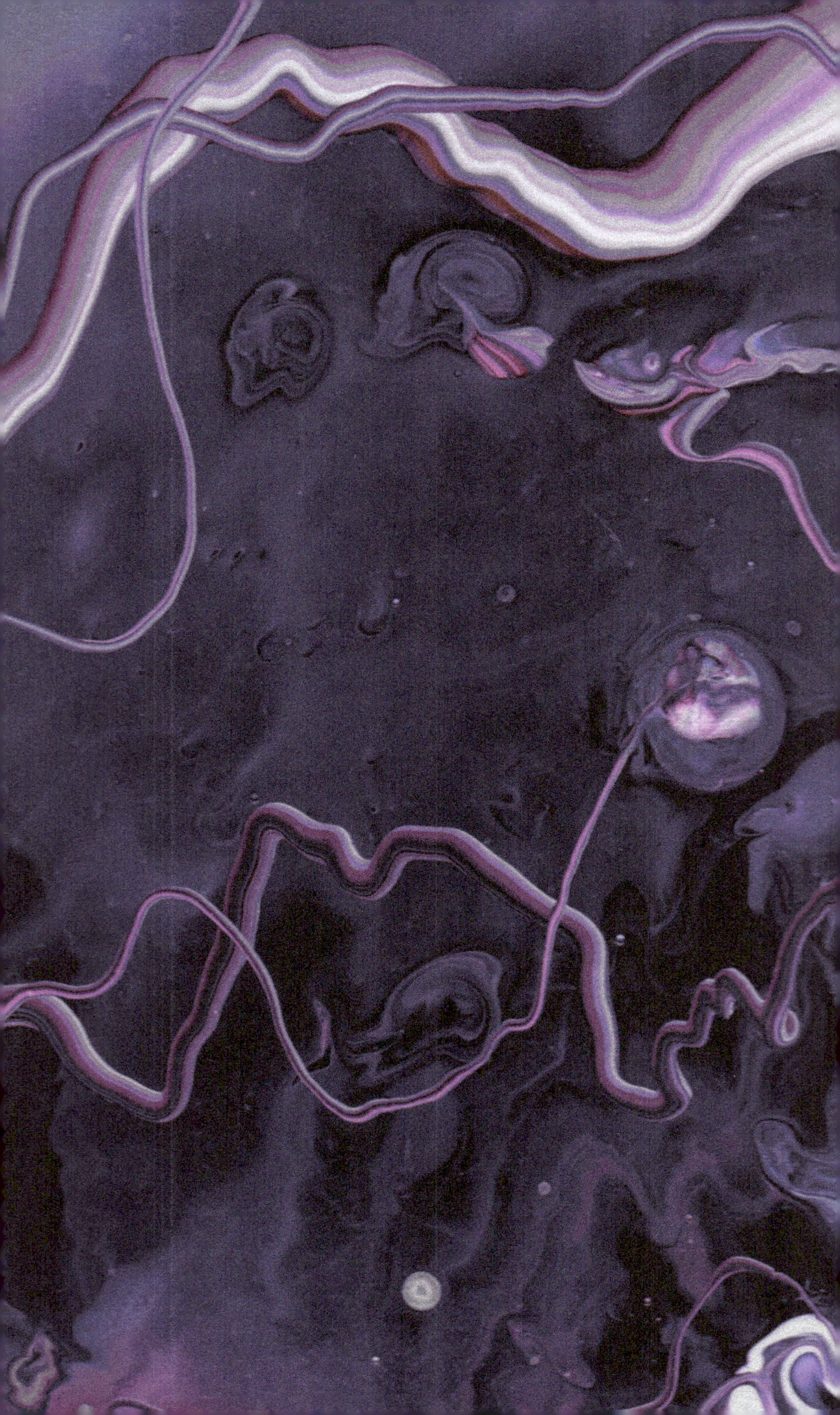

Object Permanence

During the harmattan, a film of white covers the Cordyline. The Ixora
and Red Acalypha are quiet and satisfied like mothers on the front porch.
The albino neighbor sings an Igbo carol in the yard, laying clothes on the
heaps of granite stones bordered by bricks the color of red earth. His
voice firm as scripture. It was as though there was a playground in his
throat, children the height of little trees clapping loudly in ululation of a
looming absence. It is evening in his voice and the playground is littered
with torn slippers the color of yellow bush and climbing ivy. In his song,
there was the year of hymns and in the hymns, there was the year of
recollection and in recollection there was memory, the body's echo. In his
song, decades sat like worshippers in the pew of an old church. Outside,
the wind crackled like scars. In his song, there was a skyline of children
with laughter loud as dream chasing pigeons and failing to catch them,
which really is the game—the sublimity of looking at the world in failure.
The birds perch on the children and like wheat in a field they run into
one another giggling like rain. This is the closest I have been to under-
standing Kafka's philosopher who ran into the playground seeking to
seize the top of a child just to capture the ephemeral. Except when I run
into the playground, the children are already gone. The silence, small as a
punctuated sentence. The sky, a femur of blank page. The world silent as
waving. I have seen years carried abroad like coins in the teeth of but-
terflies and the language I have is not the one I crave. I have watched my
childhood awake like dawn and christened it joy because it did not stay
long enough. I only wield semantics large enough to entomb what I want
alive. I, who have lost in transmutation the potency of my name. I, name-
less protagonist of a threnody.

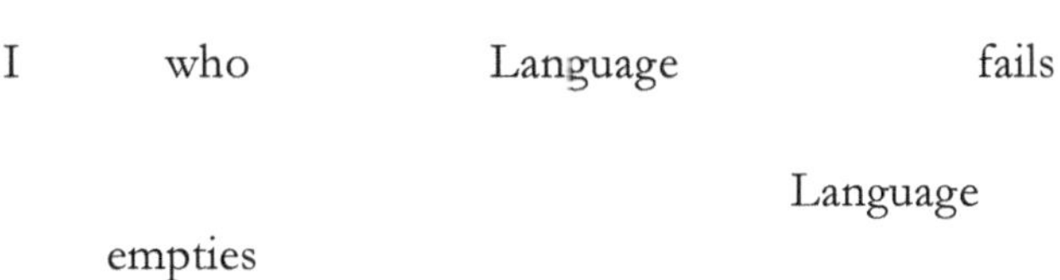

Language   demands

of   a   body   I

          cannot   give.

In the beginning was Language.

          In the beginning, Language.

In Language, a beginning.

In the beginning, Language was a half-opened eye exiled to the lonely center of life.

Our reader describes what it was like to find Maryhilda Obasiota Ibe's "Object Permanence"

I am in the woods, and although they—the woods—are emptied for the winter cold, the taller trees' tangle—and the air there—holds its sounds, and what it's given it holds, it sustains, and "Object Permanence" knocks, knocks against what I throw it at, and it roots about where it lands. But it cannot throw itself. We know this about language, however reticent or moved we are by it. Hymns, the pre-imbued chants, sustain memory, held as if outside of us for us; what I want alive is occasioned by it, and in being read to the tangle, alive not to untangle it, but to caparison there, a thrown but unthrowing livery, as chaff in the wind. Childhood is a chant, or its nine letters are. The conjured spirit visits; that which can urticate can salve. This close, the volta—unbound by choice—wings past lines of sight, becomes an apeiron. Syllables promulgate. Things decohere. Language is not a thing. Anything less would be to miss the forest for its wood.

—*S. G. Mallett*

Our reader describes what it was like to find Jona Whipple's "Why Are You Still Here"

When I read the first line of this story, it got me on board immediately. One sentence, I was catapulted into the middle of a strange situation, and I felt compelled to continue reading just to find out why. The setup is clever, but not gimmicky, because it is justified—as the story progresses, we learn that the father character has dementia, and the mother and the daughter are caregivers. These topics are often difficult to write about because of the intimacy and the emotional weight, but this story achieves a great balance between being honest and showing restraint. As I finished reading, I felt a complicated sadness, which to me is always a sign of good writing. I'm glad that this piece gets to be shared with more people, and I hope you enjoy it as much as I did.

—Xueyi Zhou

Why Are You Still Here

On the day my father promised me to the neighbor, my mother cried. It was all the sound of ritual, something no longer worth looking up from my breakfast plate for. My father banged through the side door, his unsteady metal sword clattering against the frame. He landed his proclamation, then demanded some ale. He glanced around, eyes glassy and unfocused, settling on the syrup bottle. The sword fell to the kitchen floor as he took the bottle in his hands, turning its curves over between his palms. My father: guzzling maple syrup from a glass bottle in the shape of a woman. My mother: elbows on the table, the curtain of a stained cotton napkin spread across her face, shoulders contracting with sobs.

"What it is," she told Mrs. Tobin later that morning, "is that he wants to see her get married before he—before he *goes*." She wrung the napkin in her hands, dabbed at her eyes, yellowed orbs, red-threaded. "Before he *really* goes," she whispered low, leaning into Mrs. Tobin for conspiratorial effect. Mrs. Tobin leaned back, protecting her airspace. "It's a very sweet thing if you think about it," my mother continued, smiling cautiously as she became ever more certain that Mrs. Tobin was a wall to be removed one brick at a time. "It means he's still in there somewhere."

My mother sighed, glancing toward the kitchen window to draw Mrs. Tobin's eyes and thoughts to my father, who stood at the sink staring over the blank expanse of the backyard, digging his fingers into his beard and thinking of nothing. Mrs. Tobin's polite smile blinked on and off like a broken neon sign, she rubbed her elbows under her crossed arms and said she'd discuss it with Mr. Tobin, who had been hiding in the garage pretending to sort bolts into tiny jars ever since earlier that morning when my father chased him out of his patio chair with shouted promises of a hefty dowry and healthy sons. My mother nodded and did that thing with her brows where she tilted them up until the lines in her forehead formed a perfect peak, a cathedral roof.

"What do you think of all this?" Mrs. Tobin asked, looking me up and down, the first time she'd ever said anything to me that wasn't shouted across the lawn. I looked up to meet her gaze, and her eyes weaseled tight and small, as if she was trying to sort out some kind of pattern printed on my skin, decide if I was bruised fruit, just as crazy as my parents. "I think," I said, aware of my mother's hands, how they held the fabric of the wadded napkin so tight they looked like they might bleed, "I think it's fine, it's whatever." I was not yet used to the way adults had begun look-ing me in the eye and asking me what I thought about things, expecting me to answer. It was like I had been standing in the shadow of an eclipse for fifteen years, and then the Earth moved and they could see me in a place where there had been nothing before.

I scratched at the skin behind my ear. I felt my mother relax. But Mrs. Tobin's tiny eyes had found me, and they would not let me go.

My father's dementia began like a secret, a bloom of black mold behind the walls. The first few times he'd lost control of his bike on his way to and from the university where he worked, he reasoned it to be due to the dizziness he suffered when he took his heart medication too late in the day, or without enough food, or any number of other things he said could affect a body "after a half century of living."

"Drink plenty of water," he said, winking at me from under a gauze pad he held against his head to stanch the bleeding, "and don't do drugs, at least not the ones I did." That particular day, he'd slid sideways and crashed into the curb, grating his bald head against the pavement. Later, he complained of numbness that came and went. One night, he asked me to chop the zucchini for him because, he said, "My hands are tired." His hands were tired more often after that, then his feet, his legs—and then the university began to send spies to sit in the bushes outside our house, attach trackers to our car, tape codes to the bottom of his deodor-ant stick. At night, my parents met in the downstairs family room to talk low and serious, unaware of my presence on the top stair. "I'm here," my father said, punctuated by a soft tapping, which I imagined to be him placing the palms of his hands on the tops of his thighs, "I'm here, but I just can't…" From my hiding place, I could feel my mother leaning in to prompt him forward as his pause inflated the space between them, but nothing called him back from these moments when he disappeared into himself.

"Can't *what?*" my mother prompted, reaching with her voice into the clouded smoke surrounding my father's brain.

It had always been unlike my father to stop speaking when he held an audience, and then, he walked into rooms as if searching for something, said random half-sentences, or delivered isolated clippings of poetry. "The golden is before us, and we—and *we*," he once shouted in the produce aisle at the grocery store, so loud I saw the limes tremble. We abandoned the cart, and the three of us drove home in silence without the tomatoes and cereal.

Family time was a holy land my mother vowed to reclaim, even across the unpredictable landscape of my father's health and my persistent disinterest in being around either of them. She carried the cross of the notion through gritted teeth. Dinner with my parents became mandatory, and I was expected to be at home in the hours before and after, doing what my mother called *visiting*: sitting in the living room watching the fall darkness press down on us until someone got up to turn on a light. Hospital visits became more frequent, and then they too became family time, and my mother scheduled all of my father's appointments at times when I could be expected to join them.

My father on those days was morose and petulant in the backseat, angry because my mother didn't trust him to drive, or because he thought he was seven years old and she wouldn't let him have a Donald Duck Pez, or because fuck you lady, he was Steve fucking McQueen and knew how to fucking drive goddammit. She wouldn't let me drive either, no matter how many times I reminded her of my permit slip. "You can practice next year," she said, teeth pressed together, hissing words out of the corner of her lips and checking the rearview as if my father could have possibly been present enough to clock her tone. "We're focusing on family time." I slouched and sneered, I picked at the edges of my ragged cuticles and flung pieces of skin onto the floor of the car out of spite because she'd been sitting in the fire lane behind the B building, laying on the horn until she saw me come out of the double doors, where I'd been trapped behind an avalanche of other bodies, all of them slowing down to get a look at the crazy-faced woman peering up from behind her screeching wiper blades.

My mother and I waited in empty gray rooms with uncomfortable chairs. I picked through *AARP* magazines for articles about diabetes medications and lists of Shirley MacLaine's favorite restaurants that had not yet been torn out. Walls of windows looked out onto construction sites, buildings going up all around the hospital, and I huddled into my coat under blasting air conditioning and sketched geometry triangles. The metal chutes of bright hallways were lined with impersonal, synthetic closets. The waiting rooms always had televisions, and my mother and I pretended to watch football games and house-flipping shows, handing those crumpled magazines back and forth, until she reminded me to do my homework.

With my notebook balanced on the edge of a chair that felt like it had been carved from marble, I wrote an English paper on the theme of empathy in *Jane Eyre*. *If Jane Eyre had any more empathy*, I wrote, *she would have been living in the attic and shitting in a bucket. If she had been any more empathetic, they would have been looking for a place in the manor to put their new doormat.* In a room at the end of the hall, a doctor injected dyes into my father's head and spoke to him through a microphone. After the test, we watched as the doctor moved a mouse back and forth across the back of a small notepad. Clouds of color in turmoil moved over the outlined surface of my father's brain, ebbing in lasso strands, and then the bad part: At the end, a wall of gray, a wash of nothing.

We nodded along with the doctor as he dragged the color back and forth, into and out of possibility. We nodded along with that doctor just as we had with all the others, their exhausted monologues walking us through the terrifying and endless process of crossing off the less serious diagnoses. We nodded along, smiling, with the specialist who suggested that we go along with my father's confusions, engage him with his stories, meet him where he was living. "Stay in the moment," the specialist said, touching his fingertips together, "and, in a word, *play*."

We smiled, we nodded, we agreed that this was the best course of action, my mother and I, and we went to the kiosk at the mall where you could buy replicas of battle weapons, all painted metal with plastic edges and jewel inlays set with blobs of hot glue. That was when we were still in the stage of observing terminal illness where you believe that if you're agreeable enough, if you just go quietly, if you move just the right way, it won't be able to see you, it will pass you by in the dark and leave you whole.

My essay won me an elegant, impressive F, and regular meetings with the school guidance counselor. I'd been assured by Mandy Jeselnik that she had turned in her *Jane Eyre* paper the year before and it was just the intro paragraph over and over, copied and pasted until it looked like a full eight-page paper, and had gotten an A. "She's not actually *reading* them," she'd said of Mrs. Phelps, blowing smoke out from between the gap in her teeth as we sat one cheek each on the toilet tank, feet up on the seat, in the fifth-floor bathroom.

"Anyway, if she calls you out on it, just pull the dad card. You don't really get to use that for that long," she warned as she ashed between our sneakers into the bowl.

The most the guidance counselor could do was scratch illegible words into a yellow legal pad in his windowless office by the cafeteria, then send me back to class. His expertise was in sudden death: Cars full of teenagers speeding into trees, school shootings, someone jumping off the roof of the L building and landing in the parking lot. No one had jumped off the roof of the L building since 1996 because they started locking the stairwell door, so he was woefully out of practice in the business of sudden loss. He'd perhaps never been in the practice of handling the kind of protracted, dissolutive exit my father had not planned.

My father managed to keep having good days until the eighth week of the fall semester. Once or twice each week, as he was able, he would sit in a chair before his class and deliver his own lectures. Sometimes, he could only manage to show up and observe his replacement, an adjunct named Jerry Yarbrough. Jerry, according to my father, stumbled through the maze of slides my father had prepared, pausing before clicking the button to check his notes on comically large note cards before each advance, as if a surprise awaited him. On the days when my father could only observe, when stuttering prevented his speech or auditory shadows confused him until he was convinced every student was talking at once, he let Jerry do the talking. In the evenings, he referred snidely to Jerry as "One-Ball Jerry," an uncharacteristically cruel nickname derived from Jerry's survival of testicular cancer. "The man's got no soul for it," my father said. "You watch. They'll tenure One-Ball and then they'll be calling me to come down there and fix it."

On what turned out to be my father's last day at work, I came home after school to find my mother at war with the bottoms of the kitchen cabinets. "Your father needed to come home a little early today," she said, glancing over her shoulder before letting me through the locked screen door to the kitchen. "He's asleep now, so be quiet, please?" The cabinet doors gaped open all around us, their contents arranged on every stable surface and filling the sink. She shook her head, lifted a rag to her face to give it a light sniff. "Do you smell that?" she said, sniffing around herself, under her arms, sticking her head into the cabinet. "What *is* that?" she said. She grabbed the lemon cleaner and huffed at its lid. "Probably shouldn't be using this anyway," she said, holding out the bottle as if to read the list of its contents, "they say it causes all kinds of crazy things in dogs."

I learned the full story about what happened on my father's last day at work from Ryan Gibbs, who was in my father's history seminar on that last afternoon. "Watch the door," Ryan said, ducking down behind the dumpsters to pick up small piles of the flattened cardboard boxes he was supposed to be throwing away. I kept my eyes on the bright yellow line of light coming from around the back door of the Best Buy stockroom where he'd jammed half a concrete block to keep it open. I avoided eye contact as much as possible as he talked, embarrassed by the puckered spots around the neck of his Best Buy polo. There were wrinkled dimples around the necklines of all of his shirts where he obsessively dug in his fingers and wiped at the corners of his mouth, so they were sometimes wet with spit or dirty with whatever grime was on his face. It wasn't the spit or the dirt that bothered me. I didn't like thinking about the way his fingers moved without his awareness, couldn't stand the thought of physical compulsions, like when someone pretended to be listening to you, but their eyes relaxed and focused on something like they were looking through you. I didn't like thinking about the ways that we could disappear, but still be there.

Class that day had started normally, according to Ryan. My father had been standing, moving back and forth in front of his whiteboards, engaging with students throughout the first thirty minutes of his Iron Age lecture, like his old self, except for a limp. At some point in the lecture, he'd gone quiet, stepped back and stared at the script he'd written across the whiteboards. Without a sound, he'd wandered out into the hallway. Students glanced at each other, nervous laughter rippled through the room. Just as Jerry began to get up from his seat to go and find my father, he re-entered, but without his pants and underwear. He walked in sock-footed, dangling beneath the wrinkled ends of his shirttail.

"My little eggs!" he exclaimed, raising his arms before the packed auditorium, exposing himself even more. "My little eggs, all of you! By

God, I'll sit on you one by one until you hatch!"

Someone made for the door and then they all scattered, leaves in the wind, leaving my father sitting on the floor in front of his whiteboards. I asked if anyone stayed with my father. Ryan assured me that a small crowd waited in the hall, forming a semicircle around the pile of my father's clothes, waiting for Jerry to return with someone who knew what to do. Ryan booked it down a stairwell and escaped to his car, "called it a day," a fact he was too stupid or immature to regret sharing with me. "Heavy shit, huh?" he said, wiping his mouth, but he said it in a way that could have been in reference to everything from my disappearing father to the pile of flattened refrigerator boxes. He didn't wait for a response, didn't see my shrug as he looked away to check the door.

I walked home in the pink twilight, under a swirl of birds changing patterns over me, turning and dipping along the sound waves of some distant church bells calling out the hour. The watermelon gummy rings Ryan had given me, stored in the pocket of his cargo pants, were a mildewy green, and I let them go loose and slimy in my cheek, then set my jaw and clamped it hard on my tongue until they turned softly bitter and tangy like cut grass. I thought of my father's legs, how when you saw them in the summer they seemed carved for a man of a different size, a man more delicate, paler in color. The smoothness of his calves had inspired his tormentors in school to call him *bird legs*; my mother sometimes did this too, and pinched at his thighs. He slapped her hands away, screeching like a barn owl. The light of the kitchen in those scenes seemed bright and effusive at the time, but leaked its brilliance somehow in my memory because from then on, I would think of my father's legs as they had been on that last day, exposed under the bronze lights to the unforgiving eyes of his students.

When I came in the side door, my mother tossed a handful of cutlery into the sink with a crash. She glared at me on her way back to the table for the plates, stopping to lean into the mud room and remind me that dinner time was family time. "And why is your mouth all green?" she said, squeezing my cheeks in her hand to stare at my tongue.

"My little egg," I said to her, stroking her face. "By God."

On the day of the wedding, my mother cried. She folded up the sleeves of her wedding dress so I could use my hands, held the fabric together at my elbows and shoulders with metal binder clips. I tripped over the mildewed skirt when I walked, crushing the plasticized fabric under my feet and popping the clips in the back. She found a belt in her closet and used it to hoist up the excess around my waist, a backwards hem job. She stepped back to look at me and then it came, the tears, her eyes two swollen slits, the crying some kind of permanent condition. I looked like the top of a rotten mushroom. She said "I'm so glad your father can see this day. I just wish you had washed your hair."

Outside, the News 7 van parked on the corner. All down the winding driveway to the street, neighbors stood in their sweatpants and bathrobes, my mother's invited guests. Mr. Bankhead held a cup of coffee. Even though Mrs. Stafford didn't live nearby anymore, she had shuttled both twins over in their matching white Sunday dresses. The little girls held plastic sandwich bags filled with bruised handfuls of petals from Mrs. Tobin's azaleas and stood still and wide-eyed on the side of the driveway, their mother's hands flat on their sternums, drawing them into her hips, eyeing the sword on my father's belt. The scratched tip of the sheath scraped the ground as he limped past, calling "Good morrow" and gathering handshakes from the men in the crowd.

Crisp, rotten rings of tulle petticoat scratched at my knees as I dragged the weight of the dress down the cracked pavement. My mother played the wedding march on a paint-splattered boombox, the sound smearing around us as the tape squeaked along at the wrong pitch and speed. "O joyous day," shouted my father, unsheathing his sword and lifting it to the gray sky, wobbling on his right side, his foot turning in. The gauntlet of people beamed, tucking their newspapers under their arms to clap their hands.

Mr. Tobin waited at the bottom of the driveway, his cheeks red and puffed, disguising that same look of pity I saw in all the watching eyes behind me. He offered me his fist instead of his hand, placed it in front of me like a fence post, and I was grateful for it, the way he recognized the intimacy of putting your hand inside someone else's. It could have been that he was just aware of his wife's gaze from where she stood near the street, guarding her azaleas from further molestation, hands on her hips in her grass-stained sweatpants, ready for this silliness to end so she could get back to the yard work. The back of Mr. Tobin's hand was red and scaly, as dry as raw wood and uncomfortable to touch when I remembered that it was supposed to be flesh. I put my hand on top of his, as gently as landing on a branch, and we proceeded.

We presented ourselves to Mr. Landry, who lived on the other side
of the cul-de-sac and held a regular D&D game in his garage. He wore
a faux leather vest from a pirate costume held closed over his gut with a
safety pin. The curve of an ornate costume cutlass hung from his belt.
The News 7 cameraman changed positions behind Mr. Landry, this side
and then the other, gathering all the best angles of the manufactured oc-
casion.

Mr. Landry had only read the first few words from his wedding ser-
vice pamphlet when we heard the sword scratch across concrete and saw
the News 7 cameraman pop his head up from behind his eyepiece. At the
top of the driveway, my father lay in a heap, sword and sheath scattered
beside him, a dark stain growing on the front of his khakis. A few neigh-
bors gathered to help, leaned in and offered advice for seizures, sprained
ankles, for things that can be cured, but my mother assured everyone that
this was normal, even as she removed her flannel shirt and threw it over
my father's pants to protect what was left of his dignity. She lifted his
head onto her knees and nodded polite thanks to all of our neighbors as
they drifted away across the lawn in one wave like a flock of birds. The
news van rumbled back down the street, and Mr. Tobin's giant hand pat-
ted at the crushed lace where my shoulder might have been.

I slept under my bed that night, slid off the side and rolled under,
pulling down the blankets on all sides until I found the absolute dark.
There, I pressed into the floor, where I dreamed I could untie all the
knots of myself, gently teasing apart the ends of twisted strings as the
sky tilted sideways overhead. The silver edges of the dream rattled, first
a threat, then an intrusion. I woke, hitting my head against the bottom
of the bed, my cheek numb and cold from the carpet. The rattling sound
persisted, and I followed it out the door and down the hall.

In the kitchen, my father sat on the floor in the dark, leaned up
against the cabinets. Holding the side of an open drawer, he tried to hoist
himself into the wheelchair that had been sitting folded behind the couch
for weeks, and now stood by him empty, waiting.

"I used to have a rope here for this," he said, noticing the shape of
me in the dark, a slice of my face in the streetlight coming in the window.
He winced as he lowered himself back to the floor. "Do you know what
they did with it?"

"I don't know," I said, "I'm sorry. What do I do?"

"You can find my rope, Private! I need it," he barked, leaning back against the cabinets, breathing hard. Beads of sweat rolled down his forehead.

"Dad," I said. My voice cracked, too high, too blank. "Dad, there was never a rope there. There was no rope, Dad."

We stayed there in the dark, waiting, both of us moved by the air in the room and the pulse of our blood. I felt him crying before I heard it, and the hairs stood up on my legs at the sound, something I'd never heard, a lost and empty peal of what was left of my father ringing out into the night. I came to my knees on the tile, covered my face in the dark. He reached out until he could almost touch my hair, fingers grazing my face, both hands outstretched to pull me into him.

"What is happening?" my mother said, alarmed but half asleep, a tornado siren in a distant county. She flipped the switch on the wall and we all shriveled away from one another under the harsh light until she turned it back off. "What's happened? I'm here!" she said, sliding to her knees beside him. She cradled his face, wiped at his tears with her shirt. He held her forearm and muttered explanations and apologies about the wheelchair, but she shushed him. She began to rock him, moved him side to side until his body calmed, his breathing slowing. I had seen her leaning over him in this way that morning on the driveway, and a week ago when he had fallen in the breezeway, all the times he had come home bleeding and confused. She had assumed this posture over time—softly, afraid—learned to curve over him in this way, an impermanent shelter for what was to come.

When I moved, it was to wipe my face on the back of my arm. My father, near sleep, glanced across my mother's shoulder to see me again, sitting in the beam of white light from the motion sensor on the Tobins's garage. "Why do I still see this one darkening my halls?" he asked her, lifting his head. "Did I not see her married this day?"

"Oh yes, my Lord," my mother said, peeking back at me where I sat hunched on the floor, a breath away from them. "She will join her husband when she is of age." He spluttered, a cruel laugh.

"And you be mine, I'll give you to my friend," he said, raising a finger toward my face. "And you be not, hang."

My mother unlaced her arm from around his back, used it to make a shooing motion in my direction, waving me backwards in the dark, away to my room down the hall.

On the floor, my back to my bedroom door, I listened to them talking, hushed, then the sounds as they traveled back to their bedroom, and finally the silence of the house rang in my ears. My window stood open, the cold breeze spinning circles across the floor, winding around my toes, and if I shut my eyes it felt like I was moving on the air. I could build hidden rooms, I thought, and I began to plan them, to cover the walls with scenes of hurt. But the hours turned, and I opened my eyes to the morning pouring over the hills at the end of the street, a wall of gray, then threads of gold, again, waves of color crashing back in, night birds disappearing into the trees. I could go where they go, silent in the air, a sharpness hidden in the vivid dark. If I wanted, I could live in endless night, moving in all the ways no one hears.

But I had no desire to live behind the walls of myself, bricking up the exits and turning in silent circles. I had no desire to float unseen. My throat was full, metallic, heavy with something like rage, with something like sadness, keys to the same door, the heavy handle of an escape hatch. Down the hall, I could hear my mother in the kitchen, the clicking of the coffeemaker, the shifting of dishes in the sink, the sounds of her beginning to build the day. I looked around me, feeling on the floor for something to knock down, something to shake, some insisting noise to make so that she would know I was still here.

Leslie Birch Was Not Real

Leslie Birch was not real. He stood on the corner of Western and Polk in Chicago, Illinois, in November. It was a real place and a real time. If Leslie had really thought about it, he might have wished or even hoped for the realness of this corner to rub off on him. Gum on the shoe. Stuck. Two minutes ago, he was buying a pack of beer when he looked outside the window of the corner shop and he thought it was snowing. He swore he saw snow falling, small, dry flakes, dust or dandruff. He left the beer on the counter and the woman standing at the cash register didn't call his name because she didn't know what to say. Leslie Birch stepped outside and it was not snowing. Just cold. The grey of the sky stayed up there out of reach.

Leslie left the beer and walked down the street. On a street this cold and this grey, there was only a smattering of life. Only a few people walking, stepping out of their own corner shops, looking up at their own grey skies. A trio of boys circled the block on bikes. Once, twice, three times. Leslie didn't mind leaving the beer on the counter. He didn't really want the beer. What he had wanted was to stand in front of a cashier and hand her some crumpled dollar bills and for her to take them from him.

It was Tuesday afternoon and Leslie had missed four shifts at the package facility. When he didn't show up for the first shift, one of the floor-leads or operations managers would have called him repeatedly. Leslie's phone died on Saturday. None of the calls went through. When he didn't show for the second shift, he would have been terminated automatically and his information would have been erased from the system. By the third shift, someone would have cleared out his locker, only to find a pack of nicotine gum and a stick of deodorant. At the start of the fourth shift, it would be as if there was no Leslie Birch, here or anywhere else. Leslie Birch walked down Western Avenue and no one noticed.

Real or not, Leslie heard the bone break. He heard the snap of the bone first, and then silence. He turned and the street was empty, except for the three boys and their bikes. They were maybe nine years old. Maybe they were fourteen. Leslie had two sons who were adults now, but they had never been nine or fourteen, not in his memory. The boys in the street wore thin jackets and their cheeks and noses were red-stung by winter winds. Two were standing with their bikes still between their legs. The third boy was on the ground, his bike scattered in one direction, his body in another. Leslie saw the boy on the ground try to raise his left arm, and saw where the arm fell away from the shoulder, where it hung too low. Even through his jacket, Leslie could tell his arm was broken. The standing boys looked at Leslie and back at their friend and then to Leslie again. No one made a sound. Down the street, a dozen pigeons all took flight at the same time, as if they had planned it. One, two, three. Leslie, who was not real, who had been walking through the city for five days and sleeping during the mornings in parks and libraries, turned and walked away. Surely someone would come. Someone who could help. There was that lady at the corner store; the boys were still in the view of the window where Leslie had sworn he'd seen snow. Leslie Birch had nothing to offer.

Leslie made it only two blocks before he turned around. He picked up his left foot to take a step further way from the boys, to keep walking, and instead used it to turn his body around. Western Avenue was wide, and the buildings on either side were low. To the east, Leslie could see the downtown of Chicago blooming like a mushroom cloud in the distance, many miles away. These streets were empty and made of the same color as the sky. Grey above, grey below, sun-bleached like the posters that hung in the windows of corner shops that promoted old music festivals and strip clubs. When he turned around, the boys were still in the middle of the street. Everything was still frozen. Leslie walked to where the broken boy was laid out, and kneeled beside him.

You left, one of the standing boys said.

Leslie grabbed the broken boy's hand on the uninjured arm and squeezed. The boy squeezed back. His grip was weak and his face was drained of color.

What's your name? Leslie asked the broken boy. His voice was calmer than he had expected. It was the first time he had spoken to anyone in five days. His tone was smooth. His words didn't catch on anything in his throat.

You, you, you, the boy said. His voice was shaking and he spoke between short bursts of breath.

Where are your parents? Who's taking care of you?

You, you, you, the boy said again.

Leslie turned to the two boys still standing with their bikes. What's his name? Where are his parents? He spoke louder now, pinched the words between his teeth. The boys just looked at him. No one moved.

You left, they said.

Wind whipped down the street. Leslie tensed his shoulders as a chill passed through him. He caught a whiff of himself and suppressed a gag. He thought for a second that no one would ever again ask for his name. The thought was as quick and sharp as a needle in the eye. He leaned down to whisper in the broken boy's ear.

I'm not real. I can't help you. I don't know what to do with you.

You, you, you, the boy echoed.

Earlier today, when a cop had kicked his leg to wake him from sleeping against a tree in Humboldt Park, Leslie had decided to take what money he had on him and buy a bus ticket to Oklahoma. Leslie's father had died earlier that year and he had been a Choctaw Indian who grew up in Oklahoma and never talked about it. That made Leslie half an Indian and he had the blood certificate to prove it, but he didn't know anything more about being Choctaw than he knew about being Cherokee or Chickasaw, and when he was drunk, sometimes he mixed them up.

Leslie thought his whole life his father had been part of the Choctaw Nation of Oklahoma, but it wasn't until he passed away that he learned his father was actually Mississippi Band. It wasn't until he passed away that Leslie knew those were two different things, that there was a difference between the people who stayed and the people who didn't and that, somehow, his father had lived with both. No one from either tribe came to his funeral. Neither Leslie nor his older brothers knew who to call. His brothers had accepted their father's silence a long time ago and were now silent Indians themselves, standing like poplar trees at the edge of a field.

The funeral was just Leslie, his white mother, and his half-Indian brothers who also had white wives. There were their children, who knew even less. If he had still been married, Leslie's own white wife and his own quarter-blood sons would have been there as well. The only Indians Leslie knew were his brothers and his fathers and his sons. The only

Indians Leslie knew were the ones who made him and the ones he made. None of them knew what any of it meant. All these words, delineations, blood quantum, lines drawn between one river or another. They didn't know the language, the stories, the families, the past.

Being half-Indian with no history was like being just half-white, the other half a mystery. Not real. They had none of it, none of the stuff of being Indian, and it was Leslie's father who had kept it from them. Leslie had asked, first in quiet, timid tones and then in hollers and screeches louder than winds. His father had never answered, and Leslie had never figured it out. What did a son know of his father's behavior, of his intentions, of his choices and consequences? Or of his own? Nothing, nothing.

Leslie had tried to go to Oklahoma before and never made it. Short spells of compulsion, time that Leslie couldn't answer for. He'd come to and find himself on a highway approaching St. Louis. He would always turn around, always a job to get back to, sons he couldn't leave behind then. Leslie thought, because he wasn't real anymore, that maybe this time he could make it. In the back of his mind, Leslie knew that there wasn't anything down there for him. There would be no family, no long-lost cousins, no one who would know his name or his father's. Leslie knew that if he wasn't real here that he wouldn't be real there, but it was the motion of the thing. Leslie could be not real, but he could be unreal with movement, with direction, with velocity. That trajectory kept him solid. He had been walking for the past five days. And now, he was kneeling in the middle of the street with a broken boy and no one was moving.

I've called an ambulance! The lady from the corner store was standing on the sidewalk with a phone to her ear. A small crowd of onlookers had stopped on the sidewalk. Leslie looked up at them and saw what they must have seen. A broken boy lying there in the middle of the street. A not-real man kneeling at his side. The two boys with bikes stood above them like angels. It must have looked like a painting or an oil spill. Something like that.

After the ambulance came and took the boys away, the small crowd of passersby slipped back into side streets and the woman went back into her corner store. The boys left their bikes in the street, and Leslie dragged them out of the street and leaned them against a boarded-up storefront. When he turned around, the grey street was empty again.

There was no sign that the boys had been there, or that Leslie had either. He walked to the middle of the street where the boy had fallen. Leslie felt something twist behind his sternum, then the sensation of a string being pulled taut from his anus to his throat. He leaned over and vomited onto the pavement. The partially digested food and stomach bile that had left Leslie's body was now as much his as the street was his, as the sky was his. In the cold November air, steam rose from the warm vomit and spilled out of Leslie's mouth and no one noticed.

Wake

The last time I saw him he was smiling,
wandering around my uncle's property,
watching my cousins talk as if they were
a flock of birds changing direction. Dizzy
with the broadening space around him. His wife
only two years dead. Everything was unfolding.
For the first time, he saw mountains outside and
darkness within them. The strange patterns on the floor.
The beds that remained unmade, as if in protest.
Constellations of dust frozen in time perforate each room.
All his clothes are coated in stardust.
He was mostly cement by then, dried and driven
into tree trunks. Century-old nails made in town
by an extinct blacksmith. Walnut harvested from
the mountain property, heartwood warm
like maple syrup or blood. Like history kept in
incubation. I can't tell how much dark fire used to be
there. What kind of obscure misery compelled him
to tell his children to lie about the other, then
line them up in the kitchen and beat them until one
confessed. History becomes a dream that sweats off
like wax. The whole house still reeks of apple butter.
The pantry is loaded with small jars canned decades
ago with only the dry dark to sup on its fermentation.
The sky was clear that day. My mother sat
opposite my uncle and avoided his smile.
With decades of words buried between them,
only she knew where the gravestones were.

Thunder Thighs

In the room's thick dark, he explores me.
I say nothing.

His fingers trace my belly; below,
his hand claims a cheek.

When he comments on my slender frame,
it's implied that I should learn to stop growing—

*'cause right now you don't have thunder thighs
like other women.*

By the time my mother comes home,
I've been told to tuck myself in.

He believes there should be a line
somewhere, so he draws it at treating me

like a kid.

Bughouse

The ladybug comes first, red as a blister rubying the crown molding. My husband stretches a fingertip toward the ceiling and clicks it like an on-off button. The stink of its yellow blood is like something burnt.

"Are you leaving the windows open again?" he asks me. "I told you not to leave the windows open."

***

Ants march on us next, mapping highways and turnpikes across our laminate countertop. They are palm-heeled to a dark smudge, and my husband sprays aerosol pest-killer.

In the weeks that follow, I spot a spider ducking behind wainscoting seams.

A millipede squinches up our shower curtain and I shriek.

Vinegar flies dangle in the kitchen.

Boxelder graveyards crop up in windowsills.

"How are they all getting in?"

We scour the house late into the night. Every surface is scrubbed to shining until our elbows ache, but when we fall back victorious and kissing and undressing onto our mattress, the thump of a moth against a bulb at our bedside interrupts.

Back on our feet, my husband and I are snatching fistfuls of empty air until the thrash of wings is powder on the drywall.

The romance is spoiled, and I switch off the light and settle back exhausted.

"Love you," my husband murmurs, and when I am nearly asleep he shifts beside me. "You're not going to say it back?"

"I love you," I say.

"Why are you saying it weird?"

<u>L E N A   Z Y C I N S K Y</u>

Beautiful Fighters

Mixed medium
2022

I created "Beautiful Fighters" in response to the war in Ukraine. The art-work captures doves, which are symbols of peace, engaged in a fight. It is executed in mixed media, where I used a patchwork collage technic to manipulate pieces of magazines into a harmonious whole, which I then finished with acrylics. Despite the dark foresight, I hope the destruction of war will be over soon (not just in Ukraine, but in Israel-Gaza, too), that the peace will break in unexpectedly like rays of sunshine do through what looks like endlessly thick clouds: time to collect, rebuild and heal.

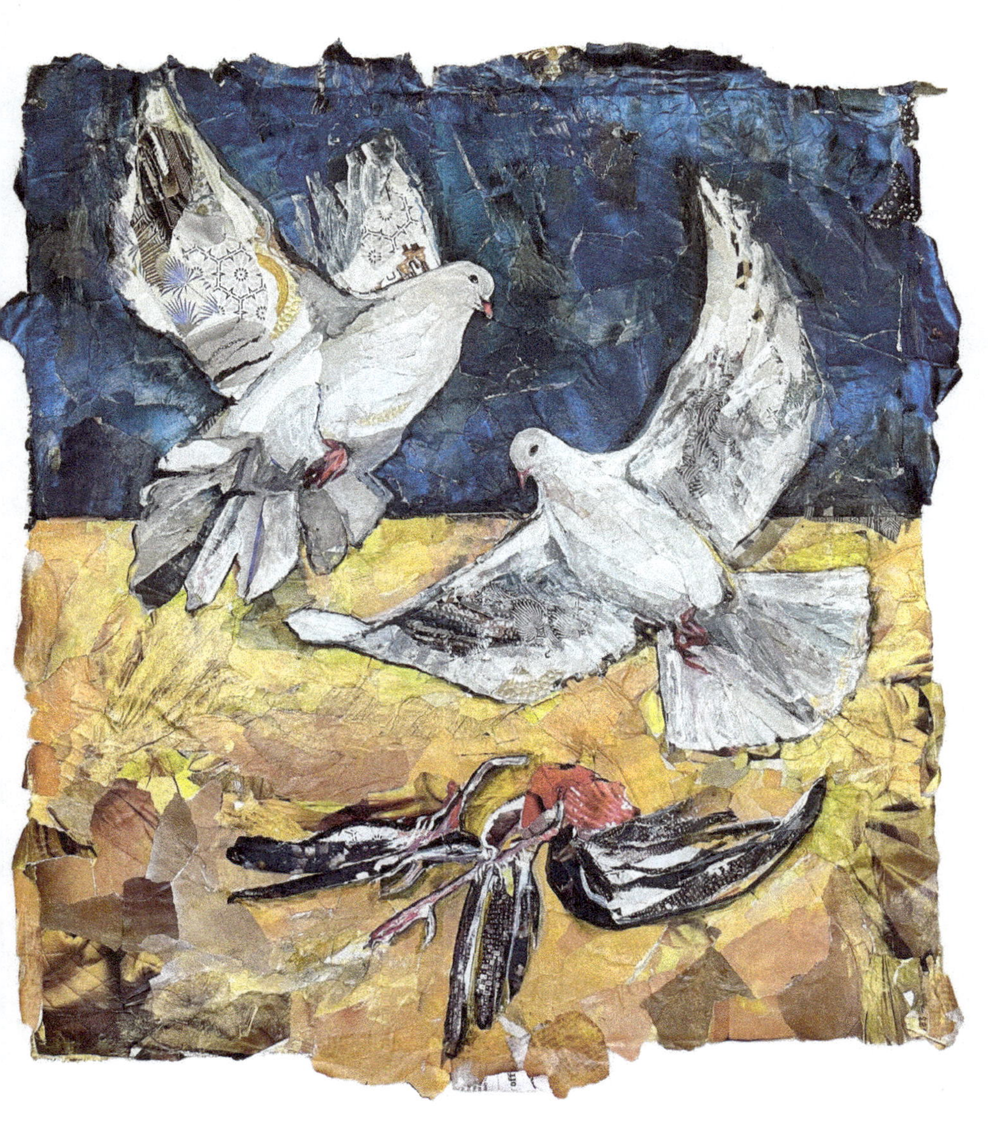

"What do you mean? That's how my voice sounds right now. It's been a long day."

"Did I do something wrong?" he asks.

"No."

"I feel like I'm always doing something wrong."

My eyes are wide open now, bolted to the dark ceiling. "Me, too."

My husband lets out a breath of frustration. "Why do you always do that? Make it about you when I'm upset."

"I didn't mean to upset you."

"I think you should apologize anyway."

"For the way my voice sounds?"

Our back-and-forth takes us in a circle, and I finally concede.

"Okay. I'm sorry."

"See? You're saying it weird," he says. "You never say it like you mean it."

"I'm super tired. Can we talk about this in the morning?"

"You always want to talk later."

"You're always upset."

My husband jerks up in bed. "Seriously?" He is talking through teeth now. "This didn't have to be a big deal. If you just apologized like you actually meant it."

I am quiet, wishing I could fold myself smaller, the same way a pill bug can coil into a ball, the way a grasshopper accordions its lace-wings tight against its flanks.

"You're just going to go to sleep, then?"

"I'm sorry," I whisper again.

"That's the best you can do?"

We hear a clack of something dropping to the floor, and when I switch on the light a June bug is on its back on the hardwood, six legs flailing.

***

Our furniture is dragged back from the baseboards so we can dust and vacuum every crevice. Cobwebs are broomed and carpet beetles are halved and crane flies are clapped in preparation for the party. Guests arrive, and despite our best efforts I still spot cutworms beating themselves against lights, a mantis perching on the sofa arm, a lightning bug winking overhead like foil confetti. Our friends are swatting at gnats while they dig in ice for beer cans, crack glowsticks, bounce ping-pong balls, bob near the Bluetooth speaker.

"Where's the birthday boy? We have to do candles!" someone shouts as midnight nears.

I find my husband alone in our bedroom. He looks like he's been crying.

"It took you a whole hour to realize I was gone," he tells me.

"Why are you in here? Are you okay?"

"It's my birthday. And you didn't even notice I was missing. No one did."

"Of course we did. Everyone's asking about you. I think we should go—"

"You're my wife. I thought you would have noticed, at least," he says, breathing hard. "You know I hate my birthday. I've always hated my birthday. If you really knew me, you'd know I didn't want a party."

"I thought you said—"

"I make your life miserable. I know I do," he panics. "Why are you even with me?"

I lock the bedroom door and hold his head in my lap while laughter and music seep in from outside. "Because before I met you, I didn't think it was possible to love someone so much," I tell him, my chest aching.

Some days being in love feels like being a longhorn ant, carrying something ten times my weight.

I am a dog tick, so swollen to bursting I can barely move, and love is something liquid red.

We sit together like this until our guests filter home, and I watch a widow gossamer her net between walls while I stroke the hair from my husband's forehead, trace the lines of his beautiful face with my thumb.

***

We fill the seams of our doors and windows, caulking gun in my husband's hands while I smooth the sticky seal with a putty knife behind him. When we don't see a single insect all day, we pop champagne to celebrate, laughing as we lever the cork, collapsing on the kitchen floor and sipping straight from the green gooseneck of the bottle.

"Do you remember the day we met?"

"The way we used to talk?"

"Until the sun was rising."

"At the top of that parking garage. Where you could see all the city lights."

"Remember our first kiss? We were so—"

"And that waterfall we went skinny dipping in?"

"Why do you always do that?" my husband mutters.

"What?"

"Interrupt me."

"Oh. I didn't realize."

"You do it all the time. You're not a very good listener."

"I didn't mean to. What were you going to say?"

"I'm not saying it now." He passes the bottle, and a pair of katydids start a chorus in a high cabinet.

***

The bugs are pouring in ten times more than before, so many that high corners are velveted black. The frosted bowls of the overhead lights fill with a trail-mix of exoskeletons. My husband and I keep our shoes on to stomp for roaches while we walk. We are shaking silverfish and moth larvae out of our clothes when we dress, washing palmettos down the shower drain before we step into the tub. Black flies float in our cereal milk and strawberry-root weevils wriggle in our rice. We are scratching mosquito bites until they bleed, tweezering hornet stingers from one another's knuckles. A fleecy egg sac bursts and spiderlings unspool from it by the thousands, so we are sucking them up in lines with the vacuum tube.

We spend a whole weekend hanging blackout curtains. We run our hands along every wall, every baseboard, every windowpane searching for cracks, spackling the smallest suggestion of one.

"It was your idea." I spit in frustration, fingernailing something bitter and winged from between my teeth. "To live in this house. To move out of the city."

"Oh, so this is all my fault?"

"That's not what I meant."

"Don't I always let you have your way? About every other thing? I'm always doing what you want." He is raising his voice. It climbs a rung with each word. "And you. Do you ever do a single thing for me? You treat me like a chore!"

"That's not true," I murmur.

"You don't get to decide how I feel."

I go silent enough for us to hear the tick of chitin against glass, the drone of house flies in the next room.

"You're always doing this. You say something you know will upset me, and then get all deer-in-headlights when it works. You're such a bitch sometimes."

I am still silent.

"Say something! Apologize! Anything!"

"I'm sorry," I whisper.

"That's it?"

I am quiet.

"You're seriously bad at making me feel better!"

"I don't like when you yell at me."

"You think this is yelling? This is what yelling sounds like to you?" he is shouting now. "You've had it so easy, haven't you? You have no idea what yelling is!"

My voice shakes. "Maybe we should wait until you've calmed down to talk about this."

"I wouldn't get so upset if you knew how to apologize the right way. It's only you that gets me worked up like this. No one else ever does." He is roaring now. "Just you!"

I am shrinking back from him, even though I know he hates when I do.

"I've told you not to do that. You make me feel like a monster. You make me feel like the worst person on earth."

I lock myself in the bathroom for hours, pressing darklings into porcelain one by one as they come up from the drain.

***

My husband knows I don't like flowers, and after work, when I've slashed my way through fresh spiderwebs to get to the kitchen, I find bunches of mint and rosemary and eucalyptus in a vase. Caterpillars are already eating holes through the leaves.

"I'm so sorry," my husband says. "I don't mean to get so angry. It's how everyone treated me when I was young. I hate that I get like that. I'm an idiot. A horrible person. You're so much better than I am." He goes on and on, kissing my cheeks and my eyelids and my fingers between words.

Water is set to boil, but for every copper-winged Indianmeal my husband picks from the penne, the next duplicates tenfold. We order takeout instead, eating on the driveway under a salting of stars, laughing at the constellations we draw.

"See?" he says, bringing a blanket when I start to shiver. "This is how you apologize the right way."

***

Later that night, I slide a hand down my husband's shorts while we watch television, but he shirks away.

"No. Not with all these bugs everywhere. We need to get them out first."

***

The next week my husband fogs the living room, and the floor is littered with legs and wings.

"I have to go," I say when I am passed a broom and dustpan. "Meeting friends for lunch. Remember?"

"You're just going to leave me? To clean this up on my own?"

"You should come with me. We could both use some time out of the house. We can do this together later."

"I want to do it now."

"I'm not canceling."

He frowns. "I feel like you're always trying to get away from me."

"I want you to come along."

"You don't mean that. You act like you hate being around me when we're with other people. And your friends are assholes to me."

I sigh. "I'm late. I can't deal with this right now."

"Me? You can't deal with me?" My husband is taken aback. "I do so much for you. Everything I do is for you. And you can't do this for me?"

"I've had these plans for weeks."

His eyes narrow. When he wheels back his open hand, it is to slap the wallpaper near my head. He shows me the smashed centipede on his palm after.

"Go. Have fun," he says. "But if it was you asking me to stay, you know I would."

***

Cocoons drip from the underside of everything like woolly stalactites, half-marinated darts and loopers and carrot seeds and wood nymphs ornamenting all the rooms of the house. There is a wasp nest chandeliering our table. Dragonfly eggs kernel our sink basins. Each step my husband and I take makes a cuticle-molting crunch, and we keep our lips pressed in tight lines as we tiptoe through the house to keep from inhaling midges and fleas.

At night, clover-mites tickle footpaths over our skin and orb weavers feel their eight-legged way down the tunnels of our throats so we are rasping and choking awake.

"I can't stand this anymore," I admit. Even at work I feel sowbugs crawling under the fabric of my uniform.

My husband frowns. "You want to leave me."

"No. I want to leave this house. Together."

"I'm not leaving. I'm not moving. I'm not giving up on this. If you want to leave, you'll have to go without me."

I try to imagine leaving him, and I cry under a heavy quilt until I can't breathe.

It would be like cleaving an earthworm down its center, and I'm sure he is the half with our shared heart.

***

The house smells of cedar and sawdust and the rotting coriander of smashed stink bugs when I enter. My husband has a mouthful of penny nails, and he hammers cuts of plywood over our windows with an enormous mallet.

"Do you have to cover them all?" I ask when he starts in the bedroom. "How will the light get in?"

"We don't have a choice," my husband says. "This is going to help."

We switch our bulbs to infrared, stick the walls with a checkerboard of baits, hang strips of flypaper like party crepe. Whole colonies gather to drink from the dish of poison we set out, their humming bodies squirming in unison like they are a single creature, a greasy, ash-colored companion come to stay with us, one we never invited inside.

"I don't think this is working. Nothing is working."

***

I go running in a lightning storm.

I take a trip to the grocery store and don't buy anything.

I pack a bag to stay overnight at a friend's.

Anything to breathe air that isn't bloated with insecticide, textured with drain flies.

"You don't love me anymore," my husband says while I empty my suitcase. "I don't think you ever did."

"I love you so much that sometimes I feel like you and I invented love," I tell him.

"Then why do I feel this way?"

"What way?"

"Like I have to beg you for it. Like I have to pull your teeth out to get it from you."

***

My husband brings home steel plates to weld over the vents, insulation stripping to stuff under the doorframes, tubes of Gorilla glue to seal the entrances. "We can keep them out of the bedroom, at least," he says, duct taping us in and plugging the keyhole with putty.

"Won't we be trapped?" I ask while I help him paint weather-proofing pitch.

"Do you have any better ideas?"

I don't have to answer.

"Of course you don't. I'm the only one making an effort," he says. "This has to work."

There is nothing else left to try, and we drag furniture to barricade the door when the bumping and clicking and buzzing outside swells to a brontide. Termites take bites of the house to get to us, and we are coating our four walls in layer after layer of sealant to cork their shafts and tunnels, lathering it so thick we lose whole inches of the room.

When they finally make their entrance, it is teeth-first, pale bodies plunking one after another onto the floor like drips from a faucet.

After this, my husband and I have no choice but to work in rotating shifts, holding books and saucepans and soles of shoes and our gritty palms over fresh chinks while the Poly-fil and paste dry.

With a blood-colored bulb as our only sun and moon, I am not sure if days or weeks pass this way.

I start to ache like a clenched fist, a body-shaped bruise.

Sleep can only be caught in snatches.

My parents call.

Friends text.

Work emails.

"We'd love to hear from you."

"Where have you been?"

"Can you please submit your sick day requests in the online portal?"

I don't answer, melded to a single joint gone Sisyphus-stiff from pressing, steeling, holding on.

***

"I don't think I can do this anymore," I say, when I am sure my arms won't stay above my head for another minute.

"Are you even trying?" my husband demands. "I'm never going to stop trying. If you want it to end, you're the one who has to give up on this. You have to say the words."

I don't have any words at all left to say, so I drop to my knees to find the mallet in my husband's toolchest. I am crying while I weigh it in my fist, while I rise to swing at the wall, while it erupts in paint chips and wood splinters and plaster dust.

My husband watches in silence.

When I have made a gape large enough to fit through, I look back at him one last time.

He nods once.

We both try to smile.

Then I am hoisting and scraping my body between studs and joists.

The walls in the rest of the house are sheets of writhing insects. Maggots squirm. Earwigs and cicadas clamber sticky from their molts. Ants have gathered to dine on the carcasses of yellowjackets. Cocoons have been peeled back like hangnails, and moths pound like a hundred hearts around me as I stumble for the front door.

Outside, a torrent of hot white sunlight scorches me.

When I lift my hand to shade my eyes, a newborn cecropia is opening and closing its silken wings in my palm.

<u>HAZELLE RACHELLE</u>

Compulsory Heterosexuality

The bartender with black curls, the blonde stalking across the road in a
houndstooth coat, ponytail girl with the white teeth, the waitress with
milkmaid braids across her perfect bare shoulders, the dykes making
out at the karaoke bar (both of them), the girl behind the counter with
upside-down lips, thighs like columns under the lathe, a waist like a neck,
a girl with a chest so pale it looked like a mess of wires for a clever spy to
snip and untangle, preferably with teeth, face inches from the explosion,
a girl with red sashiko across both knees, a girl with horsey teeth and
a news reporter's smile, the ceramics girl with ink smeared all over her
arms (all fucking over), the library employee who smiled when I returned
all my library books, the one who didn't, the bosomy one with life dedi-
cated to Christ, the flat-affect girl jittering in her daily puffer vest, whose
mobility device whirred in late behind her every day, the girl who cried
when she saw porn for the first time, the girl who would eat anything if
she thought it would make me laugh, and the man in the end because I
saw a bit of each in all of him.

Adagio for Bisexual Erasure

Another September dusk and you
think, for whatever reason, of him as
he rarely was, composed and sober. Buttons
freed, undershirt loose against the
plumpest parts of him. In his left hand, a plum

bitten, waiting, a book spread, being read
in the right. La nuit de l'homme spritzed
across his neck, a silver chain hung
there, where you were thinking of sinking
the sharpest parts of you, as if to reach

a pulsating sadness in his jugular. So why
were you, those years ago, so scared,
when he took you down Vine, over
the night's shadows and their silence,
brought you closer, close enough

to see yourself atop his space dust
irises? And you cowered. What is
the word for when the blood grows
ever slightly colder? When we lose
some hidden part of ourselves?

Cling

and so we made love or maybe just talked about it in the dimmed light of
your bedroom. My kitchen. Your face flickering like a static of light from
a dream of almosts. We were always up against it. The wifi. Your flight
schedule. My mother. The guilt of not being enough. Time, a chip on
our shoulder—the future hunching over itself like a man who outlived
his spine. I don't like remembering most of it. The specifics wear me out
and memory is a carve in the bone. Angles converging in the rib. Scratch-
ing and rehashing themselves like a novel going nowhere. But nowhere
scares me so I try to name things to contain them. Map them out on the
floor beneath my feet. Smash the slant of light clean on the concrete. My
therapist says none of what I tell her warrants a prescription unless I am
lying and I don't know how to translate the aftermath of want—which
is still want—that a guy going nowhere wants it all, all at once. And I
am supposed to write it down. Not the all, but the specifics. Clutch the
velocity of thought. Seize the panic in a procedure of breath. Block the
escape routes. Yield nothing to the slatted light dream in the back of my
head. So the fore of my skull and the eyeballs burning. Skyline a gesture
in the vague. In the cut of my heel the smashed glass glittering—gullet
a clog of mucus and language. Language loyal to itself, slithering in the
nerve, inching for some debris or dream to scatter its syntax on. So we
did make love because I know we talked about it—your sun bleeding
on the brackish water, my moon scattered on the reeds by my kitchen
window. Across three time zones you said you're kissing my forehead
and I said you're only doing it because you have to. And you said *hush
and crawl outside the mind and its mirror and lick this breath of light with a naked
nib, beyond word beyond thought*, a curve beyond intention, a sort of death
and the time goes nil. My finger unknotting the tangle of your hair. Our
limbs tugged in each other like the comma of a lost language. I asked
you how long will it be like this, this litany of words in the wake of flesh,
this gouging of oblivion—this gesturing at the throat of want and never

quite breaking it open. Whatever you said next dissolved in the static, then a curl of wind and your voice quivering *I am coming I am coming I am coming*

VINCENZO COHEN

The Way to Hammamet

Watercolor on canvas
50x100 cm
2000

The painting was created through the encounter of large color spots and represent scenes of life in North Africa by expressing love for exotic and distant places. The artwork focuses on the gradual disappearance of natural spaces and civilisation and testifies, like in a living crib, the tradition of the Berber Bedouins. Landscape shapes blend in the background through the encounter of colors. The chromatic background that comes from the combination of stains of watercolor recalls the weaving of oriental fabrics and the wear of time.

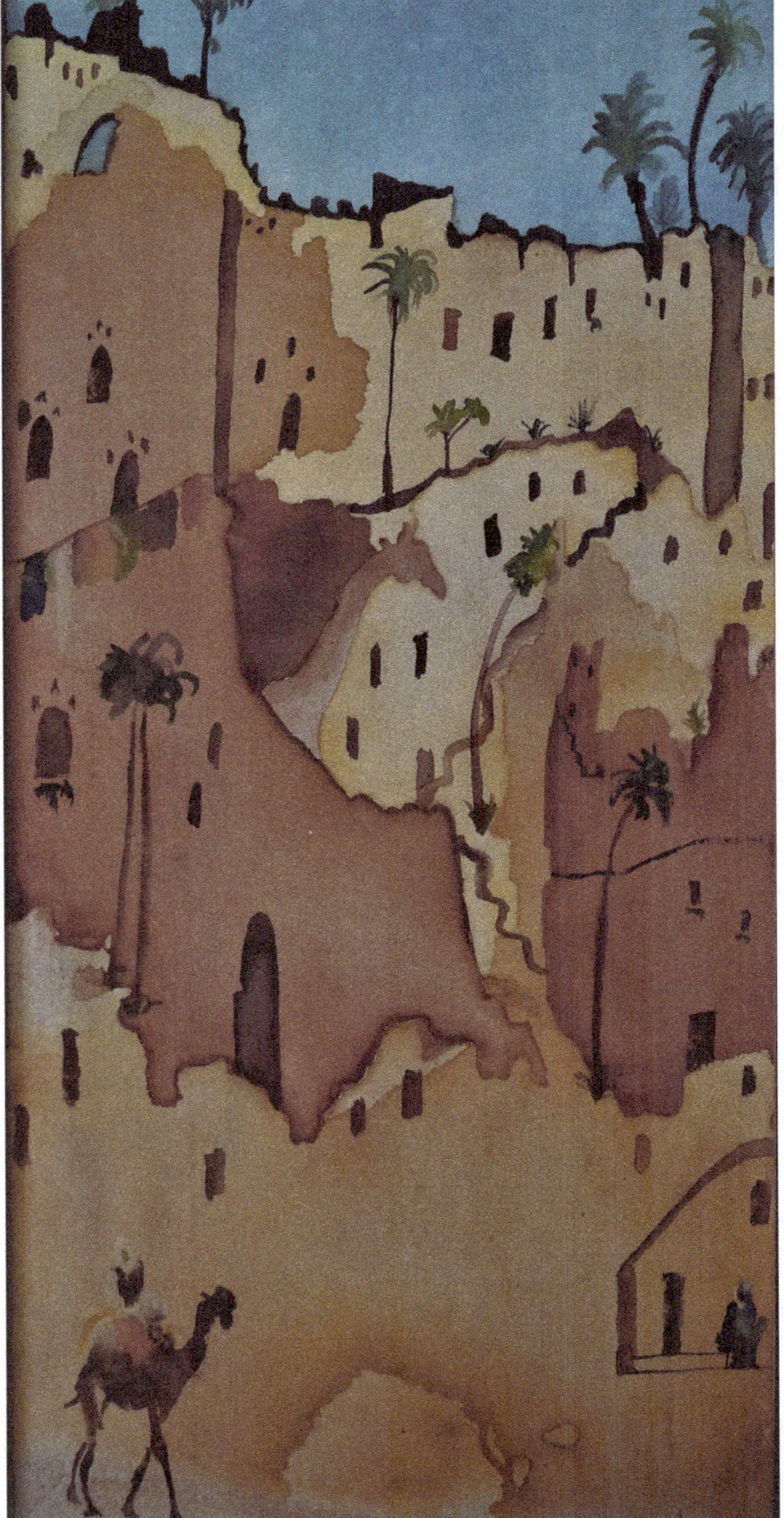

The Genie & Me

I go to the garage sale because all the lamps moved out when my roommate did, and the apartment's never been darker. An old woman with a face like a used tissue sells me the oil lamp for thirty-five cents, and it comes with me to the Dunkin' Donuts on Seventh. I like Dunkin' because they write my name on the cup. Most of the time, they spell it wrong, giving me y's and e's I haven't earned, but sometimes they get it right, which is even worse.

I tell all this to the Genie, who takes occasional sips from the caramel Coolatta I bought him. He's wearing a gray plaid vest and matching fedora that makes him look like a DJ from a Disney Channel original movie. His lamp, from which he emerged spectacularly about twenty minutes ago, sits between us, forming an avant-garde centerpiece with my empty cold-brew cup. Today, the barista spelled my name Kattrina, with two t's instead of the correct one, so I don't have anything to worry about.

"I'm nervous," I say to the Genie. "I don't really do this."

I give the Genie a tour of my apartment and try to figure out if he seems impressed. When we get to my room, he scrunches up his nose. "It smells like latte in here," he says. I open my closet door and show him the stack of empty coffee cups, the ones with my name smelled right.

"I can't figure out what else to do with them," I confess.

I show him to Angela's old room and invite him to make himself comfortable, a suggestion he accepts with a mordant smile. He's a small man, five-four if you're being generous, with a pouf of hair nearly as big as the rest of his head that bobbles when he walks.

"You can stay here while I think of my wishes," I tell him. My eyes drift to the far wall, where a solitary Wicked poster still hangs. "It's empty right now."

I make chicken roulade for dinner, and the Genie tells me the rules.

"I don't kill anyone, firstly," he says, examining his plate. I've taken my mother's good china out of storage, and I'm not sure how effective the cursory rinse I gave each dish was. "Making people fall in love, no. Wishing for more wishes, God no, three is plenty." He purses his lips. "Can't change the past, either. And no world peace."

I think for a long time, then wish to be three inches taller.

The Genie snaps his fingers and I feel three extra inches of leg sprout from beneath my knees. The Genie stands, sending his chair backward with a noise like a throat clearing. "This chicken," he says with a flourish, "is dusty."

I go to work for another week before I remember I have a Genie and wish to be a billionaire. Two minutes later, I get a fraud alert from Wells Fargo.

"I found a Genie," I explain to the customer service representative over the phone. "So I wished for a billion dollars."

"Ah, okay!" says the woman. "So I'll just check off Genie, then." She congratulates me on my good luck and asks if I want to upgrade to a platinum checking account.

Try as I might, I can't come up with my third wish. I make lists of possibilities and cross them all out. I have no need for a beautiful singing voice; no interest in being smarter; no real desire to travel the world or the galaxy. I'm nearly set on the ability to fly until Google tells me how many people get sucked into jet engines every year.

"That's exaggerated," the Genie tells me with an eye roll when I read him the statistic, but I decide to play it safe.

With the promise of free coffee, the Genie begins to accompany me to the Dunkin' on Seventh every morning, where I order a caramel Coolatta for him and a cold brew with sweet foam for me. The baristas must be learning my name, which is bad news; I add five cups to my collection in as many days.

"Things with your name on them are sacred," I explain to the Genie on the walk home, empty Dunkin' cup still clutched in my hand. "Great to have, but awful, awful luck to get rid of. I might as well walk home in the street with my eyes closed as throw out this cup."

"I don't know if that's true," says the Genie.

The Genie shorts the power by running his hair dryer and space heater at the same time. The Genie eats an 80-gram edible and orders two hundred dollars of Wendy's. The Genie drops hints.

"Most people," the Genie says pointedly one sunny Saturday afternoon, "don't take longer than a week to make all their wishes. Some people are done in an hour." I tell him I want to be sure, then ask if he wants to come with me to the farmer's market; the Genie thinks for a minute, sighs, then puts on his shoes. "We're out of bok choy," he tells me.

One night, the Genie comes home drunk and climbs into my bed.

"Ka-tri-na," he purrs, chopping up my name like sashimi. "Katrina, girl. Girl, you are so fucking weird." He falls asleep with his head on my shoulder and we don't talk about it in the morning.

The Genie borrows my lipstick for a date. He puts it on; takes it off; puts it on; takes it off; puts it on again.

"Some guys get scared if you're too femme," he tells me.

"Fuck them, then," I respond.

"Mm," says the Genie. He takes the lipstick off and doesn't get back from his date for a day and a half.

My birthday rolls around and the Genie buys me a monogrammed necklace.

"Oh wow," I say, holding it to my chest and tucking in my chin so I can see how it lays on my collarbone, "Oh wow, this is great, seriously." The Genie smiles.

The Genie asks for his eggs without the yolk. The Genie asks if I can buy vegan egg substitute instead. The Genie invites me to go clubbing. I hem and haw for a day before saying yes. Friday night comes and I put on my sluttiest dress and a pair of shiny red shoes.

I like the club. I like being part of the pulsing fog of movement that isn't quite any of the people who make it up. We are music and sound and movement in a moment that lasts forever. We are every thump of the bass in "Turn Down For What" by Lil Jon and DJ Snake. We are love, asking for ourselves in return. We are a seventeen-dollar Aperol spritz.

I jump up and down with the Genie for a while, and then he's gone, and I jump up and down alone for a while, and then there's a girl in front of me wearing a shiny leather dress, and she yells something at me that might be "you're so pretty," and I yell something back that might be "thank you," and then we jump up and down together for a while until she leaves, too. Everyone leaves, I think to myself as I jump, and I am impressed by my own profundity. The Genie finds me again, and we do tequila shots, which sit nicely with the half-dozen tequila shots I've already done, and then we jump some more.

There are only a few seconds between the realization that I'm nauseous and the realization that I'm about to vomit; I barely make it outside to throw up in the street. A passing Audi honks at me and I give it the finger. It must have rained while we were inside because the whole world has turned slick and shiny like vinyl. I drop into a crouch and rest my head on my knees, praying for the spinning in my head to stop, for me to be somewhere else, to be someone else. Right after Angela left, I'd catch myself staring at the peak of Mt. Rainier and wanting to be there because somehow I felt that would make everything better. It took me a long time to realize that what I actually wanted was to be away from myself, from my brain, just quiet consciousness completely separate from my existence. It took me even longer to realize that, unfortunately, I am wherever I go.

"Hey girl," I hear the Genie say, and realize he's followed me outside. "Are you good?"

"So good." I move to stand, but that makes something in my stomach plunge like it's fallen down a mineshaft, so I stay down. "Ough."

Tonight, the Genie is wearing a silver scarf and patent leather pumps I think might be mine. His hair is gelled into an inverse tsunami. "How much did you drink?" he asks me.

I shrug. "Enough," I say thickly.

"Do you want to go back in?" he asks. I shake my head and rest it on my knees again, which helps for a second but then makes things much worse.

"I miss Angela," I say.

"Oh, no, Kat. Come on, no you don't."

"I keep thinking she's going to come back," I tell him. "Every time I get a text I think it's going to be her wanting to talk." Angela hated clubs, but I made her come out with me once; I remember how she spent the whole night hovering by the bar and then apologized to me when we got home, and suddenly I hate myself so bad I can't breathe.

The Genie shakes his head. "Don't shit where you eat," he says. "I always say that."

I shake my head. "I wish I hadn't," I say. My fingertips have gone numb and I feel like I'm going to throw up again. "I'm so fucking dumb."

I feel a hand on my shoulder. "I'm sorry, girl," says the Genie. I look up at him. The pumps combined with my low vantage point make him look unusually tall and sharp-jawed, and for a second I'm almost strangled by the urge to kiss him. I settle for vomiting again, this time all over my shiny red shoes. I close my eyes.

"Jesus Christ, girl," I hear the Genie say from what sounds very far away.

I wake up naked in my bed the next morning with little idea of how I've gotten there. There's a vague memory of a taxi, or maybe that's a microwave, and my mouth tastes like a rotten lemon. I discover that I've tried to message Angela, three texts consisting of eleven words and a blurry picture: I hate this place without you, then I have a genie now, then a flash of beige and black that might be me and might be the sidewalk. The texts haven't gone through; I guess I forgot I'm blocked. I go back to sleep, and then I wake, and then I go back to sleep again, and when I can't sleep anymore, I lie in bed feeling cold even though I'm under too many blankets.

Dusk has settled over the room like snow by the time the knock comes. I've called "come in" before I can even think to consider feigning sleep. The Genie opens the door carefully, like it might be rigged, and I push myself up onto my elbows.

"Hi," I say.

The Genie steps into the room and quickly shuts the door behind him as if he thinks someone might be listening in. It's the first time I've ever seen him nervous.

"Kat," the Genie says. "You need to make your third wish."

I settle back down. "I'm still thinking," I say.

"You've been thinking for a month and a half."

I shrug. My eyes are fixed on the ceiling. "It's a big deal. We both know I'm not going to get this chance again." I wait for the sound of the door, but it doesn't come.

"Katrina," says the Genie.

"Why?" I ask him. The ceiling is a slightly different shade of white than the walls, I realize. "Don't you like it here?"

"That's not what this is about," he says.

I lay my forearm over my eyes like a blindfold. "Maybe that's my wish," I say to him. "Maybe my wish is for you to stay."

The Genie is silent for a moment before he answers. "You aren't a bad person, Katrina," he says, and then the door opens and closes and I am alone again.

I find the Genie sitting at the kitchen table, thumbing through a months-old Lululemon catalog I can't throw out.

"Hey," I say.

He looks up from a spread of leggings. "Hey," he says. I take the seat next to him. For some reason it's hard to look him in the eye.

"I get too close," I tell my fingernails. "I get too close too fast. I tangle myself up in other people and when they go, they take parts of me with them."

"Mm," says the Genie.

"I've been thinking about my wish," I tell him. "I feel like I have to make it count."

"I could make you forget about her," says the Genie, and I can't find the words to tell him why that would be the worst thing, so I just say maybe.

Three days later, I put the lamp up in the free section of Craigslist. A man named Bareth answers the ad. "I've always wanted a Genie," he tells me excitedly over the phone. I give him my address and tell him to come at half past two. Bareth arrives in an old Grand Marquis that's the exact same shade of beige he is.

"This is a nice place you've got," he says, looking around my apartment. "Smells like latte."

"I think I'm going to be moving out soon," I tell him. When I give him the lamp I don't feel anything at all.

I do not watch the Genie go. I wait until I can't hear Bareth's car anymore and then I wait some more. I walk down to Dunkin' Donuts on Seventh and order a caramel Coolatta. The barista spells my name right, but it doesn't matter anymore; my last wish took care of that. I threw out all the cups in my closet. I won't have to worry about any kind of luck ever again.

I use my straw like a spoon and dab whipped cream on my tongue, and I think of Angela. I told her I loved her so I could hear her say it back and one day I will die so they carve my name on the tombstone. I tilt my cup to admire the strokes of the Sharpie and I smile, very small. I love having my name on things.

Quiet Spring

Acrylic on acid-free canvas paper, using golden heavy
body & fluid acrylics
8x10 inches
June 29, 2023

I enjoy painting scenes from Nature in semi-abstract ways. Because my
medium, acrylic, dries quickly, I create a lot of texture in my pieces. It
helps the painting stand out from the page as if it is living art, like the
environment that inspired this painting.

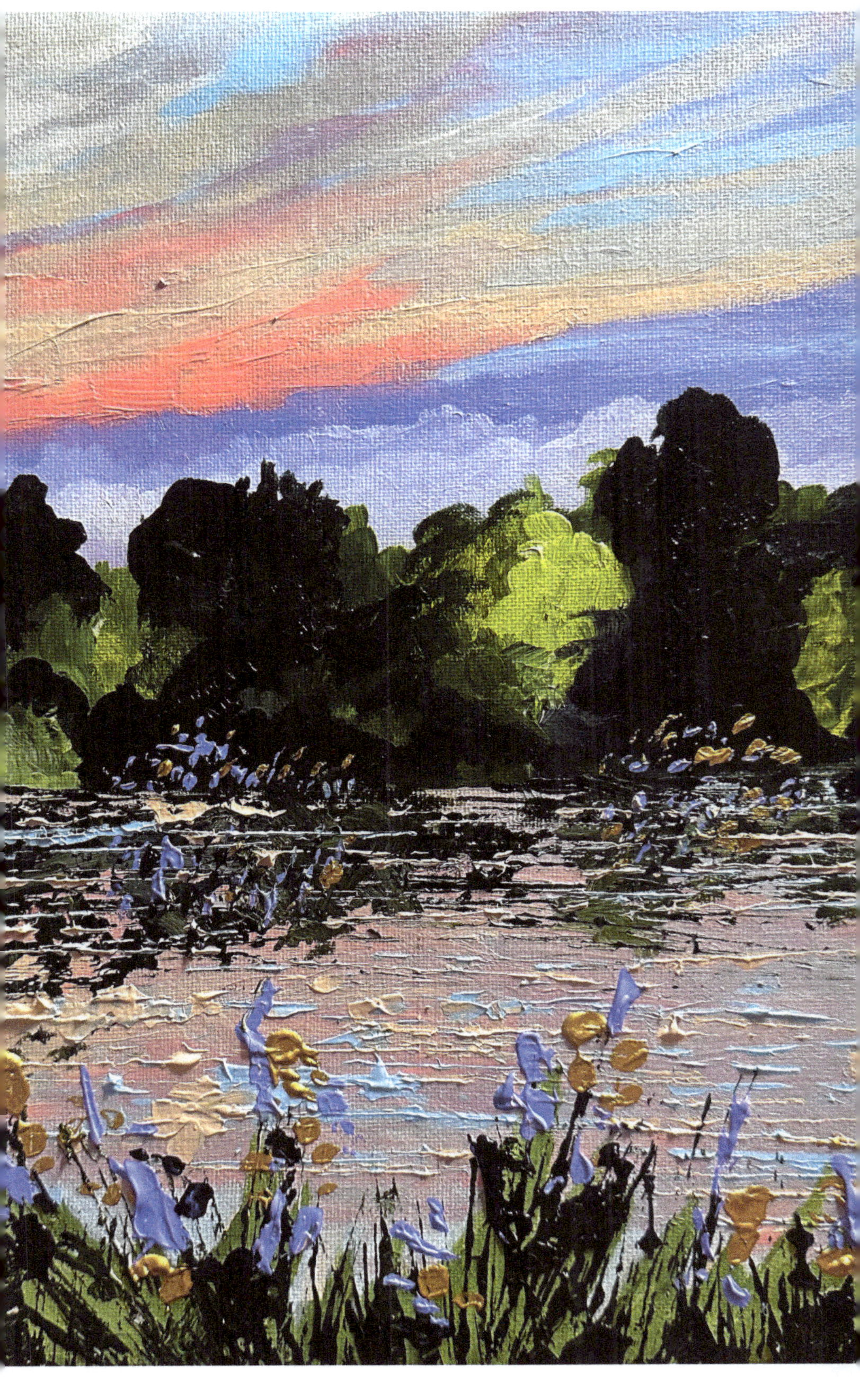

The Recipe—Joy As An Ingredient For Cooking Grief

***

I.   measure the grains of joy with a tin of milk.

II.   pour water into it & let the dirty particles come afloat.

III.   sieve them out.

IV.   add salt & turn on the heat.

V.   let it seethe & become tender.

VI.   stir.

VII.   add rosewater & tomatoes.

VIII. add cubes of sugar & one spoonful of honey.

IX.   grind calcium out of wet skeletons.

X.   stir, again, until every grain is red.

XI.   joy is ready, serve your countrymen & observe how they feel.

***

In the kitchen, I measured our joy with a fifty grams tin of milk. Not because the country is small. But, one spoonful of this joy equals the weight of a cadaver on the shoulder. A burden. Beneath the running tap, dirty particles emerged on the surface of the water, dancing to the ebb. My eyes, dancing, running—too. When I sieved them out, I found tiny rocks from tombstones, bullets of a trigger-happy cop, debris from the bombings in the North, a cupful of bloodstains & etcetera. Because I want you to eat & be healthy, I wash again & again until the grains were white as a snowdrop. Then, I added salt & turned on the heat. Inside the pot, our joy seethed into something soft. Say, a baked *flower*. & when I stirred, the steams rose to my eyes & condensed into a clean spring. The grains now white & impure, I added rosewater & tomatoes, for colour. Hoping to add to my joy, a red affection. But, I remember that three lay-

ers of skin & a fibrous sheath is how narrowly into the body, an arrow
must travel to taste blood. The body, not proof enough. Brother, because
I want your last supper to be mouthwatering, I added thirty-six cubes of
sugar, each for a state in the country. & two spoonfuls of honey, each
for a river. In a grinder, I crushed calcium out of wet skeletons. Because,
brother, all I want is for you to eat & be strong. Bone enough to feast
on the memories that pulleys us into the sky, where we walk on water
searching for our brothers. Hoping to find them more flesh than dust.
More blood than vapour. I stirred again, until every grain of joy was red
& sweet—like strawberry. And then it was ready. & I served the country
& listened. Spoons clattering against plates. One man, knowing how hard
it was to swallow the joy, chewed & chewed & broke the complex emo-
tional bonds into simpler bearable ones. Another man kept chewing until
the j-o-y became a love song in his larynx. Another, knowing how hard it
was to sing the songs alone. lured his little son to lay on his broad chest.
& as the boy listened to the song of his heart, he planted the joy between
his milk teeth. & together, they sang the ode.

CONTRIBUTORS

Abhinav is a graduate student residing in Delhi. His work has appeared in *trampset, The Deadlands Magazine, The Remnant Archive, Gulmohar Quarterly*, among other forums.

Abduljalal Musa Aliyu is a school teacher and poet. He writes from Zaria, Nigeria. He is the author of *Encyclopedia of Dolour* (Chestnut Review, 2024). His work appears or is forthcoming in *Chestnut Review, Vast Chasm Magazine, Brittle Paper, adda, Efiko, 3 of Cups anthology* and elsewhere. He was a co-winner of the Sevhage-Agema Founder's Prize for Poetry and the third prize winner of the inaugural Writing Ukraine Prize. He rants on Twitter @AbduljalaalMusa.

Brennan Burnside's work has recently appeared in *BlazeVox, A Minor* and *The New Absurdist*. He lives in South Carolina.

Gospel Chinedu is a Nigerian poet from the Igbo descent. He currently is an undergraduate at the College Of Health Sciences, Okofia where he studies Anatomy. He is a 2021 Starlit Award Winner, 1st Runner Up for the Blurred Genre Contest (Invisible City Lit) and Pacific Spirit Poetry Prize 2023, Honorable Mention in the Stephen A. Dibiase Poetry Prize, 2023 and also a finalist in the Dan Veach prize for younger poets, 2023. His works of poetry have appeared or are forthcoming in *Worcester Review, Augur Magazine, Fantasy, Fiyah, The Deadlands, Channel, Apparition Lit, Mud Season Review, Trampset, The Drift, Consequence Forum, The Rialto, BathMagg* and other places. Gospel tweets @gonspoetry

Matthew Church lives in the midwest with his wonderful family. He holds degrees in philosophy, Spanish, and English from Purdue University. Currently, you can find one of his poems in *New Ohio Review*, and when the work day is over, you can find him in his basement, cranking a tube amp past the edge of breakup, trying to discover the sonic limits of his pink Jazzmaster. On the best days, his son accompanies him on drums. This is his second publication.

Vincenzo Cohen is an Italian socially engaged multidisciplinary artist. He graduated in Painting from Fine Arts Academy in 2002 and held his first Solo Exhibition in 2005. In 2007, he earned a master's degree in Archaeological Sciences from ""La Sapienza"" University in Rome. Cohen' s work encompasses figurative arts and writing, reflecting his life and travel experiences while exploring various social themes. His art stems from extensive historicalscientific research, focusing on cultural and naturalistic content. Over the years, he has embraced diverse experimental styles and media. His deep passion for nature, ingrained since childhood, motivates his involvement in environmental awareness projects.

Coby-Dillon English (they/them) is a writer from the Great Lakes. A member of the Mississippi Band of Choctaw Indians, they currently are an MFA fiction candidate at the University of Virginia, where they teach writing and serve as the editor-in-chief for *Meridian*. They were a 2023 Tin House Scholar and a 2021 Periplus Collective Fellow. Their writing has received two Pushcart Prize nominations, a Best of the Net nomination, and PEN/Dau Prize nomination for best debut short story. Their work can be found or is forthcoming in *Cream City Review*, *Yellow Medicine Review*, *Salt Hill Journal*, and others.

Shauna Friesen (she/her) is a mountain climber, rock collector, and author living in Los Angeles, CA. Her words have been featured in *Pithead Chapel*, *Foglifter Journal*, *Flash Fiction Magazine*, *Fictive Dream*, and *Bruiser Magazine*, among others.

Keely Houk is an Award-Winning Art Director, Artist, and Designer. She has received over thirty awards for her work in higher education, including multiple CASE Circle of Excellence awards. In addition to her design work, she is an illustrator, painter, and author with multiple pieces being featured in publications and international exhibitions.

Winshen Liu is from Illinois. After working in tech, education, and the service industry, she is currently pursuing an MFA at the University of Mississippi. Her poems have appeared in *Cincinnati Review*, *Frontier Poetry*, *The Malahat Review*, *The Rumpus*, and *Southeast Review*, among others. Follow her work at winshenliu.com.

Taylor Mallay is a Midwesterner who enjoys tinkering away at poems here and there. Her work has previously appeared in *The Dewdrop*,

ONE ART, and *West Trade Review*, among other publications.

Rosalind Margulies is a writer and recent college graduate currently hanging out in Oregon. She has work published or upcoming in *Epiphany*, *Hobart*, *StoryQuarterly*, and elsewhere. You can find her on Twitter @rothalind, or visit her website rosalindmargulies.com.

Maryhilda Obasiota Ibe is a Nigerian poet. She is the winner of the 2020 Bloomsday Poetry Prize and was longlisted for the 2022 Palette Poetry Emerging Poet Prize. Her works have appeared on *Brittle Paper*, *Blue Marble*, *Poetry Column* and elsewhere. She's currently an MFA candidate at the University of Wisconsin-Madison.

Danielle O'Hanlon is a self-taught visual artist specializing in 3D acrylic sculpting and mixed media paintings. Her work is abstract and dreamlike, with color-changing backgrounds and 3D elements. Danielle also works with oil, acrylic, and charcoal. Danielle's works are internationally award-winning, have been published in multiple magazines, and have been featured in galleries all over the US. Danielle currently lives and works in Georgetown, South Carolina. More of her work can be seen at www.danielleohanlonart.com.

Hazelle Rachelle (she/her) is a writer and emergency manager from Portland, OR. Her work can be found at *HORNS*, *HAD*, *Pile Press*, *ergot*, and other places, or you can get it straight from the horse's mouth at @hazellerachelle and hazellelerum.com.

Emily Rankin is an artist and actor currently based in New Mexico. She was born in Riverside, California and attended university in Texas, where she received a BFA in 2011. Her body of work deals with the tangles of emotion and understanding, and the intuitive messages of dreaming and subconsious exploration. Her work has appeared in various publications, including *Gasher*, *Raw Art Review*, *Meat for Tea*, *Black Fox*, and *Rattle*. www.eerankinart.com

Jona Whipple is a writer, librarian, and archivist, in that order. She is currently pursuing her MFA in Fiction Writing at the University of Missouri-Saint Louis. Her stories and essays have appeared in *Hawaii Pacific Review*, *Heavy Feather*, *Catapult*, *Hypertext*, and *Bluestem*, and are forthcoming in *CRAFT*. She lives in Missouri, dangerously close to where she was born. jonawhipple.com

Linda Woolford lives and writes in Massachusetts. Her fiction is published in *Kenyon Review*, *Hobart*, *Michigan Quarterly Review*, and *Third Coast*, among others. She's the recipient of a Massachusetts Cultural Council fellowship, a winner of descant's Frank O'Conner Award for Short Fiction, and a Katherine Anne Porter Fiction Prize Finalist. Her stories have been anthologized and nominated for Pushcarts.

Lena Zycinsky is a poet and artist whose work appeared in the *New York Times*, *Poetry Archive*, *Consequence Forum* among other places. Author of numerous books and shows abroad, she holds a BA in English and is currently a low-residency MFA student at NYU in Paris. Born in Belarus, Lena lived in the USA and Greece, and now resides in London. More info: leanzycinsky.com

Chestnut Review

www.ingramcontent.com/pod-product-compliance
Lightning Source LLC
Chambersburg PA
CBHW070413310726
48977CB00003B/675